TALKING TO OURSELVES
Conversations with editors of the Irish news media

IVOR KENNY
TALKING TO
OURSELVES

CONVERSATIONS WITH EDITORS OF
THE IRISH NEWS MEDIA

Kenny's Bookshop and Art Gallery

Published in Ireland by
Kenny's Bookshop and Art Gallery
High Street
Galway

Index compiled by Jim Cumiskey
Odyssey plc 35 Dame Street Dublin 2

Cover photograph by Michael Olohan
National Gallery of Ireland

Print origination by
Lithographic Plate Plan
35 Upper Grand Canal Street Dublin 4

Printed by
Beta Print Clonshaugh Dublin 17

Bound by
Kenny's Bindery Salthill Galway

ISBN 0 906312 40 X

To the memory of my father
T.J.W. Kenny
founder, editor and managing director of the
Connacht Tribune

When he wanted to write a heavy editorial, my father would bring
home his portable typewriter and close the door. Silence was
enjoined.   I breached the sanctum and got my nose over
the edge of the dining-room table.   The typing stopped. I asked,
"What are you doing?" "I am writing an editorial."

Contents

Acknowledgements

Nineteen people helped me to write this book - eighteen editors and my friend and colleague, Gillian Acton.

The book was made possible through the generosity of Dr. M.W.J. Smurfit and the John Jefferson Smurfit Monegasque Foundation.

The book is in memory of my father. It is published from his and my home town by the family firm: my thanks to Conor, Thomas, Dessie, Gerry - and Maureen.

Introduction: The Fourth Estate

Burke said there were Three Estates in Parliament; but, in the Reporters' Gallery yonder, there sat a Fourth Estate more important than they all.
Thomas Carlyle 1795-1881

Neither in what it gives, nor in what it does not give, nor in the mode of presentation, must the unclouded face of truth suffer wrong. Comment is free but facts are sacred.
C.P. Scott 1846-1932

A good newspaper is a nation talking to itself.
Arthur Miller 1915-

The title of this book is taken from the playwright, Arthur Miller. There is a line in a play called *Jumpers* by Tom Stoppard: "The media. It sounds like a convention of spiritualists." While the word is relatively recent and carries a whiff of disparagement, it is not a bad one to describe the mediators between us and our information. Whatever we name them, they wield considerable influence over our lives notwithstanding the disclaimers throughout this book and that old flattery, the intelligence of our readers.

The purpose of the book is to add something to our knowledge of the media in Ireland, just as the purpose of the two earlier books in the trilogy was to add to our knowledge of leaders and of entrepreneurs.

I have been on the periphery of the media most of my life. My father, T.J.W. Kenny, was an editor and a disciple of the

1

great C.P. Scott of the *Manchester Guardian*; a sister, Peggy, who married the writer, Walter Macken, was news editor of the *Connacht Tribune*; a brother, Jack, after a colourful career, was editor of the *Waterford News and Star*. My first job was in Radio Eireann; my first job in the Irish Management Institute was as editor of *Management* journal. In more recent years I have written fairly regularly on management and economic matters. I have for seven years been a member of the board of Independent Newspapers PLC.

My father served his apprenticeship with the Hulton newspaper syndicate and, during the Great War, was a correspondent with the British and Belgian Armies. He came from Sheerness to Galway and founded the *Connacht Tribune* and the *Connacht Sentinel*. He died on May 9 1940 when I was ten years old. The *World's Press News* said, "He had that golden gift, a hawklike nose for news". Following his scoop on the landing near Clifden of the transatlantic fliers, Alcock and Brown, he was offered a job by Lord Northcliffe but refused to leave his adopted city. In tributes to him it was said, "He had an uncommon quality among businessmen in Ireland that he never told a lie - or half a lie which is worse".

This book, like its predecessors, makes no judgments. Judgments are for the reader who has, no doubt, definite views about what constitutes bad and good media and who, if the experience of the two previous books is anything to go by, will exercise that judgment with even-handed inequity. Ask your friends for their views on the relative merits of *The Irish Times* and the *Irish Independent* and you will see what I mean.

Like the companion volumes, the conversations took place in the participants' homes or, occasionally, offices. They lasted on average three hours. I have long lost any misgivings about assuring the subjects nothing will be published without their consent. There is always, I suppose, the danger an anodyne script will be returned, the blood rinsed out of it. That has not been my experience: on the contrary, you get a more relaxed and revealing result from the safety of the relationship. I have to pay particular tribute to the participants in this book who exercised saintly restraint with their editorial pencils.

They are all male and range in age from 29 to 55. Their length of service in their present jobs ranges from months to 17 years. Only four studied journalism at third level - the small number probably reflecting the availability of media studies rather than personal preferences.

Ten came from, by Irish definition, middle-class families, eight from working-class families. Kieran Walsh's father was an editor-proprietor, Keith Baker's was an editor, and Hugh Lambert's was a printer. Otherwise there were no family connections with journalism.

The average length of apprenticeship served, i.e. the time between their first job in the media and their appointment to their present job, is 18 years. Keith Baker and Edmund Curran served the longest apprenticeship, 27 years; Tom Collins, Damien Kiberd and Brian Looney the shortest at ten. While several of the longer apprenticeships included editorial positions, the conclusion is this is a job you don't walk into.

The abiding impression is of dedicated professionalism. They have all spent their working lives at their trade - and there is nowhere else they want to be. For the majority of them it goes back to their schooldays: "As far back as I can remember", "As soon as I could read", "The only thing I could think of was newspapers". Many of them ran school or college magazines and most were "good at English". Journalism is, in the quasi-religious sense, a vocation: journalists, like policemen or doctors, are a priesthood. It would not cross their minds to move *outside* the priesthood.

The Irish News, Belfast, Catholic and Nationalist, was edited for a time by Nick Garbutt, a Mancunian from the Dublin *Sunday Tribune*. He is now deputy editor of the *Belfast Telegraph*, a paper seen, despite protestations, as firmly in the Unionist camp. (To complete that set of musical chairs, Tom Collins moved from *The News Letter*, unequivocally Unionist, to the *Irish News*, unequivocally Nationalist.)

That is not to convey the impression that these men are mercenaries - guns for hire, value-free. First, the personalities of their media come through these conversations and are entwined with their own personalities. Secondly, they are clear enough about their values, which they describe almost to a man as liberal: "Liberal, tolerant, a broad church, my values and the paper's are one", "I regard myself as a classical liberal", "*The Sunday Tribune* does reflect my values, hinging around the notion of equality". But Joe Mulholland, in television, admits that, while he would be seen as a liberal, he questions a lot of things. And there is some questioning about the liberalness of the newspapers themselves: "Papers are trying to ram through a social agenda", "Mainstream is not broad church", "There is a hostility to business and to traditional Catholic values". Finally, "We espouse market economics - making money is a good thing".

Several participants are sensitive about the fact they (now) lead middle-class lives - leafy suburbs - and may not therefore be capable of reflecting the needs of the less privileged and the young.

Some are more conscious than others of their readers' values: "What the ordinary person would think, justice and fair play", "While your own values come across and while common sense is the key, you learn from your readers", "Friendship means nothing: our obligations are solely to our readers".

Readers are more than just people who want their prejudices reinforced or who get mad at coat-trailing columnists. They are people who spend up to £260 a year for a daily paper and £62 for a television licence. They are not simply a critical audience, they are the *market*: "We live or die by the market", "The most competitive in the world", "Not the 1000 Dublin 4 people fortifying their own delusions", "If you don't deliver the ABC1 reader you can't sell ads", "Serving the market does not conflict with good journalism - the opposite in fact".

There are different opinions about what constitutes news. Vinnie Doyle says he was advised young was better than old, pretty was better than ugly, TV was better than music, music was better than films, films were better than sport - and anything was better than politics. Michael Brophy says all news is comment.

Content moves along a spectrum. At one end is *news*: *what* happened and *who* did it, conveyed primarily through radio and television: it may not be necessary to read the front page any more. Then there is *analysis*: *how* and *why* things happened and what their consequences might be. Finally, there is *comment*: that is what *I think* about what happened or about the issues of the day and, perhaps, what should be done about them. The distinctions along the spectrum are imperfect. Add to them the constant need to please the market and the picture gets blurred. To illustrate: lay three or four newspapers side by side on a day when there is not an overwhelming story. You will see an interaction between what the editor thinks is important and what the editor thinks his readers think is important. It is his choice but it is hardly a moral one: it is not a stark precedence between truthfulness and deception. It comes nearer the view of an eminent physician: "Far older than the precept, *The truth, the whole truth, and nothing but the truth*, is another that has always been the guide of best physicians: *So far as possible, do no harm.* You can do harm by the process that is quaintly called telling the truth. You can do harm by lying. But try to do as little harm as possible."

Edmund Curran thinks Ireland is well-served by its newspapers. Conor Brady believes they compare favourably with their international counterparts - even the "less serious" newspapers where, despite occasional errors and excesses, there is never conscious distortion. The Irish Press Group in its heyday is seen as the nursery of Dublin journalism. There is sadness about its decline.

The difference between the daily papers and the provincial or regional press is one of intimacy. The editor of a Dublin daily when he is going home is unlikely to meet someone he has just been writing about. When Michael Brophy was working on the *Kilkenny People* he was told by John Kerry Keane that he could not slag the local dramatic society - they were doing their best. John Cunningham sees no point in rehashing the details of suicides when everyone in the parish knows what happened. Brian Looney tells us that, contrary to popular belief, there is no public relations ethos in Kerry - the Tralee Racegoers Supporters Club has a press conference every year and this year no journalist from *The Kerryman* was invited. Kieran Walsh says you are not really dead until your name is in the deaths column of *The Munster Express*.

All the editors are acutely conscious of being the captain of the ship. The best journalists, they believe, do not necessarily make the best editors. Even deputy editors may not make the transition. The editor bears the ultimate responsibility for everything that goes into the paper whether he sees it or not, including the advertisements. The editor's desk is seen as an isolated one.

There is an edgy relationship between the editors and politicians. At best politicians get a reserved respect, at worst, "the highest bollocks in Ireland" - a *Sunday Independent* columnist writing about the Tanaiste, Dick Spring, TD, or "Just a Couple of Bowsies" - a *Sunday World* headline on the Taoiseach, Albert Reynolds, TD and

Desmond O'Malley, TD, then leader of the Progressive Democrats. Politicians are better "trained" for the media - a mixed blessing when what is needed is honesty. When all the political parties complain equally, an editor is sure he is doing a good job.

The "story" that overhangs everything is the conflict in Northern Ireland. There is a lot about it for two reasons: it is the big story, and many of the Southern editors worked in Northern Ireland where the experience had a profound effect on them. Colin McClelland says that coming out of Northern Ireland you go through withdrawal symptoms because the adrenaline of conflict is a drug. The editors' views on the conflict are grim. They were given, as will be clear from the text, before the Major/Reynolds Downing Street Declaration of December 15 1993[*].

The "right to know", a phrase which has never been clearly defined, is the banner of the Fourth Estate. In theory, every decision and the causes and motives behind it ought to be within the knowledge of the public. In practice, this can be extended beyond reason. There may, for example, be nothing more than differences of opinion on the merits of options needing further study: these differences can be whipped up to incite paralysing controversy. Yet out of the welter of justified and unjustified "information", perhaps a rude justice does emerge. Sooner or later the public arrives at a judgment.

The biggest stone in the editorial shoe is the libel laws. They are the greatest restriction on the editors' ability to transmit information. (Chunks of this book were excised lest they bring expensive retribution.) The media cannot win a libel action. They can either lose or not lose and, even if they do not lose, they will be substantially out of pocket. It is easier and cheaper to settle even if it involves unblushing untruths and farcical apologies.

[*] See Epilogue.

The libel laws inhibit useful muckraking - the exposure of fraud and parasites. I do not believe, however, the media have the right to prise open people's private lives: it was Beelzebub, Lord of the Flies, who went about lifting the roofs off people's houses. The media must be kept in check and the law of libel should be weighted against them, but not so outrageously as at present. The defence of *qualified privilege*, as suggested by Vincent Browne, should be open to them.

When a concerned churchman asked Aidan Pender, the then editor of a changing *Irish Independent*, what he was trying to do to the paper, the answer was, "Sell it, Your Grace". Several editors refer to their newspaper as "the product". *The Irish Times*, controlled by a Trust, "a charter for excellence", and the *Sunday World*, "a print annex to television", each in their own way have to respond to a changing market place.

Joe Mulholland talks about the competition RTE faces: 20 channels, soon 40, soon 100. The newspapers, on the other hand, with the exception of the Press Group, have shown a significant stability, illustrated by Liam Igoe of Goodbody Stockbrokers. A table from his research is reproduced here. It is worth studying: it gives a map of the territory. It covers all the papers sold in the Irish Republic over a ten-year span. (It does not cover the four-year-old *Sunday Business Post* whose story is told in Chapter 3.) A UK predator would think hard before taking on the Irish market: not remarkable if newspapers really are a nation talking to itself - an English newspaper is not a substitute for an Irish newspaper. Indigenous established newspapers that continually identify their market, that are well-managed and well-edited (two different things), will survive competition. They can never be invulnerable but English newspapers are more likely to continue to nibble at them than to bite. In any event, blaming the market place for one's own failure of anticipation is hardly heroic: you can't steer a ship by the wake.

Circulation of Newspapers in the Irish Republic - Average Copies Per Issue

	1983	1987	1988	1989	1990	1991	1992
Irish Dailies							
Irish Times	86146	88739	86337	91885	94929	94062	92797
Independent	165768	151150	154296	152513	154234	151367	149065
Press	94295	79235	79108	63904	60287	58741	50443
Cork Ex	63560	58509	57713	58002	57237	56224	55516
Star	0	47125	81169	73992	79248	79711	85154
Irish Total	409769	424758	458623	440296	445935	440105	432975
UK Dailies							
Mirror	47230	75800	58000	62000	61500	58423	56295
Sun	*	26795	26500	26000	30000	25250	31355
Mail	5396	3645	3500	3300	2610	3400	3138
Express	*	6603	3000	4400	4660	3500	4288
Telegraph	2747	3196	2500	2500	3100	2792	3054
Today	*	4850	2500	2900	3300	2750	1673
Times	4200	960	2000	1900	2100	1593	1550
Guardian	*	1400	1000	1000	1390	1325	1675
Independent	*	*	800	1200	1540	2167	1750
UK Total	59573	123249	99800	105200	110200	101200	104778
UK Share	12.69	22.49	17.87	19.29	19.82	18.70	19.48
Evenings							
Press	145031	125292	117441	105196	92246	80507	69567
Herald	118616	110015	115514	104505	96838	98288	95075
Cork Ev Echo	38401	33582	32866	32048	30022	28764	28784
Irish Sundays							
Press	319105	257461	240987	215814	207162	200571	179923
Independent	249021	222361	236299	223683	235221	236543	247198
Tribune	103000	96660	96905	96911	101100	90343	90034
Sunday World	343639	366806	361905	346757	330300	313183	301528
Total Irish	1014765	943288	936096	883165	873783	840640	818683
UK Sundays							
Mirror	74270	76350	63500	70200	65400	64018	63090
People	76840	88025	69000	82000	79100	67703	62245
News of World	155000	177400	175000	171000	155500	160000	149076
Express	41000	27250	62000	21000	19640	18500	18007
Mail	*	*	*	19000	14900	14700	13885
Times	26000	21850	17000	27000	30600	30134	40000
Observer	11000	13098	9000	12000	11930	10287	15000
Telegraph	8036	7675	6000	5500	5500	2806	5000
Ind on Sunday	*	*	*	*	6330	6282	8000
Total UK	392146	411648	401500	407700	388900	374430	374303
UK Share	27.87	30.38	30.02	31.58	30.80	30.82	31.38

* Figures not available

Januslike, the media face two ways: telling the truth and pleasing their market. There is no getting away from that duality. It will not be denied by lofty arguments about journalistic standards, or taste, or vulgarity - that is simply to shift the argument onto other ground and, in any event, what are my standards may not be yours.

Are there then no absolutes? The answer from what these men say would seem to be: very few. The boundaries are shifting and slippery.

You could take a guideline from Francis Bacon: *It is a pleasure to stand upon the shore, and to see ships tost upon the sea: a pleasure to stand in the window of a castle, and to see a battle and the adventures thereof below: but no pleasure is comparable to the standing upon the vantage ground of truth (a hill not be be commanded, and where the air is always clear and serene), and to see the errors, and wanderings, and mists, and tempests, in the vale below: so always that this prospect be with pity, and not with swelling or pride. Certainly it is heaven upon earth, to have a man's mind move in charity, rest in providence, and turn upon the poles of truth.*

Or, more likely, you could take a guideline from the *obiter dicta* of the late Frank Sherwin TD: *Like everything else, nothing is perfect.*

Plato, among others, regarded democracy as a chaotic and unruly form of government. We are a democracy, with our share of chaos and unruliness, because we believe in our right to govern ourselves. We share a belief in the essential equality of all men. This notion derived from the Judaeo-Christian concept of all men being equal before God. It was transferred from religion to politics mainly by Rousseau. In it is a strong concept of individual freedom and rights. It is a system that works when there is a balance of power.

The media in Ireland play their part in keeping that balance. They make mistakes like the rest of us. They serve God and mammon. They are impure and imperfect. By and large they serve us well.

Woodview
University College
Dublin 4
December 24 1993

1

Vinnie Doyle

Irish Independent

*When it's going right, it's like drinking champagne all day -
the most satisfying job in the world.*

The conversation took place on August 3 1993

Vinnie Doyle is editor of the *Irish Independent.*

He was born in Dublin February 9 1938.

His father was Ned Doyle, a labourer.

His mother was Kathleen Harris, a housewife.

He is an only child.

He is married to Gertrude Leech, a housewife.

They have three children: Garret (28), Conor (27) and Vincent (11).

He was educated at the Christian Brothers School, St. Vincent's, in Glasnevin, Dublin, both primary and secondary.

He joined the *Irish Press* in 1958/59, worked first in the library, then became a copy-boy. In 1962, went to *The Sunday Press* to run the show business page, then on to the first colour magazine produced by the *Sunday Independent* and stayed with it for its nine months' existence: then was sacked. 1964 freelance for *The Evening Herald* and with the British *Sun.* 1967 sub-editor on *The Evening Herald.* 1970 assistant editor of the *Irish Independent.* 1973 night editor. 1977 editor of *The Evening Herald.* 1981 editor of the *Irish Independent.*

His hobbies are reading, walking and the job.

I never knew my father - he died when I was five. I have just fleeting memories of him. I was born between the two canals in a place called Fontenoy Street. The late 40s and early 50s were difficult times in Dublin and we were poor. My mother was a housewife up to the time my father died. She tried dress-making, at which she was quite talented, but she did not have enough in herself. Entrepreneurial spirits were not thick on the ground in those days. So, coming from an acutely poor background, she did what she considered the best thing to keep body and soul together, she went out as a cleaner. I went to a primary school in Glasnevin which drew to itself a lot of the middle-class youngsters in that area. The difference between poor working-class and comfortable middle-class was astounding. There were things they did not have to do. I would have to go to a local turf depot and bring free turf home on a hand-cart - we had no other way of heating our house. That was no big deal but it does take on a significance when you see your school pals wheeling by on new Raleigh bicycles, something you could never aspire to. There were just the two of us, my mother and me, and the skimping we did to put me through secondary school was unbelievable. I rarely had new clothes. She made huge sacrifices - the school fees by today's standards were modest but they were a formidable target for her to meet. She put me into an altar-boys' society composed mostly of middle-class kids. One summer there was to be a two-week holiday in Wexford to which we were asked to contribute £6. There wasn't a prayer that she or I could meet that.

Against that background I attended secondary school, failed my Inter Cert, continued, did all right in my Leaving Cert, and then went out into the jobs market. A conviction - wrong as it turned out - that I would some day write full-time for a living and a passion for books enabled me to avoid a lot of the dead-end jobs. Then I struck lucky and landed a job in the library of the *Irish Press* under a saintly man, Aongus O Dalaigh, a brother of the late President O Dalaigh. He steered me through the clippings in the general direction of newspapers. I did not need much steering. In those days, the library had a glass window and you could look down over the case room - it was five or six years after the start-up of the *Evening Press* and the pace was frenetic. Instinctively I knew I was in the right place -I wanted to stay there.

Even in those days I saved what I could to buy the scripts of plays of John Osborne and Arnold Wesker but more than anything my early journalistic markers were set down by a remarkable and brilliantly edited American monthly magazine called *Esquire*. The golden decades were the 50s and 60s. The editor, Arnold Gingrich, assembled journalist-writers like Norman Mailer, Gay Talese, Tom Wolfe and Truman Capote - new journalism at its finest.

In the six months I was in the library, I would badger the sports department to do small markings like hockey reports at the weekend. A vacancy for a copy-boy on the *Irish Press* came up and I got it. I was absolutely chuffed. The *Irish Press* was not a robust paper - it had its difficulties even in those days, but it was a great training ground. The Irish Press Group is probably one of the great nurseries of Dublin journalism. My aspiration was that some day I would be allowed to sit down and edit copy. I never even thought about becoming a reporter. There was a certain romanticism about the subs, a certain air of "we run the show" and a definite distaste for even the best of reporters. Canon fodder they called them. There was even a real, live, published author on the desk, Seamus de Faoite, who wrote such classic short stories as "American Apples" and "Moon Road Home" for the Oxford University Press. If you really wanted to see greatness, writer Ben Kiely was only one flight of stairs above. This was for me. After a year keeping my nose clean as a copy-boy, they had a vacancy for a junior sub. I was called into the editor's office on Friday afternoon - Joe Walsh told me I had the job and, a perceptive man, said there was no point in going back to the desk at that hour of the day, I should go out and celebrate. I remember walking down the Quays and up O'Connell Street. It was twenty-to-six and people were streaming out of their offices. I wanted to shout at them, "Look at me! Look at me! I am a sub-editor!" It was probably a desire to escape from grinding poverty, from the lack of money to do what most teenagers were doing. I was 19 then. I stayed with the *Irish Press* for two-and-a-half years and was extremely happy. They were kind and tolerant. For eight or nine months they would give you little scraps to do, fillers. They would come back to you and say, "Look, that's not the way to do that. Try it another way."

If you're handed a story, and you're nervous, the story tends to dominate you. You don't know how to handle it, what to cut out. In the end, you find yourself knowing instinctively what to do with a story. I was so enthusiastic that, when my shift ended, I would wait until the senior subs, the chaps who did the splash stories on page one, had gone home. In those days, there were no computers - it was all hard copy. Any copy that was unwanted was put on a metal spike. The spiked copy was supposed to be kept for six months in case of a libel action. Breaking all the rules, I would put some of the spiked copy in my pocket, bring it home along with the first edition of the paper and compare their stories with what they had cut. I saw instantly the kind of copy that should never make it into the paper.

As I became more competent I felt there were other things I could do. *The Sunday Press* wanted somebody to run their show business page. You had to get a show business story each week, you had film reviews and you had to do the big theatre openings. I don't know what prompted me but I applied for and got it. I also gravitated towards the production end of the paper and became interested in layouts. There was a brilliant production editor on *The Sunday Press* at the time, Willie Collins, who taught me everything I know about production subbing. He had endless patience with me. The trouble was the better you got, the more they handed you. I had an horrific Saturday schedule. I would go into the office at ten o'clock having been there until one o'clock the previous morning doing film reviews. I would then go down and see the show page off the stone, make all the cuts and look after the pictures, go back up and do some production subbing and layout until four or five o'clock. I also had a City Diary to do. I'd go out and cover functions and come back in at nine o'clock, write the diary until 11.20, then run round to Mulligans for the last ten minutes to get a pint. I would come back, stone-in the diary and stay on the city edition until 3 a.m. Was that exploitation? People cynically said to me you could not buy that kind of experience - and, in truth, they were right. By the time I was finished, I was an all-rounder - I could do news reporting, production editing, layouts, theatre criticism, whatever.

The *Sunday Independent* made a spectacular move against *The Sunday Press*. They launched in 1963 the country's first colour magazine. Austin Walsh, the production features editor in *The Sunday Press*, went over to edit it. He rang me to ask would I join him. I felt I owed *The Press* a lot but, nevertheless, here was an opportunity to get in on something new - colour. It was a whole new ball-game, inspired by the success of *The Sunday Times* magazine. The difference between us and *The Sunday Times* was that we did not have their deep pocket to maintain the magazine. There was really no demand for newspaper colour in those days, it was not on TV and the advertisers didn't want it. It was successful for the first two or three weeks - we went ahead of *The Sunday Press*, then it fell back drastically. It lasted nine months. It had been the brainchild of Eddie Murphy, who was a member of the family of the original owners of the *Independent,* but we had lost £0.75m, considerable money in the early sixties. Austin Walsh came to me one day and said, "This is our last issue. I'll do the best I can for you." There just wasn't another job. Bartle Pitcher, the managing director, called me into his office and said, "I've no option but to say that you're sacked. What are you going to do?" My wife was six months pregnant with our first child. I told Bartle I did not know what I was going to do and he suggested I see some of the other editors and I knew he would have done a little lobbying on my behalf. We went off for the weekend to my wife's place in Kinvara and thought about things. I wondered if there was any possibility of getting my old job back in *The Sunday Press* but newspapers have their vanity like anybody else and, if you leave them, they are not too quick to take you back. I rang the evening paper editor, Aidan Pender, whom I knew slightly, and asked him if I could have a few shifts subbing on *The Evening Herald*. I had never done any evening paper subbing and to an extent was chancing my arm. I had worked mainly as a production sub-editor on *The Sunday Press* where there was a reasonable amount of time to edit copy, but evening papers are very, very fast. Things were extremely tight in Dublin for freelance work at that time. There were five of us competing for three shifts a week. Instead of organising a roster, they would put five matches in a box and whoever took out the longest match was not going to get a shift - this happened to me three times in a row. I had the rent to pay, my wife was pregnant, and there was no money coming in. I got a little work from *The Sun* in its pre-Murdoch days, just re-launched, and this enabled me to keep my head above water.

I had been getting one or two regular shifts from *The Evening Herald* when I wrote a long letter to Aidan Pender saying how I thought things there might be improved. A staff job came up in 1966 and I got it. I was put in charge of the foreign file which I found enthralling. Although there was a massive amount of work in it, the copy was clean and literate. The biggest story that came across my desk then was the landing of men on the moon. I stayed up most of the night to watch the television coverage. There was a friend of mine on the *Evening Press* doing the same story and I badly wanted us to do a better job. I took notes of the television and radio coverage during the night and came into the office at six o'clock that morning. Together with the foreign copy, I had a fairly extensive file and wrote what I felt was a good story, which hopefully captured the moment. It was not to be. The editor came in and told me the story had been overtaken by television - what we wanted to know was, now that the astronauts were on the moon, could they get back. I argued and argued but we came out with the headline, "Can They Get

Back?". The *Evening Press* came out with a marvellous story and heading, "The Moon - It's a Walkover". They left us standing. Aidan and I became good friends and when he got the appointment as editor of the *Irish Independent* he took me with him as assistant editor. That's how I ended up on the *Irish Independent* - the year was 1970.

The *Independent* was the intimidating flagship of the Group. A powerful paper, steeped in tradition and staffed by righteous men, many of whom were slaves to what had been Politically Correct in the 50s. Pender understood the then first iron law of our trade - what sells newspapers is news. Once in the chair he halted the circulation slide and began increasing sales. It was an extremely difficult job for him trying to move a paper which had become lifeless, without flair or style. He insisted on the paper resting in the middle market, a sort of Irish *Daily Mail*, and that is what we delivered for him. In the end it was a huge success, clocking up a circulation of 189,000. It was a personal triumph for Pender, a fitting end to a spectacular career.

In 1973 I became night editor of the *Irish Independent* - responsible for the night-to-night running of the paper. Outside of the fun and the learning curve, my three years in that position left me with some vivid memories, the nicest was having the chance to work with the most gifted person I have known, the then chief sub of the paper, Niall Hanley, who went on to become editor of the *Herald* before he died so tragically in the Bordeaux wine race air crash.

The biggest story I ever worked on? The 1974 Dublin bombings. The story has been well documented but mine is a short aside on what it was like being home alone on the big night, the editor on holidays and his deputy on leave. The first I knew of the tragedy was when the bomb in Talbot Street shattered the windows of the *Independent* building in Abbey Street. When I picked myself up off the ground my first thought was where in the name of God am I going to get extra staff on a Friday evening? The local? I rushed down and sure enough found five or six reporters there and also a talented woman feature writer with the Group. The reporters were coming back anyway so I went up and asked if she would go down Talbot Street, "Don't think about news, don't try to count the dead, just give me your impressions of what you see. It's going to be a huge story." She turned around and looked at me and said, "I'm sorry. I've got a date." And walked away. She never worked for me again. Worse - the *Irish Press* beat us on the story.

I went over to *The Herald* in 1977 as editor. The country had been through a severe recession in the mid-70s and *The Herald* had suffered enormously. The concentration in the Group had been on the daily and the Sunday. Consequently, resources were put into those papers only if it was felt they would generate revenue. Unfortunately, the flagship of the Press Group in those days was the *Evening Press*. It was powering away with six to ten pages of small ads to *The Herald's* two. The *Evening Press* was one of the most successful publishing ventures in the last two decades, it and *The Sunday World*. While the *Evening Press* had a circulation of 170,000, *The Herald* looked as if it might go under the 100,000. My first reaction on being given the job was terror. One was cushioned to a degree on the daily - we had resources and manpower, whereas, on *The Herald*, it was a scramble to get staff and a decent budget. I used to walk around among the subs, racked with doubt, wondering if the whole thing was going to go down the tubes. During my first year as editor I was at the annual Independent Group conference held that year in Killarney, attended by the Group's editors, together with financial and marketing managers from Ireland and around the world and chaired by Tony O'Reilly. I was addressing the conference, desperately trying to explain the urgent need for funds. I had a pen in my hand and I banged it down on the table in front of Tony and said, "Look, I believe in *The Herald*. It's a question of whether you believe in it or not. If you do, you'll have to give us some resources." Tony came over to me at the coffee-break, said that he was impressed by my commitment, what I had said seemed to come from the heart, and they had decided to pursue an expansion policy on

The Herald.

Some days later, I was standing with a bunch of the subs and execs in *The Herald* newsroom and someone told a funny story. I burst out laughing. When I walked away I realised it was the first time I had laughed on *The Herald* for months. Gradually we stopped the slide and even began to claw back some money. There was disappointment after disappointment but, in the end, we turned it round. I had brought a couple of people in and we put some vitality into it but we did not have any real marketing strategy. The guy who gave us that push was Joe Hayes[*]. He came in as marketing manager which is what he had been with the cigarette company, Gallaher's. We struck up a warm personal friendship. Joe is about ten years younger than me and I thought I would have difficulty working with him. He did not know anything about newspapers but he had an unerring instinct for marketing. He believed in spending a pound to make a pound. He came to us in 1978. Our relationship has been not without its traumas. I resigned once as editor of *The Herald* and twice as the editor of the daily. The last time I left it a bit close to call. I resigned at ten o'clock in the morning and it wasn't until ten-to-one that Joe came into my office and said, "Listen, you'd better come out to lunch!"

With the market research we were able to see where we were going wrong and where we should direct our editorial power. *The Herald* had always been a working-class paper. It was difficult to get it out of that groove. When I left *The Herald* it was up around 128,000 and going strong - but the *Evening Press* was still streets ahead. There was a good 50,000 between us, though we were pulling back. Both Joe and I knew that, no matter what we did, we were going to be a me-too *Evening Press*. We tried all sorts of gimmicks, attention-grabbers. We asked, "How Slow is the Mail?" and we got a chap dressed as Dick Turpin to deliver a letter to Mullingar while at the same time we put one in the post. The horse won. We both knew we had to take a quantum leap, something new, exciting and fresh. In other words, we said *The Herald* would have to go tabloid. The *Evening Press* was broadsheet as it is now. *The Herald*

[*]   See Epilogue.

would not be the first tabloid evening paper in Ireland - there had been *The Mail* before it and it had failed. We had agreed we could not go tabloid until we had established *The Evening Herald* first as a good broadsheet. We decided to put a new typeface on the paper and a new seal or masthead. We sat for ages talking about the masthead. Eventually we had so many of them we picked one almost at random. Joe Hayes and I could not wait to see what the reaction on the street would be to the new paper. When the first edition came out we walked up O'Connell Street as far as the Parnell Monument. Nobody was queueing up for *The Herald*, or for the *Evening Press* for that matter. We went over to a street-seller who had a lot of *Evening Presses* and a not inconsiderable amount of *Evening Heralds* - we had pushed up the print number. I asked him, "How's it going?" "All right." "Notice anything different about *The Herald*?" I said hopefully. "Not much, a fuckin' brutal front page, but." We turned around and walked away. It was one of those awful flat days.

In the event, it was sufficiently successful to build a base from which we could launch the tabloid. I did a few dummies but the finished product was the sole concept of Niall Hanley and it was a runaway success. The small ads came over in droves, the ABC1 readership grew each year and it was well on its way to overtaking the *Evening Press*. Then, as I mentioned, Niall Hanley tragically died in the air crash. The next editor in was Michael Brophy who is currently making a resounding success of *The Star*.[*] He continued, and even stepped up, Hanley's momentum which eventually helped its present editor, Michael Denieffe, to roll it past the *Evening Press*, where he looks likely to keep it.

In 1981 I achieved a lifelong ambition - I became editor of the *Irish Independent* which was now suffering from being out of touch with the new liberalism which had been growing in influence since the late 60s and early 70s.

When I was in my mid-20s any friends I had believed in divorce, pre-marital sex and birth control. When I was 35 my beliefs hadn't changed to any great degree. But there was this

[*] See Epilogue.

huge generation thing coming behind us again, and if we were not aware of that, in ten years we would have nobody to sell newspapers to. We took a considerable amount of flak for changing the tone of the paper. We also felt it had got too sensational. We became absolute sticklers for accuracy. The foreign coverage had been skimpy. There was no news analysis. It became increasingly clear more and more people were taking their news from the radio in their car, in the kitchen, or from television. We felt the only way we could combat this was to take a more analytical approach to news. We put in a new news analysis section. It's only in the last year we have had the resources to develop the business pages to the extent that we could not only compete with, but outperform, *The Irish Times.* It's too early yet to isolate the effect they've had on the paper, but the feedback we're getting is terrific - we are also taking in *The Daily Telegraph*, the London *Times* and the *Daily Mail* services. Those developments have secured our position and ended the huge circulation gains *The Irish Times* made in the 80s. That all stopped in the 90s: they came into the 90s with marginal gains and since then have had marginal drops. It will, of course, cost us another considerable effort to start increasing our circulation from where it is now. There are at least three or four gears left in us whereas I think *The Irish Times* have shot their bolt. Not only are they carrying losses in 1993 of £700,000 but they are grossly overmanned editorially. Their operation has become part of the culture of cosiness - never could it be said about them that their worst nightmare would be coming out second-best in the morning.

What is news? It's ephemeral - you can't put it in a refrigerator and hold it there until you let it out. The only thing worse than yesterday's news is the news of the day before. There is no easy definition of news. The old cliché is true that it is easier to edit a paper on a big night when one or two stories are breaking than in the middle of August when nothing is happening. Yet, you are always trying to draw back from over-selling - it is the kiss of death to hype news which is not worth it or, worse still, is inaccurate. There is nothing more frustrating to the reader than a huge headline which is not substantiated. If, in advertising, you over-hype the newspaper, it is a real let-down for the reader who has spent his 80p or 85p only to find the hype in the ad does not match the reality in the newspaper.

Dick Stolley, the founding editor of *People* magazine once told me that if ever I had any doubts on what to put between the sheets I could try this formula: young is better than old, pretty is better than ugly, TV is better than music, music is better than films, films are better than sports - and anything is better than politics. That sat very well on me as an apolitical journalist.

I was always a hands-on editor - I got involved in the nuts and bolts of the production. Consequently, I was never a great socialising editor and therefore have a limited personal knowledge of the political leaders of the day: Charlie Haughey I would have met perhaps a dozen times. I had a tremendous regard for him - he was my favourite politician. He had about him a whiff of arrogance, one was influenced by his sense of power, the sense that he was a hugely successful player in a difficult game. I often got depressed at the level of criticism of Charlie Haughey in the *Irish Independent* - we used to bend over backwards to try to balance it by giving him photo-opportunities and to try to emphasise the positive side of his intentions, to balance the comments of our columnists. But if you hire somebody like Conor Cruise-O'Brien or Bruce Arnold, who were ultra-critical of Haughey, you have got to give them their say - you hire them for their views and their writing. If you are going to muzzle them, you might as well not hire them. Coming up to a recent election, the Cruiser had two scathing attacks on Haughey, bordering on the personal and definitely on the vindictive. In the middle of the last week I rang him and said, "Conor, I think enough is enough. If you cannot do a positive piece on Charlie Haughey, which I am sure you can't, can you pick another subject? If that does not appeal to you, why not take the week off". Conor said that he would let me know which, of course, he never did. He just sent in his column, which was a scathing attack, mark three. I spiked it. We put in something else and the following day Conor rang me at home and said, "Vinny, I'm deeply disappointed you spiked my column." I said, "Conor, I told you enough was enough - you were not being fair to Haughey, particularly on the last week before the election." Conor said, "I'm sending the column you spiked to *The Sunday Tribune.* Is that all right with you?" I told him no way was that all right with me, he would be breaking his contract and we would probably sue him. In the end, he sent the column to *The Sunday Tribune* who, with great delight, used it.

I admired Charlie Haughey's courage, his wit and style - and his absolute cunning. Michael Brophy and I were at President Mary Robinson's inauguration in Dublin Castle. We did not want to get involved and we stood back behind a line of guests so that, when the President took her leave, we could skip out quietly. Charlie passed by with his entourage, he was going to do some other business in the Castle. He looked around and saw Michael and myself. He cut through lines of guests and catering people to shake hands with us. Of course he did it with an eye to the main chance but he did it with such style - we were impressed.

He used to come down to the *Independent* for the occasional lunch. The lunches were peaceful enough but they were never quite happy - you could always tell he was on edge with the paper. He was upset because it would not give him any outright support. I had made up my mind early on when I became editor the best way for the paper, which had been aligned with the Fine Gael party, was for it to be as apolitical as I was myself. We would not give our support to any one particular party but we would support a good leader with good ideas, or a good coalition with good ideas. Once, when Charlie was in opposition, we had barely sat down to lunch when the hooded eyes looked across the table and he said, "I can't for the life of me understand why, when you are writing headlines, I'm always *Haughey* and FitzGerald is always *Garret.*" Our style of layout is a three-column headline. I said, "Deputy Haughey, you try putting *FitzGerald* in there - count the letters. It won't go, but *Haughey* goes perfectly. That's the only reason." He said, "I don't . . . believe you, but that takes the biscuit!" He was capable of being slightly vindictive. We once ran a picture of Kinsealy taken from an aircraft. It's a spectacular mansion. He was extremely upset and protested to Tony O'Reilly that we were setting him up for potential IRA or UVF hits - to which I could only reply the IRA were hardly dependent on us for information about Kinsealy. Other than that, we had a fairly reasonable relationship. When he retired, he sent me a message via a third party, "Tell him he wasn't the . . . worst". I don't know whether that's a seal of approval or a grudging return of the sword to the scabbard.

It's impossible to develop a long-term friendship with a senior politician or minister or opposition spokesman. You always know that there is going to come a time when you will be ferociously critical of them. A case in point was Brian Lenihan. I have met him only four or five times but I found him an extremely nice man - you could sit there and listen to him talking for hours. During the Presidential election, when he committed the awful "mature recollection" faux pas, we ran a comment piece across page one of the paper saying that he would not be a fit person to hold the office. I was upset that we had to do it but I knew it was the right thing to do. If you get too close to politicians or indeed to business people, you find it's impossible to take a detached view when circumstances demand it.

The bane of my life as an editor has been the draconian libel laws in this country. There has been an increasing clamour for a press council and for the range of codes that would come from it. I feel the paper is being strangled by gagging writs and by what is now becoming the galloping greed of the legal profession. There has been a huge surge in litigation. At a lunch recently, I was told *The Irish Times* libel bill was £1m - ours would have been about three-quarters of that for the three papers. I presume *The Irish Times* paid it out to protect its image, to avoid being dragged to the courts 50 times a year, or to be seen as a paper that's constantly making mistakes. We have got to the stage that we regard it as a victory where the other party have simply got to pay their costs - it costs us £10,000 a day to go to court. When we go into court, the jury does not see the editor in the dock, they see Tony O'Reilly, mega-money. The standing of journalists is so low in our society that juries find it difficult to evaluate realistically a set of damages. We once examined in detail the composition of a jury in a libel case in which we were involved. After the case we asked them how they arrived at the £40,000 damages awarded against us. They told us they set a figure between £10,000 and £100,000 - they simply picked a random figure in between. Some of the British papers are awash with lies and cruelty and deserve to be punished but, here, libel cases have become a lottery or a blood sport, rich pickings for winners. A casual remark in a newspaper or magazine and a lawyer will claim that his client's reputation has been irretrievably damaged. You would have to ask yourself, do these libels really damage reputations? Do people lose their jobs, their incomes, their friends? When the law becomes a lottery, it falls into disrepute. The time has come when judges should be the arbitrators of what damages should be awarded. It is my considered opinion after 30 years in the business that juries do not have the intellectual capacity to evaluate a complex set of issues.

The future? I see a very positive country, a country that has a great entrepreneurial spirit. I feel more than ever we are establishing ourselves as Europeans with a wonderful set of values. Unfortunately we have no riches like gold or coal - but our educated youth is our new raw material. We have never produced so many well-educated young people. In the 40s and 50s you were forced to emigrate with, if you were lucky, an Inter or Leaving Cert. If or when people have to emigrate now, at least they do so with tremendous skills - they are computer-literate, with master's degrees in business. Even the Northern problem does not lessen my optimism. We are one of the last outposts in Europe with a great set of moral values and a great work ethic. Aside from the occasional business scandal, when you compare us to Japan or to Italy, we are not anything like as corrupt or morally deficient as they seem to be. I am very hopeful. I'd love to be back in my 20s - I don't think I'd have done anything else - but I'd love to be back with the technological changes and the unique advantages they bring to my business.

But now that I am here, how could I have ever arrived without the stimulus of a great companion, Gertie? She always believed in me, was forever the support that saw me through the bad days, even though sometimes she felt our marriage was playing second fiddle to my job. Despite the pressure, we have survived together for 30 years during which she became my wife, my lover, my best friend.

What are the rewards for editing the biggest morning paper in the country? The only real reward is the pleasure of the task itself - that ultimately it was better to have been an editor than not to have been one. You need tenacity, energy, commitment and above all, resilience. You need to live, eat and drink newspapers all day long. When it's going right, it's like drinking champagne all day long - the most satisfying job in the world.

You ask me if I've left behind the little boy pushing the turf cart while he watched his friends on their Raleigh bicycles. No, how could I? But, the fact that from these disadvantages I was able to compete successfully, has left me content. I don't need riches or the trappings of power. I am happy with a nice but small home, a reasonable car, enough to pay the bills, to get around and enjoy a reasonable lifestyle. I am still extremely competitive, the need to achieve is still strong. Journalism has been very good to me but it was Churchill who said that journalism is a young man's game - you should be out of it by 40. Andreas Whittam Smith, the founding editor of the London *Independent*, refused to have anyone on his paper over 40. Now, at my age, I think it is probably an unpardonable vanity to be telling 24-year-olds what they should read. There should be something else to do. When I was in the honours English Leaving Cert class in school, there was a terrific

English teacher called Keane. He was not too impressed with my efforts to join the honours class and had said so to me once or twice but I insisted. He was a Kerryman. About two weeks coming up to the exam, I was sitting in the middle of the class and he asked me to address the relevance of Banquo to Macbeth. I wittered on through ten stumbling minutes and, at the end of it, he looked at me sardonically and said, "Well, Doyle, I'll tell you dis: if you're ever hanged for your knowledge of English, dey'll have hanged an innocent man. You are going to have great difficulty in amounting to something." Ever heedful of that good teacher, and probably driven by vanity and fear of failure, I hopefully did amount to something in the trade. It would be no disgrace to have said of me that I mastered my craft, reaped some of the rewards, and had a little fun on the way.

2

Tom Collins

The Irish News

I would have problems with describing The Irish News as a Catholic
paper because theologically the newspaper is an inanimate object.
You can't baptise a newspaper into a church.   The Irish News is a
Nationalist newspaper read mainly but not exclusively by Catholics.

The conversation took place on September 20 1993

Tom Collins is editor of *The Irish News.*

He was born in Birmingham on August 12 1959.

His father is Stephen Collins, a security man.

His mother is Mary Eithne Breen, a housewife.

He is the eldest in a family of three, one brother, Stephen, and one sister, Annette.

He is married to Maureen Dugan, an administrator in the University of Ulster at Jordanstown.

He was educated at Highfield Primary School, Birmingham; Tanaughmore Primary School, Lurgan; St. Colman's College, Violet Hill, Newry; New University of Ulster at Coleraine (media studies); City University, London (journalism).

1983 *Carrickfergus Advertiser* and *East Antrim Gazette* as a junior reporter; 1984 editor; 1985 *The News Letter* deputy chief sub-editor; 1987 chief sub-editor; 1990 deputy editor of *The Irish News*; 1993 editor of *The Irish News.*

He is also a music critic (largely unpaid) and a director of the Contemporary Music Centre in Dublin which encourages new Irish music.

His hobby is almost exclusively music and he is besotted by opera.

For me it goes back as far as I can remember. I was making small newspapers and selling them in the school-ground at primary school. At secondary school, I brought out class newspapers to celebrate sporting events. That was when my interest in the media crystallised and, against considerable opposition both from the school and from my family, I opted for a media studies course at Coleraine. This was in 1978 when media studies were barely out of the egg. The course in Coleraine was the first in these islands, as we like to call them. The course took in every aspect of the media: television, press, radio - and sociology right through to aesthetics. At that time Coleraine University was a sore point for Nationalists who felt it should have gone to Derry and I was from a traditional Catholic family - my father had come from Limerick. My school environment had been entirely Irish Nationalist - if we were going to see plays on the school curriculum, we went to Dublin rather than to Belfast. The 1916 Proclamation was on the school wall. For the first three years that I was there, English games were banned - playing soccer was a caneable offence. The school had been a diocesan seminary and was run by eight or nine priests together with lay-teachers. I was Head Boy in my final year, very much against the grain because the position normally went to the best footballer and I did not know one side of a ball from the other. It didn't handicap me writing about Gaelic matches for the school magazine. My decision to go to Coleraine did not go down well. The headmaster said to me, "I don't want a Head Boy of mine going to a dump like Coleraine". My mother was not enthusiastic because she saw it as an untried course. I decided the best thing to do was to make my own mistakes. That was my baptism in the media.

The course was interesting. There were television and radio studios and portable cameras, there wasn't much press in it. In my final two years I was press officer for the student union and launched a student newspaper called *Scribe*. It gave me my first experience of deadlines, of trying to get the paper to the printers on time.

The course looked at media history, particularly the use of propaganda by both sides in the Second World War. We saw all the old Eisenstein films - I still love that kind of cinema -right through to British social realism, kitchen sink drama of the 60s and 70s. I didn't do too well in aesthetics, dry philosophy, I preferred running around with the Sony portable camera. We made short films - I did an adaptation of a story by Kate Cruise-O'Brien called "Henry Died". When I look back on it, it was grotesque, no sense of pace, it ran through every possible emotion in nine minutes. In our final year, John Short, who was a sub-editor on the *Guardian*, joined the staff. He regaled us with stories of bias in the press. It's funny to look back on studying bias academically. In a busy newspaper office, against deadlines, the last thing you're concerned about is bias, the first thing you're concerned about is getting something down on the page.

When the course ended, I stayed on the dole in Coleraine for a year working in bars and that. I was keen to do a post-graduate course in journalism, but I applied for jobs too. I was always good at getting shortlisted and bad at getting the job. I applied to the *Belfast Telegraph* for its graduate-trainee scheme and I was the only person educated in Northern Ireland who got to the final board. Roy Lilley and Ed Curran, then respectively editor and deputy editor, interviewed me. It was quite an ordeal and I did not get the job. Two or three times I reached the final boards for BBC traineeships - they were UK-wide and gruelling one-day experiences in London. I did not get those either, so I was not destined for broadcasting.

Anyway, after the year, I got a position on the post-graduate course in journalism at City University, London. With considerable trouble I managed to get a grant for it. I got it on a Monday, the course began on Tuesday, so I threw my things in a suitcase and took a plane to London.

I had met my wife in Coleraine - she was a communications studies student a year below me. She told me that, in order to get a little closer to me, she had decided to join the student newspaper of which I was editor. My first words to her were,

"Can you type?" Her first words to me were, "No". It's been that way ever since.

In the early 80s, journalism studies in London were in their infancy. I had not done much academic work in Coleraine - I always tend to work to deadlines. I had found at school that you did well if you argued a position opposite to the norm. If I was writing about Mary Tudor I would write that she was a good egg rather than a bad egg - from my limited knowledge. Examiners were always relieved to see someone not giving them the line from the book and they marked you up no matter how fallacious your argument was. At Coleraine I wrote an essay on surrealism typed on toilet paper. The essay was indifferent but the toilet paper got me a B instead of a C. City University was a different ball-game. It was very competitive. They tried to build the course into a newsroom-type environment. However, journalism is essentially a non-academic trade - I like to think of it as a trade rather than as a profession. That does not sit very easily into a university post-graduate diploma course where people have to show their academic balls. Shorthand is an essential part of a journalist's armoury but the shorthand classes did not count towards your qualification. For the first time in my academic career I actually worked. Like many news operations, the course was somewhat haphazard and built on egos. There were three lecturers all fighting each other, physically in some instances, so you had us all dashing out from the shorthand class to report on the latest fracas between the head of the department and one of his deputies who were flailing at each other in the corridor.

The teaching of journalism was a damn sight more sophisticated on the other side of the Atlantic and we had a Canadian professor on attachment that year, Sandra Came. She pushed us journalistically. You'd arrive in in the morning and she would give you a slip of paper which she had taken from the Golden Pages. You'd be told to come back by midday with a story on the Association of Tinned Dog Food Manufacturers. We all did, no matter how looney the organisation we were sent out to. Her message was that, if there were nothing happening, you made it happen. Look in the phone book for inspiration and just ring someone and ask them if they are doing anything. That was a lesson that has not been lost on me. She came hard down on woolly construction. I had a piece where I had, not done my homework and tried to flannel my way through. She ripped it to pieces in front of the whole class. I had used the word "facilities" as an umbrella term - it means nothing and everything. She later told me she had picked on me because she reckoned I could stand it more than the rest of them, which I suppose was a compliment. Now any time I see the word "facilities" I go pale. However, the course was really good, as much for its non-academic nature as for the people I met on it. I was the token Paddy but I made many good friends, one of whom, from Scotland, was my best-man.

For part of the course you were attached to a newspaper and, one Christmas, I spent four weeks in Belfast on *The Sunday News*. I was to do four weeks on *The News Letter* at Easter but was grabbed back by *The Sunday News* because they were short of staff. My claim to fame (not a big one) is that I got the front page story on *The Sunday News* in my first week. I shared the by-line with Stephen Grimason who is now education correspondent for the BBC. We were sent down to cover a hare-coursing meeting at Crebilly. A crowd of students from Queen's University went to protest against it. There were people from the USPCA, and then there was largely the farming community which had come to see the coursing. Among the protestors was a group of women. One of them had turned up wearing a fur coat. I claim I was the first to spot that. It wasn't an earth-shattering story but it was just right for *The Sunday News*. After the student protest, the woman turned her coat inside-out and we got photographs of both sides. It was a typically Irish story - if that is not racist. We actually missed the real story: one of those who had turned up was Bernadette McAliskey.

The Sunday News was a lot of fun - there was none of the pressure you get on a daily paper. The other reporters have a bit of time to spend with you - on a daily newspaper, you are left to sink or swim. *The Sunday News* was owned by Century Newspapers and from the two stints there I was offered a job on *The Carrickfergus Advertiser*, a Century paper. That was three months before the course in London ended. I was told the job might be there for me at the end of the three months or it might not. I quit the course, took the job and started in May 1983. I was assured beforehand I would not have to bother with any sport. The first day I arrived there Carrick Rangers had moved into the Irish league, effectively the first division. My first assignment was to cover a friendly match between Carrick Rangers and Bolton Wanderers. I became a fully-fledged sports reporter in my first week in journalism. Sports reporting is decided in the press box where there is a certain amount of cabinet responsibility for who kicked the ball into the net. I fell into the rough and tumble of working on a newspaper in a small provincial town. I loved it. I found it easy as a Catholic working in a strongly Democratic Unionist town for a paper which was perceived to be Ulster Unionist. There were no Nationalists at all on Carrick Council. The Alliance Party was the closest to a non-Unionist group. There was a sufficient Catholic population in the town to sustain an SDLP councillor but they found it impossible to get anybody to stand. Most of the Catholics voted for Alliance. I have never found religion a problem - it's not high on my agenda nor does it seem to be high on anybody else's though we have to kowtow to its presence in our society. On a personal level, people work well together.

Carrick was a learning experience. The editor was John Rookes who had been one of the legendary news editors of the *Belfast Telegraph* and had a fearsome reputation for devouring reporters and correspondents. By the time I got him, he had mellowed. He had retired twice: once from the *Telegraph* and once from being the managing editor of a paper in Banbridge. He came out of retirement to edit *The Carrickfergus Advertiser*. If you wanted to do something he said away you go. He had a dry sarcastic wit and was good for me. He was training me in for the local council and brought me along to a meeting where

I sat beside him at a desk in the middle of a horseshoe-shaped assembly. The mayor normally sat behind us. That night the mayor had been taken ill and Molly Ardle, who was one of the old guard Ulster Unionists, got up to say how distressed everybody was by the mayor's illness. She thought the council should send him a bouquet of flowers at which John Rookes whispered loudly, "Forget about the flowers - send him a wreath". I nearly dissolved. He would second motions and tell councillors who were repeating themselves to sit down and shut up. Everybody loved him and he got away with it. There I was, sitting in awe of what was going on around me, and he would just pierce the balloon. I would never have got away with it when I covered the council by myself. He retired at the end of 1983 and I became the editor. There had been just John, myself and another reporter. We said the circulation was 4,000 - it was probably closer to 3,000. Whenever we were trying to sell advertising, it was always 16,000 or 20,000 readers. The other reporter was Jackie Thompson, a woman, whose name used to throw everybody because they expected a man to answer the phone. There were two on advertising and a woman at reception.

Before I arrived, John had run a referendum in the paper on Sunday opening. The votes were neck-and-neck right up to the 1 p.m. deadline when the local Free Presbyterian minister arrived in with 3,000 ballot papers.

During that time I started doing shifts on *The News Letter,* occasionally as a reporter but more often as a sub-editor. I said I could sub, but I hadn't a clue. The first piece of copy I got had written across it: 8/8x8 - in Carrick all we wrote on the copy was "single column". What it meant, when it was translated for me, was eight points on eight leading across eight ems. There were a lot of older subs and the atmosphere was quiet, supportive, almost bookish. They helped me out and I became more useful. Captain O.W.J. Henderson still owned Century Newspapers - he sold out in 1989. Henderson was mercurial, very much old style aristocratic Unionist patriarch. He was prone to bursts of righteous indignation. In all the time

I was there, he was always right in any rows he had with me. He had a reputation for interference in his papers but that was not my experience of him.

In 1985 *The News Letter* went strongly against the Anglo-Irish Agreement - I suspect more strongly than Henderson would have approved of. It stated its case sharply. That would have gone against the grain of the aristocratic Unionist establishment. Occasionally you'd get a story with "OWJ MUST" on top of it. All those stories were afflicted with the Curse of the Hendersons - there was always a mistake in them. The stories were relatively innocuous - about a garden party or a business venture - not the kind about which you'd get vexed because of proprietorial interference. I found him straight but then I was at a low level in the paper and not at the cutting-edge of his tongue. In the two years I was in Carrickfergus, one of them as editor, I was never told to toe a particular line, no matter how much the DUP protested I was in the pay of Glengall Street. I tried not to take sides but to run a decent community newspaper.

I became the editor of *The Carrickfergus Advertiser* on Monday January 2, a bank-holiday. The office was closed but our press day was Tuesday and I decided to go in. I went to the local chip-shop for my lunch. I was coming out of that about 1 o'clock with my sausage and chips wrapped up in brown paper. I slipped on the step and shattered my ankle. Within three hours of taking up the new job, I was testing the emergency ambulance service and was whisked off to Belfast. Sitting in the chip-shop waiting for the ambulance, with my leg going one way and my foot the other, the lady insisted on giving me back the money for the chips. The next morning I rang the office from hospital. I was euphoric having had my pre-med just before the operation and thought I could command the world - John Rookes was dragged out of retirement after less than 24 hours. Since then I have insisted that any time I am appointed to a new job, I have the first day off. I have seven pins in my foot.

Carrick, however, gave me a bit of responsibility at an early age and a chance to make my mistakes in an environment where it didn't matter all that much. I was editor at 24. It was traumatic enough - the little old lady who's been done for shop-lifting and wants her name kept out of the paper; the politician who keeps harrassing you to get his name in the paper; the DUP who had a particular downer on me and said we were just a front for the Unionist Party. They rang up to say they were sending down a five-man delegation - at one stage it was to include Dr. Ian Paisley. I told them fair enough but they had better bring some chairs with them - we did not have five in the office. The delegation never materialised. Their tactic was to keep complaining whether or not they had something to complain about in the hope that, to get them off your back, you'd shove in one of their press releases. Working simultaneously on *The News Letter* and *The Sunday News*, I would get to the Carrick office at 8.30, get the four o'clock bus into Belfast and get home about midnight. When you are 24 you can put up with anything.

The News Letter had been a broadsheet and in 1984 there was a long and damaging strike. It lasted ten weeks. It was one of those journalists' strikes over very little but it was good golfing weather and the dander was up. When people came back to work, *The News Letter* went tabloid. Its circulation had been slipping and it had begun to lose some of its sense of direction. They thought this was a way to give it a bit of a kick. The transfer from broadsheet to tabloid was badly handled. I was embarrassed by the first copy which rolled off the presses. *The News Letter* was a strong business/middle-class/upper-class paper - a classic broadsheet. It should have remained so - that's what its constituency was. The change to tabloid was disastrous and was handled just as badly as the change to tabloid in the *Irish Press*, if that is possible - that's another classic disaster story. *The News Letter* went tabloid in September and rocked along till Christmas. In the inevitable shake-up, a number of heads rolled. There was a complete shake-up in the subbing - and production-end of things - that's when I was brought in as deputy chief sub. My appointment as editor in Carrickfergus and as deputy chief sub were both gross over-promotions. My experience is people tend to live up to, rather than down to, their gain, so I did all right I think. I was moving in above people who had been subs on *The News Letter* for 20 years but I did so largely with their help. People took you at face value and supported you once you got stuck in. My job in Carrick was filled by a man who had just retired from the *Belfast Telegraph*.

The editor of *The News Letter* was Sam Butler. My dog is also called Sam. If I ever got frustrated, I had somebody to kick when I got home. However, I had enormous respect for Sam Butler - he always put the paper first. He had kept it going throughout the ten-week strike. It stopped publication only when the printers came out as well, forced out by the NGA in London. Then the strike was settled within three days. Sam had to work against the natural bitterness these things tend to generate. I found him always willing to give you a chance and always forgiving when you made a mistake. These are marvellous qualities in an editor. He used to write a lot and subs would cock up his stories just as they would anybody else's. He opened the paper up to voices which had never been heard in it before - you had people from Nationalist backgrounds writing.

During my time there I started to review concerts. My knowledge was limited but I worked on the basis that a bad review was better than no review at all. Reviewing can have its funnier moments. On one occasion the Chief Music Critic, as he liked to be known, Charles Fitzgerald, wrote a glowing review of *Don Giovanni*. I went along to the opera as an ordinary punter - it was atrocious. Since I had paid 36 quid for my tickets, I was rightly indignant. I wanted to do a review but decided not to. When I woke up the next morning I was even angrier. I battered out a review as a cathartic exercise, brought it into Sam and told him we had already given the opera a glowing review. He said we would print mine as well. It was grossly unprofessional on my part to second-guess the chief music critic. Sam liked a bit of a ding-dong and in the review went. Charlie went berserk. He stormed into Sam who smiled his benign smile and that was the end of that. The irony of it was that the company secretary was a director of Opera Northern Ireland. The opera company went berserk as well - having had one good review, they did not expect to find themselves trounced in the same paper. The story probably reflects badly on me, but well on the editor. That was the nature of him. If people came along with uncomfortable pieces, Sam tended to publish and be damned. That's something I try now to do myself. I think the editor's burden is to publish rather than not to publish - that's the business newspapers are in. Sam was editor throughout my period - he resigned two months before I left. He was an enormous loss to *The News Letter*. While he had quite rightly articulated the Unionist opposition to the Anglo-Irish Agreement, he was not afraid to listen to other voices. As a result, *The News Letter* may have appeared a little eclectic and unfocused at times - you were never sure who was going to pop up in it but that was part of its attraction. He stimulated a lot of debate, particularly on the Unionist side, by giving a voice to people who were antagonistic to the Unionist establishment.

My main job was to try and get the production into some sort of order and over a period I think we succeeded. *The News Letter* was prepared to invest and I ended up on design courses in Germany and so on. I discovered in myself a love of typography and design. Good design, of course, is absolutely no use unless the content is right. Good content makes good papers, good design doesn't. Every time we increased the price of *The News Letter*, Captain Henderson insisted we add some extra pages and do a bit of redesign to make the paper look brighter and breezier. That is the empty kind of design that does not work. Readers expect good value for money regardless of the price.

While I was there, *The News Letter* celebrated its 250th anniversary, an event which should not go unremarked. It's a historic newspaper. The phrase was, "The oldest newspaper in the English-speaking world published continuously under its own masthead" - this knocked out papers such as *The Times*. In the period 1985-90 *The News Letter* began to rediscover some of its roots. It was founded by Francis Joy and was a United Irishman newspaper. It was at the spearhead of the great movement of Presbyterian Nationalism which at one point set the Nationalist agenda in Ireland. To that extent, *The News Letter* had anti-establishment beginnings but throughout the nineteenth century and right through to the twentieth it was very much the establishment newspaper. It was seen as the organ of the Ulster Unionist Party, the establishment elite. The advent of direct rule turned the establishment on its head and turned *The News Letter* into being an anti-establishment paper. The signing of the Anglo-Irish Agreement was another watershed. It wrenched even the Unionist establishment away from Government. That is something that is only now being rebuilt with things like the voting pact with John Major. Once again the Unionist establishment are attending the garden parties at Hillsborough.

Following the 250th anniversary, Henderson sold out. There were protracted negotiations to sell it to the *Belfast Telegraph* but that was knocked back by the Monopoly and Mergers Commission. It was then sold to a consortium of venture capitalists based largely in London. A son of Barbara Cartland was involved in the consortium. The paper went through a dramatic change trying to get it on a firm business footing. One of the steps taken to arrest the decline was a freesheet. *The News Letter* always sold well outside Belfast, not so well in the city. The idea was to tap into the city advertising market. The costs of a freesheet were considerable - £1m in distribution alone. The freesheet was a boiled-down version of *The News Letter* and I was given the job of designing it. The regular *News Letter* lost 6,000 circulation when the freesheet was launched - people were not going to pay for two of the same newspaper. There was a steady decline in circulation down to I think 31,000 - it's now back up to 33,000. *The News Letter* is beginning to turn the corner and there are more resources going into it, particularly editorially where there is a lot more imagination. It's beginning to give the rest of us something to think about. I'm not so sure how it is going to arrest the financial decline.

As I told you, Sam left in 1990 and a number of people applied for the job, including myself. At the same time *The Irish News* was appointing a new editor. As part of the reshuffling in *The News Letter* I became night editor in succession to Mike Chapman, an enormously resourceful journalist who had been chief sub. He was a hard taskmaster - you would do a page, he would rip it up and tell you to start again. He was of the old school that believed you had to get something right first time. The tendency now is that you get something out anyway, right or wrong, and worry about it tomorrow. That lasted a month. I was interviewed for the editor's job in *The Irish News* and did not get it. Subsequently I was appointed deputy editor. My background in design complemented Nick Garbutt's, whose background was in news. We were portrayed as the dream ticket. As editor, he was the content man, I was the design man. It's a bit of a crude definition. He had been assistant editor of *The Sunday Tribune* before he moved North. He's a Mancunian - it was quite a brave appointment, an Englishman editor of the Nationalist newspaper in Northern Ireland.

The Irish News is owned by the Fitzpatrick family - the chairman and chief executive is Jim Fitzpatrick, the deputy chief executive Dominic Fitzpatrick. It's a family-owned independent newspaper - 102 years old or 138, depending on which way you look at it. The Fitzpatricks have controlled it since the early 80s - for a time Jim Fitzpatrick was editor, he is a newspaper man. He, too, is quite a hard taskmaster. We are *The Irish News* and *Belfast Morning News*. *The Irish News* was established in 1891 and *The Belfast Morning News* in 1855. Towards the end of the 19th century *The Belfast Morning News* was a pro-Parnell newspaper, which mightily upset the Catholic church at the time when Parnell was having his liaison with Kitty O'Shea. The Catholic bishops launched *The Irish News* as an anti-Parnell Nationalist newspaper. Eventually *The*

Irish News overtook *The Belfast Morning News* in circulation and swallowed it up. The paper's birth took place in the whole row over Parnell and Home Rule, its legacy is a church-based one. The masthead carries the legend, *Pro Fide et Patria* - that gives you a sense of both its Nationalistic and religious ethos. It's problematic and a matter of continuous debate whether or not a newspaper at this end of the twentieth century should be carrying on its masthead a slogan like that. It's one of the sticks with which we are beaten. You can't deny your history and to remove it could be seen as facile and cosmetic. There is a sense in which in Northern Ireland we're all being forced to rewrite history - the Allied Irish Bank is in the process of becoming the First Trust Bank because the word Irish in the title is not liked by some of its potential customers. We are told by our market researchers that we can't hope to expand into the Protestant community because they find the word Irish in the title offensive. We are not in the business of changing our name to get rid of the word Irish.

I would have problems with describing *The Irish News* as a Catholic paper because theologically, and in every other sense, the newspaper is an inanimate object - it can't have a religion. You can't baptise a newspaper into a church. My favourite description of *The Irish News* is that it is a Nationalist newspaper which is read mainly but not exclusively by Catholics. So far as the wider community is concerned, our political position is more important than our religious one. I would like to produce a newspaper which can be read by everybody but not a newspaper that is anodyne. We are a paper with strong opinions of our own but not by any means immune to the other sides of the debate. Since I took over on July 5 of this year (1993) I have introduced columnists that would not normally be seen in a Nationalist newspaper. One of them is Rhonda Paisley, daughter of the Reverend Ian. She writes every Monday - her debut was last week and in the run up to it we had about 30 phone calls, mostly well-reasoned, objecting to her. The day she appeared we got two phone calls. Now if we get the Lotto numbers wrong, we get 30 or 40 irate phone calls, so perhaps our choice of her was less adventurous than we thought. She will be writing mainly on social and women's issues - she does not want to be seen only in a political context - but there is no way she can, with a regular column, completely avoid political issues. This morning, for example, she was writing about prisons as a deterrent and she ended it by arguing against internment. On Tuesdays Peter Bottomley MP writes for us. He's a former Northern Ireland Minister and his wife is a member of the British Cabinet. He's seen by some as having gone native - he played a strong part in the recent extradition case of John Matthews, a Derryman, who had been on a Prevention of Terrorism Act charge. He has taken Bernadette McAliskey's part in her row with the BBC when it silenced her - they inserted sub-titles when no sane person would have seen her as coming within the remit of the Government ban. From the Nationalist side we have Brian Feeney, a former SDLP Councillor, a strong, outspoken public figure. We have James Kelly, the former Northern editor of the *Irish Independent*, the doyen of journalists here. Bob McCartney, a Unionist with a small u and a distinguished QC, writes a monthly column for us. His first one addressed in stark terms the Hume-Adams talks - the paper would have been uncomfortable with the views he was expressing, effectively that the SDLP was in cahoots with Sinn Fein to push a Nationalist agenda. Going back to Sam and his publish-and-be-damned, I think McCartney went too far but we published him nonetheless. We did a leader which addressed his article in blunt terms. It was a way of balancing things but also of stimulating debate.

There is a conservative atmosphere about *The Irish News*. People have been here for a long time and their way of doing things becomes ingrained. Nick's brief was to enliven the newspaper and my main brief, when I was deputy editor, was to redesign the paper, to bring it up to date. You tend to lose rather than gain sales when you redesign a newspaper, thankfully ours have continued to improve. Readers are even more conservative than the people who work on papers. Our redesign tried to be sensitive to them. I am a bit of a purist on design and don't like all the tomfoolery that accompanies redesigned newspapers - I believe the design and typography should be as unobtrusive as possible and the copy and content of headlines should be what hits the reader and, of course, pictures, which are an essential element in how a paper looks - that's where the eye goes first. The redesign I have done is a traditional broadsheet - even moving to that was a great cultural change. The serif typeface we went for was *Cheltenham*, one which has fallen out of favour, and we use little variation, except for light and bold. We needed a good strong typeface - we were using *Times* up to then and it was just fading off the page. We use devices which have now become the vogue such as quote-outs and stand-firsts which bring the eye in to the story and give scanner-readers things they can pick up. We use a lot of briefs to make pages busy while allowing us to concentrate space on bigger stories. The broad thrust of the design was to make it a traditional newspaper. Thankfully it was relatively well-received. The biggest change we made was in the masthead from a quaint *Old English* face which had been deliberately designed to make the paper look traditional. The masthead we have now is *Rockwell*, block-serif, rugged, almost brutal, but *The Irish News* was competing with eighteen other titles on the news-stand in the morning and was disappearing into the ether. We needed something that was going to hit people between the eyes. The chairman had to be persuaded to make the change. I had taken ill with a bad chest and was wheeled in from my sick-bed to make the presentation to him. The only reason I got it past him was because I threatened to expire on the boardroom table if he didn't concede. The change in the masthead was what we got the most criticism for - it lasted longer than I had expected but now things have settled down. The paper is at least presentable now though there is still lots more to do.

In newspapers there is no such thing as absolutes - you can always go that little bit farther. Once the redesign was done, my reason-for-being as deputy editor almost disappeared but even worse than doing the redesign is policing it subsequently - when you are up against deadlines, following the rules takes second place. Last August we commissioned the new colour press - my gut feeling is that there is nothing better than a good black and white newspaper but I seem to be proved wrong continually by our market research people. The colour press will allow us to produce really good black and white. *The Irish News* always had a reputation for good pictures - our reproduction was appalling. Now the photographers have a chance to shine. There are six to nine months of utter pain getting a new press to work and it hit our production very badly - we were getting lots of late papers. Then something seemed to click and we have been hitting good times. We are trying to have as long a transition as possible rather than a big bang. Big bangs mean two months with no papers. The new kit, as it is called, the new computers, will make the subs' work a damn sight easier, yielding journalistic as well as design rewards. You want to use technology to strip away the barriers between the journalists and the journalism.

Nick Garbutt left *The Irish News* in June of this year. His departure came as a surprise. I had always thought he would see me down rather than the other way round. He went to the *Belfast Telegraph* as deputy editor. *The Irish News* sells 44,000 copies, the *Belfast Telegraph* 130,000. *The Irish News* has few resources, the *Belfast Telegraph* has enormous resources. It must be the wealthiest newspaper in Ireland - it is the most profitable of all the Thomson newpapers. It made something like £7m last year. *The Irish News* is a small independent newspaper and the *Belfast Telegraph* is part of a great international chain. The move put Nick onto a new career ladder.

I have never been overly concerned about titles - I am embarrassed by my own title. I'd prefer to say I was a journalist rather than anything else. Deputies do not always make the transition to the editor's chair.

One of the main planks of *The Irish News* editorial policy has been fair employment so, while it would have been possible to appoint from within, Nick's job was advertised. I was told that if I was the best person for the job, I would get it and if I wasn't I wouldn't. There were 12 or 13 applicants from Britain and Ireland. We were asked to do an analysis of the paper over a week - I was probably more critical than any of the other candidates even though I had been editing it since Nick's departure. The interview was two-and-a-half hours long and quite gruelling. I was left stewing over the weekend, and I was offered the job on the Monday - and accepted humbly. The process was a good thing - I am not in favour of Buggin's Turn.

The adjustment from deputy to editor was not as easy as I had imagined. Even though you have been around for three years as one of the troops, people don't do you any favours. I have found that the job has to be lonelier than I would have wanted it to be. You can't unburden yourself with the freedom you could when you were the deputy. Deputy is a wonderful position because you're a bit like the court jester - you have the luxury of playing the fool sometimes and deriding the powers that be. It's not a luxury you have as editor. I have tried as editor to be as dispassionate as possible about the paper and the people who are working on it. I try to keep as fresh a perspective as I can. You try not to be expedient because you have known X for three years and you don't want to put his nose out of joint. I have tried to approach the job as if I had not been there before but obviously, after three years, you have an insight into the difficulties people have - you know their strengths and weaknesses. If you move in fresh to a place, it takes you up to a year to find your feet. An editor moving in in those circumstances is enormously handicapped - you don't know who's selling you a line until it is too late.

For many years *The Irish News* was the voice of Nationalism when the whole political structure here was very much geared against Nationalism. I see *The Irish News* in two guises. There is the paper I work for owned by Jim Fitzpatrick - it has 116 members of staff and is a business. Then there is *The Irish News* which is an entity in itself independent of the existence of Jim Fitzpatrick or Tom Collins. It has its own momentum and agenda. There is that dualism. You are conscious that you are speaking for the minority, for people who are at the raw end of life here. You are conscious of the poverty within the Nationalist community, of the high level of unemployment - your readers are twice as likely as *The News Letter's* readers are to be unemployed. You are addressing a community that has been oppressed by the state and by the law. But you are also addressing a community that is beginning to have more confidence in itself. The GAA victories for Down, Derry and Donegal have given an enormous boost to the culture and traditions of the Nationalist community. They have done more than any political act to make people feel proud of belonging to Ulster. *The Irish News* sees itself as being an *Irish* newspaper but also as being an *Ulster* newspaper - by that we mean the nine counties rather than the six. We transcend Northern Ireland but we are aware we are living in a part of the United Kingdom. We would tend to be anti-establishment. Northern Ireland itself is anti-establishment if establishment means the British and the paraphernalia of British rule here. *The News Letter* for example, does not kowtow to the Northern Ireland Office. Politics here, Unionist or Nationalist, are anti rather than pro things because the people who are in Government were not elected from Northern Ireland. They have no accountability here. If the Government is screwing people into the ground with VAT or health or education, then Unionists are as much part of the opposition as Nationalists.

There is an enormous tension between Republicanism and constitutional Nationalism. We are firmly on the side of constitutional Nationalism. We condemn in the most vociferous terms Republican violence. Because, of course, we condemn Loyalist violence, we feel we have to condemn even more strongly violence which emanates from our own community. We don't believe a united Ireland is worth the life of a single person. However, we would be in favour of Sinn Fein participating in talks - we believe dialogue rather than no dialogue is the answer. We believe people should be confronting problems rather than running away from them.

Leaders of the main constitutional parties work together on matters in which they have a common interest - John Hume, Ian Paisley and Jim Molyneux would be working together for farmers, the business community, for jobs and so on. However, an agreement between them alone will not bring peace. The only way we will get peace is by bringing the extremists in, by making them realise there is more to be gained by debate than by shooting one another. We believe, therefore, Sinn Fein should renounce violence and then sit at the conference table - one is a precondition for the other. It would be ridiculous to participate in talks while reserving the right to shoot the people you are talking to.

We support John Hume's talks with Gerry Adams though they are very, very difficult against the background of continuing violence. It is a perplexing issue. The difficulty with the Hume/Adams talks is you have to take them on trust. If Hume delivers, fine. If he does not, you have to ask what the political damage is. There is no doubt there is political damage - the talks are feeding the idea of pan-Nationalism, the demonising of the Nationalist community, to use a phrase of Sinn Fein. That in turn is feeding the Loyalist violence which has now become one of the main security headaches. John Hume has proved himself as a leader over the last 20 years. His position on violence and the IRA has been unequivocal. We believe he has to be given a chance.

We firmly believe in the three-strand approach to a political settlement. First, build trust between the peoples of Northern Ireland; second, build a relationship between Northern Ireland and the Republic; third, between the people of Ireland and Britain. The difficulty is in deciding whether you are best served by approaching this in stages, whether you go down the line of "nothing is agreed until everything is agreed". But trust has to be built up between Northern Nationalists and the South as well as between Northern Protestants and Southern Nationalists. I believe there is a considerable number of Northern Nationalists who, if push came to shove, would be dragged kicking and screaming into an Irish Republic.

It disturbs me that Nationalists spend a lot of time talking about the necessity for Unionists to come to terms with Nationalist culture, with bilingual street signs, with Irish music and dancing, with the Irish language and so on while, at the same time, there is a resistance among Nationalists to Unionist traditions. It's a bit strange to have Nationalist politicians complaining about Orange marches through mainly Nationalist towns. If you're looking for one thing, you have to take the other.

There is an awful lot of work at a personal level to bring the two communities into contact - people meet daily in the workplace and there, there is trust. It is when you look at the tribes rather than the individuals that things become more difficult. The media, including television, have had a large part to play in this. Until very recently, Gaelic games did not get any coverage on either BBC or UTV. Now they do. The All-Ireland final was on live on Sunday afternoon on BBC1 rather than BBC2 and it was on unapologetically. That does a lot to make the Nationalists' position acceptable in this society. Politicians will have to find a form of government which reconciles people's Nationalism and people's Unionism. How they do that, I do not know. It will require an act of statesmanship like Arafat and Rabin. Somebody is going to have to say there have been too many deaths, that we have to do something, that doing something is better than doing nothing. Some politician is going to have to make that gesture, take that leap of faith. My feeling is that that has to be a Unionist rather than a Nationalist. If there is going to be a settlement here, it will have to command the support of Unionists. I don't think jumping generations is going to do us any good - I remember at school walking down the avenue having animated discussions about politics, saying we were the generation that would get away from all the old conflicts. Now, at age 34, I see coming across my desk reports of 24-year-olds up on a bombing charge, a 17-year-old up on an arson charge for burning down in their home a Catholic or a Protestant. The generations are repeating the mistakes. The younger politicians beneath Hume and Paisley and Molyneux show no signs of thinking any differently. I do not believe, as some people say, that when the old guard goes, people will have a chance. If there is a solution, I think we'll trip over it some day by accident.

3

Damien Kiberd

The Sunday Business Post

If journalism is to be perceived as just polished writers sounding off about something, you don't even have to get out of bed in the morning.

The conversation took place on June 21 1993

Damien Kiberd is editor of *The Sunday Business Post.*

He was born in Dublin on November 17 1955.

His father is Frederick Kiberd, a retired salesman/agent.

His mother Eithne Keegan, a civil servant.

He is second in a family of three, one brother Declan, and one sister Marguerite.

He is married to Terry Griffin, a journalist. They have two children: Roisin (4) and Emmet (2).

He was educated at St. Paul's School, Raheny and at TCD (Economics).

1977 Industrial Credit Company as lending executive. 1979 joined the *Irish Press* as a reporter on the business page. Then became senior reporter, assistant financial editor, financial editor. 1987 business editor *Sunday Tribune.* 1989 helped establish *The Sunday Business Post* and became its founding editor.

At school I was quite good at English and got a scholarship to Trinity College. You choose one subject for the Trinity Scholarship entrance exam and I chose English but, strangely enough, when I got to college I was more interested in mathematics. However, I soon found that the idea of studying mathematics for four years was a bit rarefied so I decided to combine the literary with the mathematical and chose economics. Economics purports to be a science but a lot of it is based on subjectivity. The more I studied academic economics the less I became interested in it. I had a chance to go on and do academic research and I spoke to Professor Dermot McAleese. He said employment prospects were not really enhanced by further research in economics. In those days there were 120,000 people out of work and we all thought unemployment was terrible. Anyway, I got a job in the Industrial Credit Company. I had also been offered one in the diplomatic service. I felt work in the banking business would be more interesting - and it was. I worked for Foir Teoranta, a State rescue agency. It was wonderful to get away from the academic life and go into something practical. I went out to factories that had got into difficulty and wrote up reports about them so that lending decisions could be taken. I spent two years doing that. As I understand it, a lot of banking now is done in a rushed way - that's why you've got so many bad debts. Foir Teoranta, on the other hand, devoted a lot of time and attention to each case. The board was composed of experienced business people, some of whom devoted an inordinate amount of time to reading the reports - they based their decisions on good commercial criteria. It was an impressively-run organisation. There was no evidence of political interference. You could quarrel with the rationale, the whole concept, of an organisation such as Foir Teoranta - in a lot of instances perhaps it would have been better to let the firms go into receivership and get new owners through that route. We may have been delaying the inevitable, but, provided you accepted the idea of a lender of last resort, the organisation was run professionally. For a young person, you got a great insight into business, how family businesses went wrong after generations when, say, a strong family member died and the business was handed over to a weak generation. You saw people take on too much, not having the financial wherewithal. You encountered an array of problems. Foir Teoranta also became involved in a number of large rescues, important from a macro-economic point of view. I felt what I was doing was useful.

I had always wanted to be involved in journalism. I had edited student magazines. The *Irish Press* advertised a job for a business reporter. I applied, did an interview and heard no more about it. Luckily the person to whom they gave the job did not want it and the second person was from England and got a job in the BBC. Months after I applied, I got a phone call asking if I was still interested. I joined the *Irish Press* knowing nothing about newspapers and found the whole atmosphere very strange that first day. There were 1100 people working there compared with 600 today. You had hot metal technology. The case room was dirty and noisy. You had a huge newsroom with legions of reporters from the three *Irish Press* newspapers - 50 reporters working with old typewriters. The noise level was terrific. It took me a few weeks to get used to it. I grew to love the place. There was a great sense of camaraderie among the reporters and little evidence of people trying to climb into a better position on the backs of others. When a big story broke, everyone was expected to row in. Even though the paper had been set up by the de Valera family who were linked to Fianna Fail and who had retained control, it had developed a reputation for fairness. It sold itself on the basis of hard news reporting rather than commentary. That was seen in those days as the great strength of Burgh Quay. It is not fashionable now. Almost all the great reporters on the other newspapers had done their initial training in Burgh Quay. Douglas Gageby had worked there. There was no cult of the personality such as you have in some of the more successful newspapers now where you have named writers with picture by-lines who give opinions on everything under the sun. In the Press Group, we were expected to work hard, get the facts and report accurately and, if possible, beat the other papers to the draw. To do that, we would work often into the small hours. It gave you a great sense of achievement to walk out at 3 o'clock in the morning, get the early editions, and find you had a better page one story than the other newspapers. The next day of course, they would get a better story than you and you would be back to square one. It eventually gets into your bloodstream and you eat, drink and sleep newspapers. I was proud of the *Irish Press* - it was a fine newspaper.

The editor was Tim Pat Coogan, very strong and, to this day, a personal friend. He gave the paper an image and was robust in standing up to outside pressures. He believed the paper should be kept at a certain standard - for instance, he initiated the New Irish Writing Series to bring on young authors. He wanted the *Irish Press* to be a respectable broadsheet newspaper, strongly nationalistic. The circulation oscillated between 90,000 and 110,000 in the first half of the 80s. It's now down around 50,000 having collapsed following the conversion from broadsheet to tabloid. I don't think Tim Pat would have been too happy to work in the paper when it became a tabloid. Like all editors, he could get on the nerves of his staff from time to time - you would hear people fuming about him but they respected him.

From time to time, I worked also for the evening and the Sunday papers. Evening papers are completely different from morning ones - there is little opportunity to go into anything in depth. It's a case of speed of reporting and getting your story written concisely in five or six paragraphs in a way everyone can understand.

There was a fine spirit - I met my wife there - but, after eight years, I left because it was increasingly obvious the paper was going downhill. It became depressing. You felt there was no action being taken to arrest the decline of what had been a great company. Believe it or not, the *Irish Press* made £1m profit around 1980. Then it went into loss and has never come out it. In the recent court case, it was mentioned losses are now coming close to £15m. In the mid-1980s, there was a series of industrial disputes, largely over the introduction of new technology. In 1985, they took out the hot metal linotype machines and replaced them with computerised typesetting and two of the three titles were off the streets for six weeks. The third one, the morning newspaper, actually missed three months production. Strangely enough, when it reappeared it had not lost the loyalty of its readers. In similar circumstances in France or Germany, when papers have been off the streets for months because of battles over technology, when they come back they find the readership has evaporated. The rapid deterioration began only when it converted to a tabloid in 1988. Similarly with the *Evening Press*. It was selling up to 150,000 copies a day - it's now down to below 70,000. The whole evening newspaper market has been contracting for the past decade. Whereas *The Herald* has been holding steady around the 100,000 mark, the *Evening Press* has gone into a long-term decline. This decline was accelerated when the *Evening Press* was launched in two sections two years ago - they lost 20,000 off their circulation as a result of an innovation which was designed to improve their product. The whole story of Burgh Quay is sad. A lot of their better reporters, though not all, have left to join the *Independent* and *The Irish Times*. Morale has been impaired and we now have come to the point where there's a huge court case which will undermine morale even further. Shortly before I left I spoke to Eamon de Valera, always a decent, honourable and gentlemanly person. I suggested to him that the newspaper, which was by then a broadsheet, should have a special sports supplement on Saturdays - *The Irish Times*, in particular, was gaining on Saturdays because it had gone into two sections. He thought about it but said it would be too ambitious a project. Things like that made you ask how the company was going to get out of the problems it had got itself into. If you can't take initiatives and you're only really cutting costs progressively, you're in long-term decline.

They brought in Ingersoll as a shareholder in 1989. I believe he invested £9m in the following four years. They were clearly aware what was needed was recapitalisation and reinvestment in product. I hope the *Irish Press* does come back again commercially and strongly. It's an honourable newspaper. Although some people would see them as being in favour of Fianna Fail, I think they are fairer and less politicised than some of the newspapers with which they compete. I hope they can once again become a countervailing force to the Independent Group.

The *Irish Press* has survived a decade of losses. First, because of its inherited shareholding in the Press Association which in turn gave it a shareholding in Reuters from which they got £10m and then they got £9m in investment from Ingersoll. So, in a sense, there have been £20m of cash infusions into the *Press* titles. Going back to my days in Foir Teoranta, I wonder if that really is a good thing. If they had not had the cash, they might have been forced to take tougher decisions earlier. I maintain contact with people in the *Press* and a lot of them are depressed about what's happening. They would support whatever plan was put to them if they thought there was going to be a future. Burgh Quay is an important force in Irish life. It was created by de Valera as a counterbalance to papers which he saw as being inordinately pro-British or pro-Cumann na nGael, pro-Establishment. The *Irish Press*, consequently, always had a raw or racy edge even though it was created by somebody who came himself to represent the Establishment. It had a radical streak. Historically it employed free thinkers. It was run in an honourable way - there was never any significant editorial interference from the de Valeras. In the time I was there I can remember Major Vivion de Valera coming in only once or twice on some minor topic in which he might have had an interest. At election time the paper would ritualistically support Fianna Fail but that was the end of it. Reporters concentrated on the facts and that was it.

I went to work as business editor for *The Sunday Tribune* and stayed for only two years. I went back to the *Irish Press* for a few months. Brian Bell had succeeded me as business or financial editor and then gave up journalism, so I went back to my old job. Brian has since got on well with Wilson Hartnell Public Relations. What is coming out now in the court case is that Ingersoll held himself out to de Valera as an expert in the management of newspapers, at reversing their fortunes if they were in decline, applying the magic ointment. Eamon de Valera and Vincent Jennings believed that in Ingersoll they had somebody who would not only give them money but would help to manage the paper. The founders' ideals for the *Irish Press* were that it should be a paper for the whole country. *The Sunday Press's* circulation at one stage was 455,000. Every family in the land bought it and did the crossword and entered for the competitions. It went to farmers, working class, middle class, professionals - everyone. The *Independent* at some stage decided that newspapers should be marketed and targeted at ABC1 readers. The *Press* never applied any marketing strategy to its titles - until it was too late.

There has been a general decline in newspaper sales. They are too expensive. The *Independent* and *The Tribune* target the east coast affluent readers. In theory you should aim your newspaper at all readers - one reader is as good as another. But if you don't deliver the ABC1 reader at an effective cost per thousand to the advertiser, you can't create the argument that enables you to sell the ads. That's where the *Irish Press* and the *Evening Press* and the *Sunday Press* have fallen down in their battle with Independent Newspapers. Independent has been run by people like Joe Hayes who is an expert in marketing. He came from a cigarette company where he would have studied what the most effective media were to promote his wares. Obviously the newspapers have to be interesting in themselves and the *Sunday Independent* is a roaring success. It reflects that commercial edge the management of Independent Newspapers have.

With a few exceptions, like *The Wall Street Journal* or *The New York Times*, the American newspaper market is terribly local and fragmented. There is a series of small monopolies, one-city papers, who can pretty well dictate advertising rates per column inch. They are in an unassailable position. When

Ralph Ingersoll tried to set up the first metropolitan daily paper to be established in the United States in 60 years in St. Louis, he spent $30m and lost it all in the space of a couple of months. He was up against a newspaper called *The St. Louis Post Dispatch* which had been in existence for decades and was run by the Pulitzer family. He was not going to break their monopoly. Here in Ireland you have one of the most competitive newspaper markets in the world. Walk into a shop on a Sunday and you see 17 different newspapers. Here, the advertisers are telling the newspapers what they are prepared to pay. Also in America, a lot of newspapers would not employ printers, they would contract out their printing. So for Ingersoll and his people to read themselves properly into this market would have taken months. It is no wonder to me the partnership has ended badly. This is not a criticism of the Americans. They have put a lot of money into a situation which is completely different from anything they would have experienced in North America and they have seen no return.

On to *The Sunday Tribune*. Vincent Browne, as editor, had offered me jobs over the years, he'd offered me the job as editor of *Magill* magazine. When I decided to leave the *Press*, I did not feel like going to work for one of the papers against which we had been directly competing, *The Irish Times* or the *Irish Independent*. The pace in *The Sunday Tribune* was obviously far slower than for a daily newspaper. It was a shock to the system to go into a place where you were geared to produce only one newspaper a week. And *The Tribune* was quite different from the *Press* - it had no history attached to it. It did not have the quasi-industrial atmosphere of the *Irish Press* where the newsroom sits on top of the machine-room. In *The Tribune* the printing is contracted out and there was a small workforce. At about that time they went onto the smaller companies market on the Stock Exchange and raised £0.5m. It was making a small profit every year - that was quite a change from the *Irish Press*. Circulation was around 102,000 - it's gone down a bit now. It was run commercially by Barbara Nugent, the chief executive. She instilled great motivation into the commercial staff. There was a good spirit in the place, better perhaps in the commercial than in the editorial department. The company had a momentum.

The editorial end in *The Sunday Tribune* was quite different from anything I had seen previously. I think it's fair to say that Vincent Browne does have strong views about the people who work for him and, while I was there, I witnessed a number of heated rows, luckily not involving myself. The atmosphere could be electric from time to time. Vincent seemed to have problems dealing with some of the reporters and, occasionally, I would be put in charge of them to run the newsroom as well as being business editor. I began to see at first-hand how the paper worked. I felt rows were provoked unnecessarily and bad feeling created. The motivation of the reporters suffered. They felt that on occasion they were being unfairly treated. I was dubious about the whole operation of the paper even though at that stage it was quite successful. The personality of the editor had a formative effect on the climate of the place and I didn't really like working there very much. The reporters, who have gone on to do immensely good work elsewhere, were in a continuous state of upset, feeling they were liable to be vilified or attacked at any moment. I was thankfully a bit removed from that in the business area in which the editor had no real interest. I came into contact with it only when I had to work as news editor and saw that the reporters were constantly looking over their shoulders. In the *Irish Press*, a daily newspaper, you just went in and did your story and did not worry about whether or not you got on with X or Y, you just hoped your story would emerge on the paper the following day reasonably unscathed, with your name spelt right. In *The Sunday Tribune* you could never be certain what was going to happen next.

I remember a few weeks coming up to Christmas there was a terrible row where someone was made redundant. The editor did not like the particular type of lens used to take a photograph. It struck me all this was unnecessary. Perhaps things have improved since I left in 1989. From the outside anyway, *The Tribune's* problems look mainly financial. Their decision to launch a free newspaper caused ruinous losses. It went from being a company that was generating a profit of one or two hundred thousand a year to a situation where it was losing millions. Launching 150,000 copies of a free newspaper may have been a good idea but, if it was, it should have been done by a company with deep pockets and *The Tribune* had never been properly capitalised. It did not have the resources to go with a project that was ferociously ambitious. Eventually they had to give up - the ambition broke them. It has ended up with the *Independent* owning a sizeable part of *The Tribune* and bankrolling it. I am sure Vincent Browne has always liked to think of himself as an independent publisher and would prefer not to be linked up with any of the other major publishing companies, but the ambitions for this free newspaper, which could in theory have worked, and which was an excellent product, have ended up in the forfeiture of a sizeable amount of his independence. It's sad.

I have painted a picture of considerable unhappiness among the staff of *The Sunday Tribune* but, that said, I have a great admiration for Vincent Browne as a publisher. He has done a number of good things in both newspaper- and magazine-publishing. Nobody can take that away from him. He has great flair and commands admiration but I hope I have described accurately the atmosphere and the sort of place it was like to work in. In the *Irish Press* I felt proud of a product which many people would say was inferior to a product like *The Sunday Tribune.* Almost all the people I worked with in *The Sunday Tribune* have now left. I think it was probably a mistake for me to go there but at the time a lot of us felt that the Press Group might actually close down. In fact, the *Independent* newsroom is now full of people from the *Irish Press.*

At the time I went back to the *Irish Press* a number of us had been kicking around the idea of a new publication. I was friendly with Frank Fitzgibbon. He had worked for *Business and Finance* magazine and had edited *Irish Business.* He had also done some work on television. Strangely enough, in the mid-1980s, we had examined the possibility of setting up a sports newspaper - Irish people are passionately interested in sport. France and Italy had successful sports newspapers.

Because of the recession, we had backed away from the idea of a sports paper but, by 1989, there was a different Government and the economy was growing fairly rapidly. We did not want to spend the rest of our days as PAYE workers and decided to take the plunge. Three other business journalists were also getting itchy feet. Aileen O'Toole, a fellow Northsider jacked up her job as editor of *Business and Finance*, while James Morrissey, a brilliant reporter and one of the most gregarious people I've ever met, signed up for the trip. A fifth journalist also had signalled that he wanted to be with us.

Frank devised a massive business plan for the paper - cash-flows, P&Ls, market assessments, the lot. It was exciting. We met for some months late at night hammering out the details. We sensed in our hearts that what was at one stage just an impossible dream was crystallising into reality. By autumn it was put up or shut up: beyond that point there was no going back.

I devised the editorial plan for the paper. Our fifth partner dropped out. We wanted to do the company through the Business Expansion Scheme, tax-effective for small investors. We also involved the printer in the project, John Kerry Keane, who was the owner of *The Kilkenny People*. The idea was he would print the paper free of charge for a year in that way earning his equity. We would create the product and try to make it a commercial success. We took the project to Riada Stockbrokers. They analysed the numbers and went through the business and editorial plans and questioned us on all our assumptions. They thought it was a good project and said they would raise £600,000 capital to get the paper going. They suggested a capital structure for the company with which John Kerry Keane was unhappy. Perhaps he was unhappy with them. At any rate, he seemed to baulk at the proposal. We felt the relationship with John Kerry Keane would give us strength - we were getting involved with someone who knew about commercial printing. We were just journalists, what we knew was how to write a newspaper, not how to print it. As well as owning a newspaper, John Kerry Keane is a successful contract printer and employs quite a few hundred people. He has bought a number of provincial newspapers since 1989 and has been doing well. He suggested we should go to Davy Stockbrokers to look for an alternative proposal. We went to Davy and through the same rigmarole. They said they would get the money. A problem arose: in order to be a BES company you have to have ten per cent tax status, that is be a manufacturer. We would have had to enter into an agreement with the printer whereby we leased his printing presses for a period of hours every week and made a contribution to his overheads. In a sense, we would have to become our own printer. I think John Kerry Keane was concerned this might jeopardise his tax status as a manufacturer. He was getting a lot of legal advice from his solicitor, Laurence Shields, who was cautioning him against coming into such an arrangement. I found John personally to be a polite man, a modest and friendly fellow, but I think it is fair to say he was conservative in his approach. Everything was ready to roll. We had had to leave our jobs because news of the paper leaked out. We had hired staff. We went ahead and got offices and computers with a £50,000 overdraft from our bank in O'Connell Street. On the 6th November, 1989, the first Monday in November, at a meeting in Goodbody solicitors, the guys from Davys said to John Kerry Keane if he was not prepared to sign, the whole deal was off. Finished, finito, we've had enough. John eventually said he could not sign. He said sorry in the lift and that was it - no BES money, no printer. We went to a Chinese restaurant.

Some months before I had been reading in *The Wall Street Journal* about a French company called Groupe Expansion which was involved in publishing economic magazines and newspapers and was developing a European network called Eurexpansion. It was run by Jean-Louis Servan-Schreiber - the name meant little to me except, of course, I had heard of his brother Jean-Jacques, who had written *Le Défi Américain*. I had said to myself, when we get the paper going, I'll try and do a deal with this fellow so that he sends us economic and financial stories and, in return, we can send him stories about Ireland. It would mean we could get foreign news into our newspaper at a reasonable price. I had telephoned him several times and eventually got through and he said he would like to meet us, that he would like to come to Ireland. He said he would come on the Thursday - the Thursday before the Monday on which the whole thing broke down. At that stage, we had not seen him at all as an investor - we were going to talk about swapping copy. He came to Dublin with his wife, Perla - she is from Morocco - at a time when we were giving presentations to advertising agencies even though the paper was not yet in existence. We did not even have a dummy until the famous Monday and even then it was printed by the *Meath Chronicle*, because John Kerry Keane's new Scandinavian machine did not yet work. Frank Fitzgibbon and I brought Servan-Schreiber out to the Cafe Klara which is now La Stampa in Dawson Street. We told him all about the paper and the Irish newspaper market. He said he would like to become involved. He was staying at the Conrad Hotel and we invited him to a breakfast meeting we were going to have with advertisers the following morning in his hotel. After that he had an hour or two to spare and I brought him to see the Book of Kells in Trinity College. With his wife we walked around the town, he turned to me and said he wanted to invest in a newspaper. Now this was the Friday morning and John Kerry Keane was still in the project. Servan-Schreiber said he understood the structure of the company and that he would like to buy 20 per cent of the equity. He was putting a value on the company of £2m. So he was prepared to put up £400,000. But under the scheme which had been drawn up by Tom Byrnes of Davy Stockbrokers, John Kerry Keane was to get 24 per cent of the equity to begin with, in return, as I said, for printing the paper free of charge for a year. The BES investors were to get 40 per cent and we were to get the balance between us. Then there was a ratchet mechanism through which, if we performed, we could increase our shareholding at the expense of the people who were putting up the BES money. Jean-Louis Servan-Schreiber said that, if John Kerry Keane had a 24 per cent shareholding, he would like to have at least the same. He wanted to give John Kerry Keane £40,000 at lunchtime for two per cent of the company, a company which did not exist. Here we were, told to offer John Kerry Keane 40,000 smackers for two per cent of a nonexistent company so that Jean-Louis Servan-Schreiber would have 22 per cent, the same as him. We told John Kerry Keane and Davys. Davys were impressed - they got all excited and rang up their colleagues in Paris who told them that Jean-Louis was a big name in France. Jean-Louis went back to Paris that day and we did not finalise anything. Davys were keen to get Jean-Louis on board. Kerry Keane was not so sure. The brokers spent hours trying to bring him round over the weekend. A meeting was arranged for the offices of A & L Goodbody on the following Monday night at which everybody would be expected to commit themselves on paper. That day we continued to prepare for the launch of the newspaper, meeting potential advertisers, hiring staff and preparing stories. It was a wet evening. There was great excitement when the dummy arrived from the *Meath Chronicle* at six o'clock but at 7.30 the lawyers came back from Goodbody's and said there was no deal. We had our offices, 15 staff, a dummy, and no newspaper.

We went off to have a Chinese meal and decided the only thing was to go to Jean-Louis Servan-Schreiber and tell him the truth about what had happened and see would he help us. We had no money - we had almost spent the £50,000 at this stage. We rang Paris and luckily he was available the following Wednesday. Aileen O'Toole used her credit card to buy three air tickets. Frank and I went over at the crack of dawn on the Wednesday bringing with us Anthuan Xavier, the accountant from Simpson Xavier. We wanted him to be the auditor of the company. We told Jean-Louis exactly what had happened. He seemed quite pleased that the printer was no longer involved - he said he preferred to get involved in projects in which there was not another major shareholder. After about an-hour-and-a-half he brought a lawyer into the room together with his financial controller and told them that he was about to invest £0.5m in our paper and would that be enough. We left the room and came back and said we did not think it would be enough. We asked if he could invest £600,000 which was the money we had originally planned to raise through the stockbrokers. He said that was fine, that he wanted 50 per cent of the shares for the £600,000. We would hold the balancing 50 per cent - there would be no BES. We would print the paper on an arms-length contract basis. Jean-Louis shook hands with us. We could not believe our luck. We heaved a giant sigh of relief on the pavement of the rue Leblanc, near the Quai des Citroens. He came to the door, got us a taxi to the airport and said, "I know what it's like when you have a car and you are all set to go and you have no petrol in the tank". He said he would send on the money when our lawyers had got together over the documents. From having nothing on Monday, by Wednesday we were ready to roll.

We met up on Wednesday evening to tell Aileen and James what had happened. We had a pint in Birchalls of Ranelagh. We had got some champagne on the plane which I had put in my briefcase. We were back in business. That was the 8th November and the first edition of the paper came out on the 26th November, 1989.

There were more high jinks to follow. John Kerry Keane's new Scandinavian press could print a broadsheet with ten pages of colour - the technology of newspapers was changing and the advertisers wanted colour slots. You use four times the capacity of a mono page to print a colour page. For example, the *Irish Press* and the *Independent* do not print colour in-house. They farm out their colour work to Smurfits and then rewind the reels and overprint it with news on the day. *The Irish Times* can print colour on the run because they invested about £8m. John Kerry Keane's machine was not yet commissioned but we still intended to have the paper printed by him. The pages would be transmitted by modem and printed on Saturday in the works of *The Kilkenny People*, the old Fieldcrest factory. We had tested the modems for transmission strength and everything looked good. On November 24 1989, John Kerry Keane telephoned us - this was the Friday before the first edition of the paper came out - and said he wanted to see Frank and myself. He came down to the office and told us he had bad news and good news.

The bad news was that his machine was not yet capable of printing the paper. The good news was that *The Irish Times* on an old boys basis had agreed to print the first edition. The gauge of a page in *The Kilkenny People* was quite different from *The Times* and all our computers had been programmed to fit it.

Then John Kerry Keane told us that he would be able to get our paper printed by *The Irish Times* but he wanted us to enter into an immediate five-year printing contract with him. Frank told Kerry Keane that he would enter no contract and we left the room. This really was the last straw for us.

We talked to *The Irish Times* and, very decently, they said they were prepared to print our paper. We had to change all our computers around. That was ten o'clock on Friday morning. We worked from then until breakfast-time the following morning. We had to give *The Irish Times* an indemnity for any possible libel actions and they wanted to read the entire paper before they would print it. John Kerry Keane turned up to see the first copy being printed and to push the button on the printing machine. Many of the senior printers from *The Irish Times* were there. Cross words were exchanged between John Kerry Keane and some of my colleagues and he left. We were all exhausted. We went off to Regan's pub in Tara Street which opens early for the dockers. We looked at this first edition of the paper and were proud of ourselves and happy. We had to go home and get some sleep because we were having a party that night in the Westbury Hotel to launch the paper. Jean-Louis was coming over from Paris.

The Irish Times did not want to continue to print the paper -

they don't, as a policy, take on contract work. We had no regular printer for several weeks. The second edition of the paper was printed in Navan by the *Meath Chronicle* and the size was different again. The third edition was printed by *The Sunday World* in Terenure. They have a beautiful plant up there. They printed the paper for three months and then we were printed by Drogheda Web Off-Set Printers. They were based in Ashbourne, about 40 minutes drive from here. They printed us until February 1993 when we moved for cost reasons to the *Belfast Telegraph*.

Initially we thought the paper would achieve 17,000 sales weekly, rising to 20,000 as we became better known. We felt we would lose money the first year and break even in the second. In the event, we achieved sales of 24,000-25,000. To begin with, there was a surge of interest but we averaged out at around 25,000. We have been building the sales of the paper progressively into the upper 20s and we are now at 29,000 to 30,000. The paper was always to be a fairly low-cost operation. I was the editor from the start. Frank Fitzgibbon wanted to give up journalism and become the chief executive of the company. I have not spoken to him since June 6th 1991, the day he left.

Frank was a great person to get things going - he put together the business plan for the paper. He began to run the commercial end of things. We lost money in 1990 but not at a massive rate. We were achieving our circulation target but were not getting sufficient money from advertising. We got on with each other very well throughout that year, the four of us. James Morrissey was the deputy editor and Aileen O'Toole news editor. We had an advertising staff of five or six. We had an accountant and reporters and a few office staff to do clerical work. We were constantly trying to work out ways to generate more advertising revenue. We put together a number of plans to make the paper profitable. One was that we would change the nature of the paper and put sport into it. We felt we had established its credentials - it was seen as respectable and conservative, a good broadsheet paper, but we felt that, with sport, we could achieve 50,000 sales. *The Tribune* were doing about 90,000 and *The Irish Times* daily circulation is about 90,000. Another plan was to corner what is called direct advertising, that is, not through agencies but by telephone selling to businesses. We conceived the idea of having a thing called *The Industrial Post*, a third section of the newspaper. *The Industrial Post* would concentrate on regions and industrial sectors and we would sell advertising linked to those. Obviously the costs involved in producing *The Industrial Post* would have to be less than the revenue it earned. We were to go to Paris to put these ideas to our shareholder. There was an air-traffic controllers' dispute and we never got there. All we could do was speak to Jean-Louis on the conference phone from Dublin and he didn't like at all the idea of sports being in the paper. We were told to drop that and proceed with the idea of *The Industrial Post*. It involved our hiring more advertising staff. We had to bring in £30,000 a fortnight on it - we did that and it was costing us only about £16,000. We had the whole paper at break-even in the final quarter of 1990, a year after we launched it.

Then things began to go wrong. Disputes arose primarily because *The Industrial Post* was successful. Frank decided this was the way forward, that what we needed to do was to expand the paper completely in terms of overhead. We moved to bigger offices and Frank had got a guy experienced in trade magazines to manage *The Industrial Post*. He wanted to be the boss of advertising and marketing for the whole paper and quickly he did become the boss of the advertising department. Initially, as I explained, we had five people selling advertising - a rather staid, laid-back set-up. Frank and this fellow began hiring large numbers of people. James Morrissey and Aileen O'Toole were both upset at the way he was expanding the overhead and he was not consulting them too much. They raised the matter with me. I spoke to Frank - we did have a board: two Irish directors and two French directors, but it never met. We should have had outside non-executive directors to advise us and to act as arbiters to resolve tensions that arose.

I am a diplomatic person by nature -I don't lose my temper much and so I was the intermediary in all of this. Frank believed you had to achieve some critical mass, a market presence. We now had 38 people in advertising and 70 people on the newspaper. We had taken on the new offices and had invested in new machines. Frank put a second business plan together at the end of 1990 and had managed to secure a further £0.5m in bank borrowings.

We began producing huge newspapers. One had 64 pages in it and a colour magazine. That was in March 1991 - it was an exhausting period. The tension between Aileen and James on the one hand and Frank and the commercial manager on the other was becoming more pronounced. Whereas the four of us had all been together initially, Frank was spending more time on his own. He worked phenomenally hard as chief executive, he never seemed to rest. At night he would be poring over spreadsheets in his home. He gradually found that his view of the world was different from that of Aileen and James. He felt they were too conservative and did not want to expand and take things on like he did. Their argument was the overheads were too high and we would go bust. I was in the middle. There were a couple of rows and I told everybody to go back to their desks and do their jobs and we lurched from one dispute to another. In May 1991 the company ran out of cash despite the bank facilities of £0.5m - we were just trading at too high a level. Frank decided he was going on his holidays to Portugal. He called us into a meeting on the Friday night before he went and told us we were to close down a section of the newspaper while he was away: that was the second section which he saw as costing a lot of money and not generating enough revenue. *The Industrial Post* was generating revenue and that should be carried on. We just said no, that we should carry out a study before taking such a precipitate decision. Frank went off and we did not close down the second section and, when he came back, things went from bad to worse. We were on a cash knife-edge. We had got the investment from Jean-Louis and the bank borrowings and that was it, we just could not meet our liabilities. We were trading at a high level and generating a huge amount of advertising on the back of this huge sales force. As we found out later, we were also going to have a sizeable bad-debt experience stemming from the hard sell that was going on. The situation became untenable. James and Aileen said they could not work with Frank. Having had no board meetings for 18 months, we had to call in our shareholders and say to them, "Look, we have reached the end of the road". I had to take sides and I supported James's and Aileen's view. Frank was able to present a coherent argument for what he was doing. He was generating a lot of advertising and the paper was selling rather well. He confidently expected to make a lot of profit - it was just a matter of financing it. Anyway, we confronted our French partners with the problem. They got upset. The upshot was that they bought Frank out. He had 14 per cent of the company. I was wondering if things could be resolved in some amicable way, could we wind things down a bit, go back to normal, but feelings were too high. Frank agreed to sell, for an exceptionally good price, and left the company on June 6th. That was the day I shook hands with him and said goodbye, the other two were not talking to him at that stage but did shake hands. The French then had 64 per cent of the company and the three of us had 36 per cent.

A new chief executive was sent in by our shareholders: Jane Tolson who came from England. She was careful, attentive to minor detail and probably did not have the entrepreneurial side of Frank's character. Where Frank was ebullient, she was severe and cold but straightforward. In the gap between Frank's leaving and her entering the company, management was handled by myself and James Morrissey. We started to cut overheads immediately. We just did not believe a paper of our scale was sufficient to carry that weight. We analysed the performance of the people who were selling ads and found we had quite a number who were no good at it, so we got rid of them. It was a new experience for us - we had no experience as commercial managers and we were in doing the dirty work. We brought the advertising staff down from 30 to 15. The guy who was in charge of it left, and that was quite another day in the history of the newspaper - I remember having to get him his briefcase and his coat and say goodbye. That was all done in five or six weeks and James ran the advertising department. He got into the swing of it and managed to hustle deals. We still had overheads that were far too high.

Then Jane Tolson began to hire more people - she seemed to feel the company could break even and make a profit at a high level of overhead. We put our case to the people in France and I suppose they felt they should back the judgment of their own new chief executive. The result was that in 1991 we were going nowhere fast: the losses were severe and the French were losing patience. In December 1992 I wrote a business plan which suggested a massive reduction in overheads and trading at a much lower level if we were to survive. I put it to the board and the French people agreed. We reduced our overheads by one quarter the next month, January 1992. We pressed on and, that year, we were not losing as much money, but the losses were still unacceptable. In the summer of 1992, our chief executive from England left us and Barbara Nugent, who had left *The Sunday Tribune* and had gone to work in advertising, joined us as chief executive. James Morrissey had left in August 1992 to join a tax consultancy. Barbara has done a superb job. She has further reduced the overheads and we are now able to make the paper commercially viable. We are three-and-a-half years down the road and we lost money in 1990, in 1991, in 1992, the worst year being 1991. We hope to break even in 1993.

Just as our commercial fortunes began to look up, with Barbara cutting costs and circulation growing steadily, problems were beginning to gather for Eurexpansion, our French backers.

The recession in mainland Europe cut deep into spending on advertising, particularly in France, and a re-launch of the Parisian daily *La Tribune de l'Expansion* cost an estimated £25m with little to show for it at the end. Some time in 1992 Eurexpansion began to retrench - and that included us. In our case it meant they began to look for an equity partner who would share the cost of supporting our paper and perhaps purchase part of the Eurexpansion shareholding. For some months, using London-based media consultants, they looked for a partner.

Christmas 1992 we went to Paris for a board meeting with Jean-Louis and his German partners (from the financial daily *Handelsblatt*). It was a difficult meeting and one which could have had any outcome. We put it to them that we would stand a better chance of securing an outside investor than they, since our lives were intimately bound up with the paper. *Handelsblatt's* boss, Heik Afheldt, together with Jean-Louis, conducted the most thorough analysis of our business plan. We were able to show that our costs were in order and that our projections were realistic. After the burdens which Eurexpansion had carried for our paper, they may have been a little sceptical that we could make it commercially. Our arguments were sound, but I believe it was Jean-Louis's strong sense of commitment to our newspaper at an intellectual level that saw us through. After much discussion and various meetings in private rooms, they agreed to support us as we set about attracting a new backer. And they set out the terms on which they would agree to reduce their shareholding.

It was three days to Christmas. As we left the lit-up offices of Eurexpansion on rue Leblanc, Jean-Louis's number two at Eurexpansion, a man called Pierre Jeantet (who now runs a huge newspaper chain in Bordeaux called Sud Ouest), called me aside. He said, "We have been very tough. But look at it like this. It could be the biggest Christmas present you will ever get". Aileen, Barbara and I laughed, but we knew we had been put through the wringer by the Germans. We adjourned to the Georges V for a glass of champagne.

We set about getting a new investor without delay. It was not an easy task. Many well-heeled backers had been burned by their involvement with *The Tribune* and the newspaper sector had a bad name. Though we had made enormous strides commercially, we felt it was possible that we would have to look outside the country. And we did. Six months later we had agreement in principle from two international groups that they would back the paper in its new era. They were the British multinational Pearson and a German publishing house called Verlag Norman Rentrop.

Pearson own the *Financial Times* as well as *The Economist,* Royal Doulton, Lazards, Madame Tussaud's and Penguin. We liked the idea of being associated with such a prestige name but we knew that we might be entering the whale and could disappear without trace. We knew they would drive a hard bargain, and sure enough they wanted a large controlling stake.

Rentrop on the other hand had a more hands-off approach. He seemed to want to back people intuitively and he was prepared to move fast. We went with him. Now Verlag Norman Rentrop controls 40 per cent of the equity, with Eurexpansion at 10 per cent. Aileen, Barbara and myself have the other 50 per cent. The balance sheet has been cleaned out of its debts and we have fresh capital. In a way I feel that I have been twice blessed. In 1989 we were at the edge of the cliff and were redeemed by a French publisher and intellectual with a sense of adventure. In 1993 we were re-capitalised by a no-nonsense German who perhaps saw we had been through the worst. Certainly we had seen good days and bad days. They have a saying in Germany: if it doesn't kill you, it makes you stronger. And we feel much stronger right now and ready for greater things.

It's taken three-and-a-half years. It's been a tortuous trail. It's cost the French a lot of money and it has been hard going for us to maintain the editorial momentum of the paper. We had the emotional hassle of falling out with each other and of coping with commercial reality. As a journalist, it has given me massive sympathy for business people! That is the significant difference between us as journalists and the sort of people who might be editors of other newspapers - they have worked in large organisations but they have hardly come into contact with the commercial end of things.

There is, in fact, significant hostility to business in a lot of papers, a presumption that everybody involved in business is up to some sort of skulduggery. It's also an ideological thing. We have been attacked in other newspapers because of our sympathy with businessmen - sympathetic to, say, Dermot Desmond and Larry Goodman. We feel an affinity with people who are underdogs, who are pursued by the hounds. There must be another side to the story. We have sought to defend such people and that is not Politically Correct. At the same time, we have been quite critical of other businesses. We are not all pandering to the business classes but we are less inclined to make the kind of assumptions other papers do about business.

We have also tried to avoid the conventional media thinking on moral issues - sexual morality and all that kind of thing. We have given prominence to views that might be styled traditional Catholic. It's not that we have a particular line on this, we're not all staunch church Catholics, but we feel that, just as papers don't have a proper balance in their relationship with business, so do they not have a proper balance in relation to these issues. They are pushing an agenda: divorce, abortion and a load of other things. There are two sides to all those arguments. Newspapers are trying to ram through a social agenda. People are entitled to hold traditional views and to be respected for them.

At the time of the X case, papers like *The Irish Times* were lecturing the public and saying that Ireland was like Iran under the Ayatollahs, living in a dark age of fundamentalism. The reality is that the argument about abortion is going on in every advanced country - in Germany and North America there are huge debates about whether abortion should be legal and, if it is to be legal, what parameters should be set. The Germans export their abortion problems to Holland just like we export ours to Britain. I believe the arguments against legalised abortion are very strong but there is an assumption in the newspapers that people who do not support abortion are fascist fundamentalists. It could be argued that people who promote abortion are being most illiberal. We try to give space to people who hold different views. We try to get a bit of a balance and are quite proud of that, of not having swum in the mainstream. Mainstream is not broad church - it means that you are liberal if you agree with me. It reaches its high point in the *Sunday Independent* where anybody who does not agree with its agenda gets lifted out of it in no uncertain terms by one of their columnists. My own view is that you probably will have civil divorce in Ireland because it's just something that has been festering there for years - tens of thousands of marriages have broken up and people want to put order back in their lives. But time and again the electors of this country have shown that they don't like ideas being rammed down their throats. Opinion polls claimed that people would vote by a majority of two-to-one in favour of divorce - they actually voted two-to-one in the opposite direction. The politicians and the media were clearly wildly out of touch. The underlying assumption when Garret FitzGerald introduced his divorce referendum was that it would be passed - the media never examined themselves about why they called that one so wrongly. Perhaps they should have given more space in the papers to views they did not themselves hold.

There is a degree of caricaturing in mainstream newspapers. When they deal with a topic like abortion or divorce and they have their own views, which in the case of the *Sunday Independent* are quite overt, when they have an agenda which they don't even bother to conceal, they construe the opposition to that agenda as Alice Glenn and Padre Pio. They do not see reasonable people in the middle who do not agree with abortion and who are not particularly fanatical Catholics. That middle ground is not represented anywhere in the media. They just don't like the fact there is a huge mass of the population that does not like their agenda and is quiet-spoken and gets on with it.

That's why I think newspapers are out of touch. There's been a huge drift away from the hard news type of journalism and into commentary. We try to stay away from that - we try to keep our paper as factual as possible and have, OK, segments of it for commentary but clearly labelled as such. An awful lot of what passes for journalism nowadays could be written without ever having contact with real people. If a journalist has only got to give his views or the views of the clique in which he mixes, he does not really have to find out what the man and the woman in the pub over there think about probate tax or what Mrs. Mullarkey in Castleknock thinks about divorce or what somebody down in Sneem thinks about interpretive centres. If journalism is to be perceived as just polished writers sounding off about something, you don't even have to get out of bed in the morning. Seriously.

4

Keith Baker

BBC Northern Ireland

People often ask why it seems that only one side of life in Northern Ireland is shown across the water. My answer to that is news is news, not image-building. I don't see BBC News and Current Affairs in Northern Ireland as some ex officio branch of the Northern Ireland Tourist Board.

The conversation took place on October 14 1993

Keith Baker is Head of News and Current Affairs, BBC, Northern Ireland.

He was born in Enniskillen on April 16 1945.

His father was James Baker, also a journalist, who retired as editor of *The Impartial Reporter*, Enniskillen.

His mother was Bertha Pitcher, mother and housewife.

He is the elder in a family of two with a sister, Claire.

He is married to Jo Pelan, a teacher.

They have three children: Louise (16), Simon (12) and Rose (10).

He was educated at Enniskillen Model School and Portora Royal School, Enniskillen.

1962 joined *The Enniskillen Impartial Reporter*; 1965 joined *The East Antrim Times* in Larne; 1966 worked briefly in a PR agency in Belfast; 1966 joined *The News Letter* as a reporter - at various times was news sub-editor, deputy features editor; 1969 joined the *Belfast Telegraph* as a sub-editor - subsequently television critic and features writer; 1982 joined the BBC as a duty editor on radio news; 1986 became editor of television news; 1989 head of News and Current Affairs.

He is chairman of the People of the Year Awards.

His hobbies are his family, literature, music and work.

I suppose like most people of my generation and the generation before it, journalism was something you fell into. My father was a journalist of long standing so journalism was always in our house. Provincial editors do a bit of everything and he would read proofs at home - there was always a kind of inky feeling to domestic life. After school I would call into *The Reporter* offices to see my Dad and I can still smell the ink and the paper and what it was like on a hot day. Those evocative images are there to this day. There was something terribly comforting about it all. At school, in my academic field, if you could call it that, I was always interested in communicating, in English, in writing. When I came to the end of second-level education I debated whether or not I wanted to go to university. In those days there was no real careers guidance. I chose to go into the newspaper. I loved it. I have never regretted it.

The Reporter is still owned by the Trimble family, Joan and Valerie Trimble, as they were, and before them Egbert Trimble, who was the managing director when I was there. He was a sort of Edwardian figure, someone who, in my eyes as a teenager, was from another era altogether but someone, along with my father, who had high standards. Their approach to journalism has stood me in good stead with concern for things like syntax and grammar and accurate presentation, things which nowadays are not always held in high esteem. When you are working for your father, you are never quite sure whether or not you are there on your own merits or indeed whether you have any. I knew, that having had that early grounding, I had to go and sort things out for myself. An opportunity came up in the *East Antrim Times*, an offshoot of the *Belfast Telegraph*.

That was another great experience - I made friends there who are friends to this day. I shared a flat with a friend who is now head of current affairs for CBC in Canada. That was 1965 and I was 20. When I got away from the cosy domestic environment I found out that I was not as good as I thought I was. I had a lot to learn. It was a bit of a road to Damascus for me in terms of my abilities and my approach to the job, and I discovered I was among journalists who were streets ahead of me. It was a lesson I'm glad I learned early enough to be able to do something about it.

In those days - I make it sound like a lifetime ago and maybe it is - newspaper journalism was very much the Senior Service. BBC Northern Ireland then had a lightly-staffed newsroom even though there were some distinguished people working in it. It had nothing like the staffing levels we enjoy today. Ulster Television was only a few years old - it came on the air in 1959. The older journalists felt that broadcast journalism was not journalism at all - newspapers were the real form of journalism. Broadcasting journalists were viewed with suspicion. There was no local or commercial radio in those days. There was no Radio Foyle such as the BBC has now in Derry.

I joined *The News Letter* in 1966 as a sub-editor. There was a terrific staff there, many of whom are still friends. It was a great grounding. You could work nights - I had a flat in the Upper Newtownards Road at the time and often used to walk home at four in the morning through east Belfast. There were no troubles then - you could call at the bakery and get a fresh loaf and a pint of milk. It seems hard to envisage now. How quickly things changed. Indeed, people think you're pulling their leg when you tell them that one of the barmen in *The News Letter* local was a man called Gerry Adams.

I was offered a job in the *Belfast Telegraph* - there is a kind of Belfast Fleet Street which is around Donegall Street and people get to know each other and what is on offer. Those were days when you got hired in pubs. Somebody liked the cut of your jib, next day you were summoned to see the editor and offered a job and that was that.

I joined the *Belfast Telegraph* in 1969 when the troubles were starting - it was a hell of a time to be working in any form of the media. We were seeing the place change before our eyes and the headline type just kept getting bigger. You would come in in the morning to deal with the litany of the night before when countless people had been killed, countless places had been burned and bombed. When I go back through old files or scripts, it was on a scale then that you would now find unimaginable but we got through it and came out the other end. For those of us working on the *Belfast Telegraph* there really was no other story - and you never thought about things such as careers, you were so absorbed. It was all-consuming. During the Ulster Workers' Council strike, people who lived near my flat would join me and we would all walk to work together through the barricades. When I tell my kids about things like that now, it sounds almost heroic, a touch of "What did you do in the war, Daddy?" That is not what I am trying to convey at all. My children have no concept of what it was like compared with today, bad though it may still be from time to time.

Those days were professionally demanding, personally quite difficult. Belfast was dead at night. The place has improved by leaps and bounds. Social life in Belfast is now invigorating and lively. The commercial heart of the place is buoyant. Belfast was a bleak old industrial Northern city, shabby at the best of times, and those were the worst of them.

There are huge advantages in being a journalist in times of strife. If you're in the office and you hear a fire engine going past you probably have a good idea where it's going to or you can find out quickly. It's different if you are working in an insurance office or the civil service or a shop where people are more vulnerable than those of us in the trade. We had, and still have, a sense of being in touch with what was going on and there is a bonding among journalists which crosses all divisions. You are slightly apart from the events, not personally involved, observers looking on. You were not personally at risk, though people have had some narrow escapes during riots. While I was safe enough in an office, some of my colleagues were hit by stones and on occasion plastic bullets during a riot but there was no widespread direct threat to the media from either side. That largely exists to this day. However, it was not watertight - the *Belfast Telegraph* office was bombed and so was the BBC in 1974.

Rightly or wrongly, I have been noted for a degree of wit and, in the *Telegraph*, I got involved in writing about television.

In this, I succeeded Alf McCreary, who is now in Queen's University. I wrote the television column for six years and enjoyed a little notoriety - people bought the paper on Saturday to read the television column, or so they told me. When I left the *Telegraph* I had a lot of nice letters which I have kept to this day. People tell me they still miss it. While I was writing that, I began to rub shoulders with people on the broadcasting side of the business and it gradually became a bit of a magnet. I did some programmes for BBC World Service on radio, small newsy things like *A Letter from Belfast*, the poor man's Alastair Cooke. I enjoyed going off with my tape-recorder to do special programmes as well - that was my first real taste of broadcasting. In the early 80s, I went down to RTE on Fridays to do a series called *Week In, Week Out* - I looked back on the week in a light-hearted way with filmed inserts and newspaper cuttings - I did about 36 programmes over a year. The scripts make me cringe now. My kids found some of them recently and recite them at moments of maximum embarrassment, like when someone's visiting. I then knew I wanted to try my hand at the broadcasting business. When an opportunity came up with the BBC I was lucky to get the job and have been locked into broadcast journalism ever since.

Now, instead of being directly involved myself, I am involved as an editor in the direction of others, taking as careful custody as I can of the BBC's journalism in this part of the world. Since much journalism is about people, it's not surprising that I remember people more than incidents, wonderful characters like the late Ralph Bossence, a very distinguished and very funny writer on *The News Letter*, and sadly someone whose writing is probably lost to the new generation. Every age says there are no characters left in journalism - I don't believe that for a second. We ourselves become the characters of journalism. Each style breeds its own characters. My own newsroom is full of them. They are a salty lot. Journalists retain an individuality and a sparkle to this day despite economic demands, business plans and strategy reviews and all the modern business parlance and practices.

Journalists are not awed by office, nor should they be. Well, we may have a respect for certain institutions or offices but not always for the people who hold them. Journalists have a great belief in accountability - equally we have to be accountable ourselves. I happen to work in an organisation which firmly believes in accountability. At a simple level, if you work in an organisation that is publicly funded, people have a right to expect good value from you for the money they are paying. If a listener writes to me with a criticism - or indeed a compliment - they deserve the courtesy of a reply. But what should guide all public service journalism is getting it right - that is particularly important in Northern Ireland where you are dealing with a community at odds with itself. Your journalism has to be objective and trustworthy from whichever perspective it is viewed. People may not always like what we're telling but they recognise our right to tell it - they have to see us dealing with issues straight down the middle. They have the right to expect us not to have a particular political allegiance but to deal as impartially as possible with some difficult and sensitive things. So far, touch wood, we have carried out that task with some distinction. I am not singling out the BBC - I think all our broadcasting colleagues have honestly fulfilled a difficult and sensitive remit.

I was sitting around with some friends who are in the teaching and medical professions and I said in a moment of self-examination - probably late at night - that I envied them the worthwhile jobs they were doing. They all turned round to me to tell me that I was doing one of the most worthwhile jobs there is. I had never thought others saw it quite in that way, nor appreciated the value. Being able to communicate information to people when they desperately need it is quite a task and a hell of a responsibility.

You cannot become unmoved by the things that happen in this community but you have to deal with them dispassionately. The community will always need to know more about itself and what's going on and it pleases me to be able to bring things to people they might otherwise not know about.

When I became a "proper" broadcast journalist instead of just a dabbler, it was the second time in my life I realised that, professionally, I didn't know as much as I thought.

If you missed by four or five minutes your deadline in a newspaper, it did not really matter. When you got to broadcasting journalism there was a whole new set of circumstances. The news went out on the hour, not one minute before and not one minute afterwards. You learned a different concept of time, a different style of writing, a new form of communication. I just could not get used to the relaxed attitude of the seasoned broadcasting veterans I was dealing with. I went in as a duty editor - that involved supervising news bulletins. At 10.50 people would say there was plenty of time before the 11 o'clock news bulletin - they'd still be typing furiously. They'd make it into the studio with ease 15 seconds before the time. That took a wee bit of getting used to and caused a bit of hair loss. I thought you'd be at least 20 minutes getting ready, sitting down, coughing, straightening your tie and your hair - it doesn't work like that in broadcasting. It's skin-of-the-teeth stuff - an exciting, fantastic buzz about it that one never loses. The buzz of a newsroom of any kind is a hell of an experience - I had that thrill the day I walked into the organisation and I still have it. I like to see programmes going well - I like to see the enthusiasm people have about their job amid the stresses and the strains. They work hard. They make demands upon themselves and I make demands on them but there is a great spirit about it, an enormous exhileration.

When you're part of the BBC's news machine here, you have two related functions - one, to broadcast to Northern Ireland and two, to feed into London. I am a focus for consultation for all news and current affairs programmes which are made by the BBC about Northern Ireland. If *Panorama* want to do a programme about Northern Ireland they have, by statute as it were, to talk to me about it. If *Newsnight* want to do something they come knocking on my door. There is scarcely a day when an English voice doesn't come on the phone with, "Can I pick your brains for a moment?" - with the usual reply, "What's left of them." I am delighted the advice I give is, more often than not, taken.

People often ask why it seems that only one side of life in Northern Ireland is shown across the water. My answer to that is news is news, not image-building. I don't see BBC News and Current affairs in Northern Ireland as some ex officio branch of the Northern Ireland Tourist Board. If the news is bad, then the news is bad. The only yardstick we must go by is, is it interesting? That can be a story about the first bank on Rathlin Island or the latest atrocity, although we all remember the atrocities, not the banks.

Among the programmes I am responsible for, both on radio and television, is *Good Morning Ulster* which sets the agenda for the day and which won the Sony award this year for the best radio and current affairs programme in Britain bar none. One remarkable piece of reporting which helped us win the award was by a member of the staff who was in a restaurant in Belfast when a car-bomb went off outside it. He captured all the panic and the chaos.

Radio is a much more instant means of communication than television. There's less paraphernalia between you and the audience. You are broadcasting radio bulletins on the hour and there are the programmes that go behind the news bulletins - they will probe and reflect and, I hope, ask the questions that people want to hear us asking. It's good to hear a lively interview, intelligently conducted with a newsmaker of the day being made accountable.

You always have to be aware of the competition. Downtown Radio do hourly news bulletins. Listeners have a choice. Ulster Television provide a news service. You have to be aware of the marketplace in which you are operating. You can't arrogantly ignore it. That's something that the BBC is learning. You may be providing a valuable public service but what you provide has to be distinct from what others are doing, with a value and a reputation of its own, rather than more of the same.

I did find a cultural change joining a public service institution from a commercial one - it is a place full of acronyms, almost like some branch of the Secret Service, although I've yet to find anyone called M. It is an acronym itself - nobody would call it the British Broadcasting Corporation. It's just the BBC. When memos come around you become remarkably skilled at deciphering them. Who is HDPWSTN? The amount of paperwork that goes round the entire organisation is awesome. Of course, there was one great difference between the *Belfast Telegraph* and the BBC. Any newspapers I worked with were little self-contained entities. I was joining *the BBC in Northern Ireland*, rather than something which was entirely of the place itself. The BBC's base is London, not Belfast, although our regional identity is crucial. I agree with you, Ivor, that it is a large and complex organisation but it is surprisingly small in many respects - if you want advice about something, you know exactly who in Bristol to ring up, or Leeds or Birmingham. There is a club-like atmosphere. The phone can ring at night and it can be the Director General - it's not a frequent occurrence, thank goodness, but it has happened. While it is different from a newspaper, the people are much the same - they have the same belief in communication, the need to *tell* people, which all journalists share.

I could understand how some people in the Republic might have seen the BBC a number of years ago, rightly or wrongly, as representing just one side of the community. But it isn't true. We broadcast to the whole community. Let me give you one example, there is now a hell of a lot more broadcasting in the Irish language on BBC than there ever has been, both on radio and occasionally television. The fact that the BBC has Gaelic football would not have been the case ten years ago - and it's us who show the Ulster Championship every year. Our function is to provide a service for all the people who pay a licence - from whichever side of the community they come. But it's a complex cultural picture with many different traditions and we want our broadcasting as a whole to reflect that.

We are running up to the renewal of the BBC's Charter in 1996 and we have paid a lot of attention to what are called focus groups, people who have an interest, be they the farming community or business people or the sporting fraternity or people involved in youth and community issues. We listen a lot to what they have to say about what we do. Apart from that we have the equivalent of a board of governors - the Broadcasting Council. It is a group of people from all arts and parts. They are remarkably representative of the community at large and very quick to point to any deficiencies in our output. They also tell us when we've done something right. They don't mince their words - they are the year-to-year arbiters of our programme strategy. It comes back to accountability - you can get too locked in to an organisation, unable sometimes to see the wood for the trees. What we have to provide is a *public* service, short and simple.

There have been so many events in my time here that it is difficult to single out one but there were some remarkable ones like the Enniskillen bombing. That was my old home town and the pictures of the blown-up war memorial and the people in their dress uniforms picking their way through the rubble went across the world. I knew some of the people involved. That Sunday I was in the hallway of my home watching a Remembrance Day parade coming up the street where I live. My sister rang me from Enniskillen to tell me she thought she had heard an explosion "up the town". I remember looking out and seeing a little Boys' Brigade band coming up and putting two-and-two together and being horrified. I rang the office and they said yes they were getting reports of an explosion at the war memorial in Enniskillen, a couple of people injured. I put the phone down and said to my wife that I thought I would nip into the office to see how things were going on. Her parents were coming out for lunch and I said I would be back in plenty of time - I got back on the Tuesday. Being in the BBC here, as I said, we are not dealing with just the local reports - you have the vast weight of the BBC descending upon you. We put in long hours but so what? That's our job and we did not suffer like the people in Enniskillen did. There is nobody in this community, including those of us in the media, who has not suffered a trauma of some kind.

Organisation is a big part of this job - getting an OB unit down to Enniskillen, organising camera crews, deploying staff, all the technicalities that are difficult to deal with but nevertheless crucial - otherwise the story does not get on the air. It's only after you have dealt with something like that and you sit down with a cup of tea or a drink that it descends on you. In many ways our periods of intensity mirror those of the security forces - while they are busy, so are we.

Every so often an interview will touch you. Gordon Wilson's interview was particularly moving. I remember seeing it as it came in to our video-tape area from an OB unit in Enniskillen and there wasn't a dry eye in the house. We stood there looking at it and we decided to run the whole thing. You never forget those things but you may forget you actually played a part in putting it on the air. That has now gone into history.

Very often it's an image you see on the screen rather than an interview. An image can have a devastating effect. I remember the Teebane massacre where workmen were killed in their bus in County Tyrone. One of the shots we had was just of a lunch-box amid the wreckage. It was not a gory image but it was poignant in its simplicity. Things like that can linger. I am not sure whether those things have an effect on those of us who deal with them - I guess they are bound to. I am fortunate in that I am the person in the office at the hub of it rather than somebody who is out there in the field. Nevertheless I feel very acutely the responsibility that places on me. I am always anxious I don't put people at any more risk than needs be.

The reason I do not like to recall incidents, that we do not dwell on them an awful lot, is because you do not know what can be around the corner, what atrocity we shall be contending with tomorrow. And then the output is so vast. Yet only the other day I saw seasoned journalists gathering around a television set and starting back as if they had been struck when Martin Smyth said, in however qualified a fashion, that he would be prepared to talk to Sinn Fein. There is always the sense of surprise in this job. That's one of the things that keeps us all attracted to it. Every day is different from the one that went before.

There is a very good code called *The Producer's Guidelines* - available at all BBC shops! It tells producers how to go about their business, how to deal fairly with people. It deals with all sorts of areas - things like surreptitious reporting and when the BBC will approve of it and when it will not. And it deals with the Government's restrictions on broadcasting people from certain organisations - that remains the single most difficult area. We take a fairly robust line on it. We try to make the restriction as narrow as we possibly can. Of course I am against it - we should be arbiters of our own programmes. If people say to me that it is our job to nail these people, whoever they may be, I tell them that, no, it is not actually - our job is to be as impartial and dispassionate as we possibly can. We have got to be clinical. The worst interviews you hear are those that generate a lot of heat and there is not much light at the end of them. Any journalist who imagines he would give an unfettered Gerry Adams a run for his money has another think coming. He, like a great many people in this community, is very seasoned in dealing with the media. You are dealing with people on all sides who are extremely professional in espousing a cause. You remember when the Rev. Ian Paisley said to a young interviewer, "Let me smell your breath".

I may be interviewing you and thinking I am giving you a hard time and you will say, "Well you know as well as I do, Keith . . ." Using my name in an interview creates an impression of intimacy which can completely deflate the interviewer. When you see that on television you see what might look like a kind of cosy relationship. What it really shows is that there is a huge professionalism in the media here, on both sides of the microphone.

Yes, I suppose I do miss making programmes myself but I love the moment when somebody comes to me with a problem with a programme - I love editorial dilemmas, having to exercise my judgment on an issue or a shot or an interview. I love the moment when the buck does stop here. That focuses the mind, gets the brain-cells working. I don't know that I necessarily miss sitting down at the desk and getting into the technicalities of programme-making but inevitably, as you get into management, you get more distant from day-to-day, hands-on programme-making and become more involved in future strategy, business planning, budgetary control, staff appraisal, performance reviewing and all those things any organisation of the size of the BBC has to be constantly involved in. That has its rewards - part of it is seeing other people do well.

Only if it's absolutely vital would I see a programme before it goes out. The BBC is an organisation which runs with a fair degree of internal autonomy, on the basis that you don't keep a dog and bark yourself. You could not see or listen to everything. You are broadcasting from 6.30 in the morning till midnight - and that's only the radio. We're doing hourly bulletins on television and *Inside Ulster* in the evening, plus *Spotlight* which is a current affairs programme, and then many programmes go out live. There is a command structure in the organisation which has key figures within it such as my two senior deputies, one who is editor of current affairs programmes and one editor of news. In their own way they are the equivalent of newspaper editors. They in turn have senior producers working for them. Every morning in life we have an editorial meeting in my office. Everyone attends it. We discuss that day's agenda and bits and pieces of what was already done. We will discuss an issue of the day - the Hume/Adams discussions, the unemployment figures - people who are involved with those things will tell us how they are going and what we should be doing. I keep it as unfocused as possible - the kind of meeting that encourages everybody to join in. We also have programme review sessions, as informal as possible. Individual editors will be doing that with their own teams anyway. They will go over an interview before and after. I will sit down individually with my political editor and have a long natter about where political paths are leading. We talk a lot, and a lot of tea gets drunk.

You tell me that when you flick from RTE to BBC you will see the same story covered from different angles. I feel at times the BBC deals only with stories in the Republic that are embarrassing - scandals of various kinds. I think there is the risk that, as you say, you get a faint colonial whiff. We, BBC Belfast, maintain an office in Dublin and we give more news from south of the border than anybody else in the northern media does. We try to reflect those things that are on page three of the newspaper - not thinking of *The Sun* - rather than on page one. It does not have to be today's hot news story but things that might have a more relaxed feel to them. I think it is right that people in the North should have a feel for what is going on in Dublin because it does, whichever side of the divide you sit on, have a bearing on things which happen here. Whether you like it or not, there is an Anglo-Irish Agreement and a Secretariat in Maryfield. There is a relationship between London and Dublin with Belfast in the middle. We would be utterly blind to ignore Dublin as a centre of influence on what happens here.

We are a region of the BBC but a thing that makes us different from any other is that only this region deals with relationships between countries - with the relationship between Prime Ministers, with events of international significance as well as purely regional. When people come here and see what we do, they say it's like running a national news programme, the events are so big. We also have to reflect the events that are not so big - we cannot give people a diet which is solely politics and security, however crucial those things may be. We have to give them a wider agenda - the environment, the arts, health, education.

I think RTE covers Northern events well but it covers them from a Dublin perspective. Forgive me if that sounds a bit obvious! I would find it hard to articulate what a Dublin perspective is - it is something that's happening "up there" in a way. Obviously they have their own editorial priorities and

Northern Ireland may not always be part of them and that's fair enough. That's the case of the BBC in London as well - but then I am not having to try to balance Bosnia or events in Russia.

What we cover has changed as the community changed in the North: Stormont went, a great many of the things that the civil rights people campaigned for have been achieved - one man one vote, allocation of housing, those things that were such bitter bones of contention in the early 60s and beyond.

Looking at the future, it's easy to become pessimistic or agnostic. We have seen a lot of false dawns. I often wonder what it would be like if we had a pre-1969 Northern Ireland where you could walk at night without concern from one end of the city to the other. My children have never grown up in a Northern Ireland that did not have soldiers on patrol, wrecked buildings, vehicle checkpoints. They have no sense of what it would be like without that. To an extent, that to them is normal life. I have to say it is not to me. Often, when you see a ray of hope, you have a vision in your mind's eye of what it would be like to have this heavenly thing called peace. But then you think that the world has changed anyway - society is different, there's more crime of a casual nature, there are a great many social problems unresolved, life is tough whether there is a security problem or not - and you realise that there is no turning back. Even if there was not a security problem, and there was a degree of stability, I don't know how stable that stability would be. It would have inherent tensions in it anyway. We would always have something to worry about. Life on the other side of the Irish Sea is not a bed of roses either.

There are certain things you cannot erase and television plays a big part in that. You cannot erase the picture of David Andrews when he was Foreign Minister sitting in Windsor Park, the home of Loyalist Protestant Linfield. 20 years ago he could not have done that. You cannot erase the image of members of the Unionist Party going into Dublin Castle. You cannot get over what Martin Smyth said. Whether all these straws in the wind mean anything substantial, I don't know -

but they must signal some change. But we have a responsibility not to get too wildly excited. That can manifest itself in the public eye as pessimism - the wet blanket, but I come back again to objective, evaluative journalism that points out that we may have seen all this before, that allows people to put brakes on their enthusiasm if that enthusiasm is ill-founded. Equally, you have to say that something may be significant, that it is the first time that so-and-so has done that, that and that - but we will wait and see. It is not our job to hold out false hopes to people nor is it our job to dash them. There are other images you can't erase - the rubble of bombed buildings and the endless funerals and scenes of grief.

I was driving home on the weekend that Hume and Adams said they had come to the end of a particular stage in their talks and I was listening to Radio 4's *Midnight Newsroom* and they said something to the effect that there had been a breakthrough in the search for peace in Northern Ireland. I stopped the car - I have the luxury of a car-phone - and I rang up and said, "Please, please, who says?" That kind of wording can confer on an event a significance it might not be worth.

Yes, in radio and television, we do see ourselves as cooler than the newspapers. Papers depend very much on their appearance as well as their content. If you see a banner headline which says, "Breakthrough", as *The Sunday Tribune* had on the Hume/Adams talks, you might be more persuaded to buy that paper.

You ask me if we are the better for being relatively free of commercial constraints. I don't know that I would use the word better but it is easier for us to plough that objective furrow - there's no doubt about it. We don't have advertisers, for example - if one of our programmes turned up a business scandal, we would not have to worry about their withdrawal of advertising. We can do a critical programme on the GAA and two days later broadcast the All-Ireland final.

I think Northern Ireland can be a big turn-off for a lot of people. The Republic is not unique in its attitudes. In many ways we are the skeleton in the cupboard of this island - keep it locked up and don't let anybody know about it. I am sure there is a bit of that deep in people in the rest of the island. I think it was *Private Eye* that said the greatest turn-off was, "And now another play about Northern Ireland . . ." We do not seem to be able to get to grips with our problems and it goes on and on. I remember the late Billy Flackes, who was our political correspondent and who died earlier this year, being asked what was the solution to the Northern Ireland problem and he said, "Have you ever thought there isn't one?" As time goes on one sees how right he may have been. A great many things have changed in the last 20 years but a lot of things have not - some have got worse. People look at our problems, like Bosnia, and ask themselves what can they actually do about it and turn to something else. There is a limit to the threshold of interest people from outside can have in the North. As we speak, people are excited about the Hume/Adams initiative and that will wane. How do you deal effectively with the longest-running story in the British Isles with anything more than sporadic success? How can you realistically expect to keep it on the agenda in every household in the British Isles night after night? You can't. It can't be a constant editorial priority.

On the other hand, I believe Conor Brady in *The Irish Times* has a policy of putting every murder in Northern Ireland on his front page - once you relegate it, you are consigning it to ordinariness. We could have that here. Once you put a murder to the bottom-half of the news programme, you are decreeing an illusory state of normality. There is a terrible risk of becoming inured to what's happening here but I see no evidence of that among my colleagues. I have never failed to be surprised by the degree of caution and sensitivity and sheer human decency that exists from day-to-day in circumstances like that. You can't go to the scene of a murder or an explosion and treat it as routine. You are not a human being if you can do that. One of the things about broadcasting and television is that you actually have to go there and be there. "Sources close to . . ." does not work in broadcasting. Newspapers have several ways of being that wee bit distant from the person to whom they speak - we can't do that. We have to show the picture of the stretcher being carried to the ambulance and hear the mother.

5

Vincent Browne

The Sunday Tribune

The widespread public perception of the media as arrogant and exclusionary is understandable. The problem lies in the grossly unequal access to and unequal control of the media. This requires editors and journalists to behave as surrogates for readers, rather than as representatives of the owners or advertisers or, perhaps more relevantly, of their own sectional interests.

The main conversation took place on June 28 and was concluded on November 18 1993

At the time the conversation took place Vincent Browne was editor of *The Sunday Tribune*.[*]

He was born in Limerick on July 17 1944 and was reared in Broadford, Co. Limerick.

His father, Seamus Browne, was a shopkeeper in Broadford.

His mother, Kathleen Burns, had been a teacher in the St. Louis Convent in Monaghan.

He is second in a family of four: one sister, Mary, two brothers, David and Malachy.

He is married to Jean Learmond.

They have two children, Emma (12) and Julia (3).

He was educated at the national school at Broadford; at Ring College, Co. Waterford; St.Mary's Secondary School, Dromcollogher, Co. Limerick; St. Vincent's College, Castleknock; UCD (BA in economics and politics). He is currently completing a minor thesis for an MA in UCD on political philosophy and has recommenced studies at the Kings Inns.

1967 RTE television summer programme, *Roundabout Now* and a researcher with *The Late Late Show* from October 1967 to April 1968. He reported on the Soviet invasion of Czechoslovakia for *The Irish Times*; 1969 became editor of *Nusight* magazine. 1970 Northern news editor of the Irish Press Group, based in Belfast. 1974 joined Independent Newspapers. 1977 started *Magill* magazine. 1982 involved in the relaunch of *The Sunday Tribune* - editor 1983.

---

[*] See Epilogue.

My parents were a major influence. Being the first son in the family, it is not surprising in Irish circumstances that growing up I was closer to my mother. She was a classic victim of the unfairness of our culture towards women. She had come from a modest background in Ballybay, County Monaghan. Her father had died in Glasgow where she was born. When she was just three or four her mother brought the family of five back to Ballybay where with the help of her brothers she opened a small grocery shop. My mother won a scholarship to the St. Louis convent in Monaghan and then a scholarship to UCC, where she did a BSc and a master's in science. That was unusual for women in those days. She did a HDip and returned to the St. Louis convent to teach. She met my father in Bundoran in the mid-30s and they married in 1939. She went to live with him in a remote west Limerick village, Broadford, where she knew nobody. She told us later that in those first few years she sat at home, often crying of loneliness, writing to her mother, sister, relatives and friends.

I think her unconscious sense of frustration was transferred on to me, her first son. She was ambitious for me. She hoped I would go for the priesthood and, in my early adolescence, I thought I would. She then hoped I would join one of the "great" professions such as medicine or law. She was disappointed that I joined one of the "low" professions but became reconciled to this before her death.

She got Alzheimer's disease around 1982 and died of it in January 1987. In October 1986 we went down to Broadford, having been warned that she had deteriorated greatly. I was shocked and distressed to see her then. She talked rubbish for a while and then she and I were alone in the kitchen and for about three minutes she spoke with absolute clarity. She said she knew she was dying and that these were perhaps the last sensible words she would speak to me. She said she loved me and was reconciled entirely to the fact that I had "lost the faith" - she herself was deeply religious and had been greatly worried about my agnosticism. She asked me to promise her some things in relation to other members of the family and when she had finished she reverted immediately to incoherence. It was very moving.

My father was much involved in the local community, in Muintir na Tire, the community council, the handball and tennis clubs and the like. I think I got a strong sense of "community" from that. I was close to him growing up but then was not close at all in my teens and early adulthood. However, particularly in the last ten years of his life - he died in February 1992 - I think I got very close to him. We started to work on a history and his reminiscences of Broadford - I have still to finish the book. We went to Australia together to visit relatives he had corresponded with all his life. He came and stayed with us quite a bit, although not at all enough, and we went down to Broadford regularly. He was cautious and this used to infuriate me at times but he was also gentle, especially in his later years. He had a mischievous sense of humour and was committed to all his family. 16 months after his death, I met a woman who had met him on a train about a year before he died and she told me he had spoken a lot about me and was proud of me. I was touched - I had no sense of that at all. Neither am I sure what it is there was to be proud of. He had a miserable last few years and in a way looked forward to death. His health disimproved, his friends had all gone, and he became progressively depressed. I thought it was unfair for someone who had lived such a good life.

I found his death extremely difficult. I suppose I had simply got closer to him in the five years after my mother's death and his passing meant the end of the family as we had known it. I miss him greatly. I miss both of them. They are still the points of reference for me on almost everything. I think what would they think.

Yes, I am an agnostic. I find absurd the idea of an omnipotent all-merciful God who intervenes directly in our lives and with whom one can have a personal relationship. It is absurd on the basis of the old argument that, if there is such an omnipotent God, then it must be a callous God to permit such awful suffering. Therefore God, if there is one, is either not omnipotent or not all-merciful or not all-just, which proves the point. I also have difficulty in understanding the belief in Jesus Christ, that he was God. The fervour of religious belief is surprising given the fact that so many people believe in conflicting religions. Why should one attach to Christianity any more or any less credibility than to Islam? But I miss religion and find some religious services greatly comforting. I loved the idea of my mother or father being led by angels into paradise and of us all being reunited - but I don't believe it.

I was not particularly good at English at school - my strong subjects would have been Irish (a lasting legacy from Ring College), maths and history. I don't think that proficiency in English is essential for journalists. I feel those who are gifted writers often cease to be good journalists. Perhaps, because of their writing skill, they manage to get away with not doing the hard reporting graft. I can express myself coherently and adequately, I think, but I do not have descriptive or "writing" abilities.

The national school in Broadford was fairly primitive but there was an excellent teacher there, Phil Jones, who was a friend of my father. Ring College was also primitive and, at times, brutal, but it gave me a great grounding in Irish and maths. St. Mary's School, Drumcollogher, was an extraordinary place. It had been founded by a Mrs. Savage and without it literally hundreds of young people in the Broadford, Drumcollogher, Milford, Tullylease, Feoghanagh and surrounding areas would not have got a secondary education.

I have ambivalent feelings about Castleknock College. I wasn't happy there for the first year or so and, in general, I do not think that the standard of education there at the time was impressive. I think it is improved since. However I got a lot out of it. First of all I made friends with many people: Tom Foley of Killorglin, Co. Kerry, now living in New York, Dick Nash from Newcastle West, Co. Limerick, Noel Broderick, Ollie Egan, Jim Dorgan, Denis Hanrahan, Fergus Armstrong, Paddy Rothschild, John Griffin, all of Dublin, Tommy Greally of Roscommon, Tony Moore, who has since died, Larry

Cheevers, Liam Reynolds, and many others. I have remained friends of many of these over the years. Then several of the teachers and priests were major influences. There was Fr. Paddy O'Donoghue, perhaps the most forceful personality in Castleknock in my time there. Overall I don't think it was much of an educational establishment at the time - certainly, compared with St. Andrew's where my daughter Emma is now going.

I remember UCD primarily because of the friends I made there, rather than any impact upon me academically. I met Gordon Colleary through student politics at UCD. He was running for President of the Students Representative Council in May 1963 and I had just been elected to the Council. He was running against a Gerry Collins candidate, Peadar Lennon. Collins spent about eight years at College involved almost exclusively in student politics. The cynical among us used to say that some day Gerry Collins would become a TD. Gordon was defeated by Peadar Lennon but was elected shortly afterwards President of the Union of Students in Ireland. I got elected to the executive of USI at the same time. We went to New Zealand together to a student conference in June 1964 - paid for, it turned out, by the CIA. Gordon and I have remained close friends.

He brought me into the current affairs magazine *Nusight* in 1969 and he became involved with me in *Magill.* When Tony Ryan withdrew from *The Tribune* in 1984, Gordon became the linchpin of the operation. He borrowed money himself to invest in *The Tribune,* he devoted a huge amount of time to it, without a penny's recompense. *The Tribune* would not have survived without him. He has been good humoured, generous and fair throughout.

My friendship with Gordon has been one of the great legacies of UCD but I made other friendships. Among them was with John Kelleher, who later worked with me for a while in *Nusight* and then went on to join RTE, where he became controller of programmes and might well have ended up Director General had he not left to join *The Tribune* as managing director. Many people assumed his appointment as managing director was my doing but, in fact, it was the doing of Tony Ryan, who, understandably, wanted his own person and ended up appointing a close friend of mine. But John Kelleher's role in the relaunch of *The Tribune* was crucial and I think the failure (including my own) to acknowledge this has been unfair to him.

I made friends at UCD with a group of people, many of them in medicine, and, for the most part, we have remained close since then. These include Dermot Lavery, a solicitor in Dundalk, Paddy Boland, a surgeon in New York, John Donoghue, a consultant in the Mater and Beaumont hospitals, Trevor McGill, another consultant working in Boston, Michael Tarpey and Michael Nee, dentists in London, Liam O Flanagan working in RTE, Frank Daly, a doctor, now in Paris, Gary FitzGerald, a doctor in Waterford, Sean Whelan, now in the Department of Foreign Affairs and several others. I also became close friends with Declan Burke Kennedy, who had been at Ring College with me in 1955/56. He was perhaps the major intellectual influence at the time, along with Mary Elizabeth Archibald, whom he later married.

I joined the students' branch of Fine Gael, in part because of my father's associations with the party through his childhood friend, Denis Jones, who was then Fine Gael TD for West Limerick, in part because there was nothing else to join other than Fianna Fail. Actually I joined Fianna Fail also for a period but this was solely to have Collins voted out of the chairmanship of the branch. The Labour Party was almost dead at the time, so if one were to be anti-establishment, the only political option was to join Fine Gael, however unlikely that might now seem.

I became editor of a party newspaper, *The Citizen*, the main purpose of which was to hold the leadership of the party accountable to the rank and file. This was unpopular with the leadership, which wasn't much into accountability. The paper was put paid to. I knew John Bruton well at the time and, frankly, did not then have a high opinion of him. I changed my opinion in later years and thought he had become one of the most formidable and serious politicians on the scene. I don't recall Alan Dukes having anything to do with Fine Gael then but I do remember him as being one of the most brilliant students at UCD. It was through this connection that I got to know Garret FitzGerald. I used to go to his house in Eglinton Road. I got to admire him greatly: his intelligence, dedication and, above all, his energy.

I had more sympathy with the politics of Declan Costello. He was a socialist and should have been a member of the Labour Party - an option he long considered. I thought it was a great pity he did not become leader of Fine Gael when James Dillon stood down following the 1965 general election. I and others tried to manoeuvre him into the leadership afterwards but without any success - obviously. His defection from politics was a pity. He has been a great judge - why he was not appointed to the Supreme Court I do not know - but his influence could have been far greater had he remained in politics.

I got a poor degree in UCD in economics and politics and started to study for the Bar at the Kings Inns. I had been writing UCD Notes for *The Irish Times* in my last few years at UCD - I was also writing for the student newspaper *Awake* edited by John Boland and later by Michael Keating, both subsequently Fine Gael TDs. While at the Kings Inns, I started to write more for *The Irish Times* and for other publications, including *Business and Finance*, then edited by Nicholas Leonard.

In the summer of 1967 I got a job as a researcher/interviewer on a programme called *Roundabout Now*. The producer/director was Mike Bogdanov, who later became director of the National Theatre in London. The presenter was Terry Wogan. You might think this line-up should have ensured the programme's success, but no. It was probably the worst programme ever televised by RTE. I contributed handsomely to that achievement. I was asked one afternoon if I was ready to travel to a stud farm in County

Kildare to interview a gentleman named Sir Gordon Richards. I enquired who Sir Gordon Richards was and the person replied, "Oh no, not another week like last week". He advised me to go down the corridor to speak to Michael O'Hehir. Michael O'Hehir was almost of mythological significance to me. He was aghast (a) that someone would not know who Sir Gordon Richards was and (b) that RTE was hiring such people. I travelled to the County Kildare stud farm with a film crew, the production assistant, Nuala Naughton, and the director, Charlie Scott. In a field at the stud farm I interviewed a short, stocky man with a Yorkshire accent. I could see Charlie Scott and Nuala Naughton over Sir Gordon's shoulder out of camera range. Both were mortified by the questions I was asking. Charlie was holding his head in his hands. At one stage I asked Sir Gordon a question which inferred that I thought there were jumps in the Derby. He replied in a broad Yorkshire accent: "You don't know an awful lot about racing, son".

Following these triumphs I got a job for six months as a researcher on *The Late Late Show*. I did very little work on *The Late Late*. I started to go out with another researcher there, Dana Hearn, and she, Gay Byrne and I used spend a long long time discussing the meaning of life. I got to know Gay and Kathleen well then and have remained friends.

In the summer of 1968 I persuaded *The Irish Times* to allow me to go to Czechoslovakia. The Soviet armies invaded the day before I was due to go but I managed to get in just before the borders were closed. It was an extraordinary experience, not at all frightening. The demonstrations on the streets of Prague convinced me initially that the invasion could not possibly work. The Soviet troops took without retaliation massive provocation from the people of the city - the contrast was striking between those troops and the behaviour of the British army I was later to witness in Northern Ireland. Communication with the outside world was difficult and not helped by my inability at the time to type, which meant that my telex messages to *The Irish Times* took an age. But also I had no idea what I was supposed to do. I should have simply described what I was seeing on the streets - instead I sought to explain what was going on, which of course was rubbish. I stayed there for over three months and greatly enjoyed it. On coming back I resumed at the Kings Inns but again got involved in journalism, this time with *Nusight*, a current affairs magazine which had grown out of USI.

Together with Gordon Colleary, John Kelleher was also involved and so too were Declan Burke Kennedy, John Feeney, who was later killed in an absurd aeroplane crash on a Beaujolais run, and Kevin Myers, now with *The Irish Times*. Garret FitzGerald and another friend whom I had got to know through Fine Gael, Michael Sweetman, were also involved. We did some issues of the magazine of which I remain proud. In September 1969 we did a full issue on the Northern troubles. We did a huge issue on poverty, another on the Catholic Church. Many people still tell me they have kept the back issues of *Nusight*. All contributions to the magazine were anonymous - I was into that at the time but now I believe this to be entirely wrong. Journalists should be as fully accountable for what they do as they try to force others to be. Michael Sweetman was an extraordinary man. He had great intelligence but, most of all, he was wonderfully eclectic. His breadth of knowledge and interest was vast. Generous, good humoured and open-minded, when he was killed in the Staines airport crash - that other awful air crash - in 1972 I was more affected by his death than by that of anybody else up to then or since, apart from the deaths of my parents and the deaths this year (1993) of two friends, Dinny O'Hearn in Melbourne and Liam Hourican, the former RTE broadcaster.

Nusight never had the financial resources it required and in the summer of 1970 it ceased publication. Shortly afterwards I was appointed Northern news editor of *The Irish Press* group and went to live in Belfast in September 1970.

I went there with a strong sense I had missed the action - Northern Ireland would drift towards a normal liberal democratic state and conflict would die out. Right up to the summer of 1971 there was a feeling profound change was underway and a new modus vivendi could be found between the two communities. But underneath the surface the situation was worsening gravely because of two factors: a determination by the newly-formed Provisional IRA to manipulate the situation into an all-out war with the British to force them to withdraw from Ireland and, secondly, and probably more critically, a decisive mistake made by Harold Wilson and James Callaghan at the end of August 1969 to commit British troops to the streets of Northern Ireland on the basis of a half-baked reform programme, agreed with Major James Chichester Clarke, the then Northern Ireland Prime Minister. This decision committed British troops to upholding a regime still inherently sectarian and discriminatory and seen as such by the Catholic minority.

By February 1971 I began to realise that the situation was drifting towards anarchy. I saw the British soldiers as out of control in many situations. I recall a major turning point: a riot outside the Protestant engineering works, Mackie's on the Catholic Springfield Road. The start of the trouble there was sectarian but it could have died out had not the British army weighed in with massive force, provoked hundreds more people onto the streets, killed a woman through the reckless driving of an army jeep through a crowd and escalated the trouble beyond resolution. That night the riot spread onto the Falls and New Lodge Roads. At that time too, three British soldiers were shot dead on a lonely road at Ligoniel outside Belfast. I and others were coaxed into believing this had been done by Loyalists, to provoke hostilities between the Nationalist community and the British army. I had got to know several IRA leaders in Belfast at the time and absolutely believed them when they assured me they had nothing to do with what, up to then, was the most horrific incident in the troubles. It transpired much later that the IRA did indeed do these awful killings. I found out quite a lot about the incident from the people directly involved - this happened entirely by mistake when I was in their midst in a Southern town some time later. They had used two women to lure the soldiers from a city centre pub to a party outside Belfast. The three soldiers got out of a car near Ligoniel to have a pee and were shot dead by two men who had joined them. One of these men spoke compulsively about the incident, at times boastful and at times remorseful. It was sickening.

I got quite close to the IRA then. It was part of my job - I needed to know from them what was going on, why they were doing what they were doing. I got to like and respect several of them, although I realise that that is far from political correctness nowadays. I thought highly of the likes of Billy McKee, the first Provo leader in Belfast, Francis Card, another old-time Belfast Republican, Seamus Twomey, who could be chilling but was incorruptible. The person I got to know best was David O'Connell. There was a strong streak of ruthlessness about him and a political blindness which was numbing. But he too was incorruptible. He was highly intelligent and had sacrificed a great deal, given his abilities. I was glad that we met for a few drinks two weeks before his sudden death. I also got to know and admire Ruairi O Bradaigh. I would have to say that the most formidable of them all intellectually is Gerry Adams. There is a strong streak of integrity to him. I have always laughed at the characterisation of these people as gangsters and as mindless killers. Certainly they have been killers, but mindless, no, and gangsters, no. The likes of O'Connell, O Bradaigh and Adams could all have done well for themselves in conventional careers. Their lives were shattered by their involvement in the cause they believed in. It is important to appreciate this about the IRA when attempting to deal with them politically or militarily. They would be far less formidable were they just gangsters.

If you express any admiration for IRA people individually, you are suspected of being a fellow traveller. Well if that is so, then I am a fellow traveller. But I also believe their campaign is fundamentally wrong for a number of reasons. I do acknowledge there is a residual injustice in Northern Ireland - by residual I mean that injustice that would remain if the violence stopped and if the reactive violence and repression of the security forces and Loyalist element ceased. There would be continued discrimination and denial of the cultural identity of the Nationalist community. But I believe the scale of this injustice does not justify the taking of a single human life.

The IRA says its justification is founded on the right of the people of Ireland to national self-determination and historically peoples have fought wars of liberation to assert this right. I agree this is historically correct but I do not agree one can draw the conclusion the IRA draws. What if the Irish people as a whole agree that the constitutional status of Northern Ireland should change only with the consent of a majority of the people of Northern Ireland? Would this be an expression of national self-determination? In my view, it clearly would and, in my view, this is clearly what the Irish people as a whole have decided. No formal constitutional expression has been found for this but is it reasonable to take and destroy lives simply on the grounds of this constitutional formality? It's absurd.

The IRA has been afflicted with a kind of fundamentalism, which is uncontainable in a normal democratic society. For this reason I have argued that in principle internment would not be wrong to stop the killing, since one cannot cope with fundamentalism through the normal democratic process. The decision whether or not there should be internment is a matter for political judgment.

I hope all this is an irrelevance because the IRA itself seems to have come through the ideological barrier of fundamentalism on the issue of national self-determination. Their acknowledgement, through the aegis of the Hume-Adams talks, that the exercise of self-determination is a matter for agreement among the Irish people and, furthermore, that any new agreement on the future of Ireland would have to win both the allegiance and the agreement of the entire community, is remarkable. As of now (October 1993) we are on the verge of the most important breakthrough in the Irish troubles for a quarter of a century and one hopes this is appreciated by the two governments involved. What seems now to be required is simply a reiteration by the British, but in formal and credible terms, that they have no strategic or economic interest in remaining in Ireland and that they will respect any agreement the people of Ireland come to, provided only that the agreement of a majority in the North is required to change the constitutional status of Northern Ireland.

There is a segment of the journalistic and political community down here that do not want any settlement that does not involve the defeat of the IRA. The defeat of the IRA is more important to them than peace and agreement. The reaction of the Northern Unionists to what is going on is understandable, given their anxieties, particularly their understandable distrust of the British. But one hopes they can be convinced the breakthrough that is on offer is entirely to be welcomed and that their interests are in no way threatened by it.

I think John Hume has done a wonderful job in encouraging the IRA/Sinn Fein to go down this road and the odium heaped upon him arises from a conspiracy of political illiteracy, led by someone whose judgment on the Northern issue has been wrong, wrong and wrong again for 20 years now, Conor Cruise O'Brien. Conor is a person of remarkable integrity and intellect. His influence in awakening us down here in the late 60s and early 70s to the sectarian character of the Southern state was important but his analysis of the Northern situation has been off-beam since he wrote *States of Ireland* in 1972. In that he predicted civil war - yes I know there has been civil war of sorts for the last 20 years but he meant hand-to-hand warfare on the streets with thousands being slaughtered in a short period of time - and he has gone on predicting civil war ever since. In addition, having usefully reminded the rest of us of the anxieties and traditions of the Unionists, he has gone on to ignore entirely the anxieties and traditions of the Nationalists.

I became acquainted not just with IRA people while I was in Northern Ireland. Before going there I had made the acquaintance of one of the most extraordinary personalities on the Northern scene, a Unionist MP and barrister, Desmond Boal. At the time he was close to Ian Paisley and through him I got to know Paisley quite well and liked him. The religious fervour of Paisley is entirely genuine and there is a great big generous streak to him. Paisley was deeply wounded by being excluded from the Unionist inner circle and much of his motivation comes, I believe, from a sense of hurt pride. He can be reckless in what he says and in his choice of associates but, above all, the key to understanding him is that politically he lacks courage. He was always obsessed with being outflanked on the Unionist right, always worried that a Bill Craig, William Beattie, Ronnie Bunting or whoever would steal the right wing of Unionism from him.

Boal is quite the opposite. Boal has loads of courage. He always said and did what he believed was right. Boal was MP for Shankill and came upon a gun battle between Catholic Ardoyne and Protestant Shankill across the Crumlin Road. He drove across the Crumlin Road in his flash E-Type Jaguar, confronted the gunmen on the other side and enquired, "Why are you shooting at my constituents?" The gun battle stopped. He is a strong civil libertarian and, when it became obvious in May and June 1971 that the Faulkner government was preparing for internment, he made known his opposition to it. I asked him if, when internment was introduced, he would make a statement to me condemning it and he agreed. As it happened I met him on Royal Avenue on August 5 1971 on the day that internment was introduced and I asked him to make the statement as promised. We went to a fitness club owned by Buster McShane - Boal was a fitness fanatic - where Paisley was waiting to meet him. Paisley was not a fitness fanatic. Boal bullied Paisley into making a joint statement with him condemning internment. Paisley reluctantly agreed and spent a great deal of the following twelve months trying to get himself off that hook.

In early 1972, I think, I was phoned by someone in the IRA whom I knew and asked to go to a house in Andersonstown. I was shown what I was told was a sub-machine gun, which, the IRA alleged, was one of several hundred manufactured in a Protestant engineering works in Belfast for distribution to

Loyalists. On getting back to the *Irish Press* office on Royal Avenue, I telephoned the British army press office and spoke to Colin Wallace - it later transpired that Colin was an MI5 agent and was engaged in all sorts of dirty tricks. I told him what had happened. He asked if I could get one of the guns from the IRA for the British army and I said I would enquire.

My article was published in *The Sunday Press* the following Sunday, along with a photograph of the gun, and got a lot of attention. Fellow journalists rang and asked about the gun and I told one or two of them I might have temporary possession of one for the British army. I collected the gun from an IRA fellow in a bar on the Falls Road and headed down towards the Europa Hotel with it under my coat to show a few journalists prior to taking it to the British army headquarters in Lisburn. The news that I would be "producing the gun at a press conference" had done the rounds of the press corps and by the time I got to the Europa there were several camera crews, 20 or 30 journalists - and 20 or 30 RUC special branch officers to arrest me. I was brought to Queens Street RUC station where I was treated with great civility by the police officers. They allowed me use their phone as much as I wanted. I watched television with them, they brought me in a meal and wine from the Europa but they insisted on charging me with possession of a machine gun.

Paddy MacRory, the Belfast solicitor, visited me in the police station that night and opened with the words, "I'm afraid there is a long mandatory sentence for possession of a machine gun and you are clearly guilty. It doesn't matter whether you had the authorisation of the British army or not. They have no power to give such authorisation." I was held overnight and arraigned the following morning in one of the Chichester Street courts. I got bail of £20 or so and was released but clearly there was going to be a problem for me as I would be perceived by Unionists as being involved with the IRA. Desmond Boal and Ian Paisley came down to the court and made statements immediately afterwards indicating they did not believe I was involved in any such improper activity, although both of them told me privately I had been reckless - choice coming from Paisley. But it was typical of Boal's generosity and also of Paisley's.

By the way there was not a mandatory sentence for possession of a machine gun. I was convicted and fined £20 by Justice Malachy McBurney. I met Malachy an hour or so later in the Europa Hotel and he apologised for fining me £20 but said he had to fine me something. He was shot dead by the IRA a few months later in awful circumstances.

I enjoyed working in Belfast, even though it was amidst disaster, calamity and grief. The *Irish Press* at the time was a great institution to work for. The news room was strong, led at the time by the best newspaper executive I have ever encountered, Sean Ward, who went on to become editor of *The Evening Press* - I always felt that Sean's removal from the pivotal position of chief news editor of the group was a major mistake. He was fully on top of his brief, always cajoling, probing, encouraging reporters to get stories, find new angles, beat the opposition on deadlines. Liam Hourican for RTE and Henry Kelly for *The Irish Times* were in Belfast while I was there. Henry was superb at straightforward reporting. He was accused at one stage of making an indecent approach to an elderly lady at a golf course on the outskirts of Belfast. I tell the story now because it surfaces again and again and there is not the semblance of truth in it. Henry told me of the charge and at first I wouldn't believe him for, knowing Henry, the details were incredible. The woman's evidence crumbled under interrogation and Henry was acquitted but, out of a streak of fussy propriety, he insisted on running with the story in *The Irish Times*. I greatly regret that Henry is now lost to journalism in the world of game shows and radio soap. He could have been a great editor of *The Irish Times*.

Liam Hourican was different in many ways. Intellectually, Liam was one of the most formidable people I have met and quite the most articulate. He too had great courage and commitment to tell the truth, irrespective of the consequences. We became firm friends during those years in Belfast. I regretted his loss to journalism when he went to the EC Commission in Brussels. I was shattered at the news of his sudden death in July (1993). I had an overpowering sense of lost potential but at the magnificent funeral service in the Daniel O'Connell church in Cahirciveen I revised that sense. Hearing Sean Duignan and others speak so movingly of what Liam had achieved in terms of the devoted family he and his wife, Pat Clery, had created, the friendships he had formed, the joy and exuberance he had brought to so many of us, I realised there was great achievement and that the sense of lost potential was misplaced.

I got married in June 1973 in Boston to Jean Learmond, whom I had known in Dublin for several years. We married in Boston mainly to avoid the fuss of a formal wedding in Ireland, which perhaps was selfish. Jean's father was in the Indian army. She was born in Burma and when she was just a few weeks old her mother carried her over several hundred miles into India, to escape the invading Japanese. The family returned to Burma after the war and, when she was about six, they came to live in Ireland, where her mother was from. People keep telling me that Jean is very different to me because she is kind, considerate and generous. She is into literature and art, which I am not. She reads widely - while I read in a narrow rut. She knows about nature, biology, medicine, whereas I know almost nothing about these subjects. But together we have travelled to Australia, Malaysia, Brazil, Peru, Bolivia as well as to the continent. We tried getting into Burma several years ago but failed because of the journalist tag on my passport.

Although my parents were initially dismayed I was marrying a Protestant, she became a second daughter to them, nursing them in their illnesses, remembering their anniversaries, caring for their needs, filling in the gaps I left.

We had no children of our own and had difficulty in arranging an adoption because we came from mixed religious backgrounds. When I tried lying about my own religious practices, I got caught almost immediately. We were fortunate to be able to adopt Emma in 1981, when she was just a few weeks old. She has been the joy of our lives. There was a time when I didn't want her to come into the office because I thought others in the office who had children of their own would be deflated by her beauty. The truth is that I still think that.

We tried adopting another child in Ireland but failed and then, through a combination of entirely fortuitous circumstances, we managed to adopt Julia in Brazil in 1990. Emma, Jean and I went there to the interior of Brazil, where the judge required us to stay for six weeks before the adoption was approved. It was an extraordinary adventure, especially for Emma. The part of Brazil we were in was like a sepia-tone picture of Ireland in the late 19th century. Men rode around on horses, pigs and cattle roamed the streets. The only difference was that there was the odd car or truck and there was television - American soap operas with subtitles. Julia is Emma's only serious rival for the title of the world's most wonderful child.

I joined Independent Newspapers on January 2 1974 as political correspondent of *The Evening Herald*. I was sitting in the news room on my first morning there talking to Michael Denieffe, now editor of that newspaper and then a lowly reporter. Michael asked me what was going to happen to the then political correspondent - it was the first I had heard that there was already a political correspondent in place. It was an inauspicious start to my relationship with Independent Newspapers. I moved from *The Evening Herald* over the following few months to work with the *Sunday Independent*, then edited by Conor O'Brien, formerly editor of *The Evening Press*. Conor had been one of the best editors in Irish journalism but by 1974 I think he had lost some of his verve because of a deal of flak he got over a series of investigative pieces on the Irish Hospital Sweepstakes written the previous year by Joe McAnthony.

Conor was replaced as editor by a friend of mine, Michael Hand, in early 1976. Michael, who now is with *The Sunday Tribune*, had great flair as a journalist but he was no negotiator or administrator and that was what was required primarily at the time in the *Independent*.

I have a great deal of admiration for what Tony O'Reilly has achieved with Heinz and his accomplishments otherwise. I admire the commercial success of Independent Newspapers. I should say no attempt has been made to influence me editorially by Tony O'Reilly or by anybody from Independent Newspapers since they acquired a 30 per cent stake in *The Tribune* and since they made substantial loans to the newspaper. I have found my dealings with Tony to be enjoyable. I like him personally. I achieved very little while at Independent Newspapers and certainly by 1976 I had begun to realise that, if I was to achieve anything, I would have to leave and do something myself. My clear objective was to establish a quality Irish Sunday newspaper but I would have had no credibility in seeking finance for that in 1976 or 1977, so instead I sought to start a current affairs magazine. I had experience with this before with *Nusight* and I felt that if I could make a success of that I would gain the credibility necessary to start a quality Sunday newspaper.

This is what gave rise to the publication of *Magill* in late September 1977. One of my partners in the venture was Mary Holland, certainly the finest print journalist dealing with the Northern Ireland issue, with the possible exception of Conor O'Clery of *The Irish Times*. The other partner was a close friend, Noel Pearson. I had got to know Noel through Michael Hand, I think, in the early 70s. Noel has great guts and flair. He was into everything at the time: bands, shows, plays, politics (especially with the SDLP as he was very close to the original six founders of that party) and even a model agency. It was not hard to tempt him into publishing. Noel is compulsively generous and wonderful company. I think that summer of 1977 when we were planning *Magill* was the most hilarious period of my life but the stories are unrepeatable.

Noel became otherwise preoccupied later that year and withdrew from *Magill* and it was then that Gordon Colleary stepped into the breach. We went through a rough patch in early 1978 and then, out of the blue, an Englishman approached us and asked to be allowed invest £20,000. This was Edward Pinelas, who had a vague connection with Ireland, had seen the magazine and liked it.

Apart from Gordon, the mainstay of *Magill* was Cecily O'Toole, who had been involved with *Nusight*. She looked after the money, the administration, the production, everything bar the editorial and advertising. It would not have attained the measure of success it did without her. She left when I became involved in *The Sunday Tribune* and was a great loss. One of the successes of *Magill* was that we brought some great talent into journalism, or at least gave some budding journalistic talent an outlet. Among these were Pat Brennan who later became news editor of *The Sunday Tribune* - she is now with RTE. She has a sharp analytical mind. There was Gene Kerrigan who gave to *Magill* a dimension I could never have given : fine writing, coupled with at times devastating analysis. Some of the stories he did for *Magill,* for instance the Kerry babies story, have been the best things in Irish journalism for decades. I did some decent work. The most memorable was the series on the 1970 arms crisis, which we published on the 10th anniversary. Another was the inside story of how Charlie Haughey became leader of Fianna Fail and Taoiseach.

I was close to Charlie at the time and was enthusiastic about the prospect of his becoming Taoiseach. I thought he had the ability and decisiveness to be a great Taoiseach in the economic sphere, I thought he had the vision (I was into vision then) to take imaginative initiatives on Northern Ireland and I thought he had the compassion to do something radical about poverty. I used to meet him fairly often, not that he was ever a good source for political stories - in fact I can't remember a single story I got from him throughout the years. Now that I think about it, that is not quite true. He was great company, outrageous and funny. But we fell out when I did the arms crisis series - he felt it was an act of disloyalty to do such a thing so shortly after he had become Taoiseach. He didn't understand or accept that friendship means nothing in journalism - our obligations as journalists are solely to our readers.

Charlie was unfortunate that circumstances dictated he had to play to his weaknesses when he became Taoiseach. One of the weaknesses was an unsuspected one at the time: indecisiveness. He dithered over what to do about George Colley's disloyalty; he dithered over when to call an election; he dithered over what to do about the economy and, in the process, he let public expenditure get out of hand and the public debt rise dramatically. His first two periods as Taoiseach were disastrous and it was only when he got into power in 1987, with the tacit support of Fine Gael, that he began to do things. That 1987-1989 government was a good one and began to undo the damage his previous governments had done.

When Hugh McLaughlin started the first version of *The Sunday Tribune* in October 1980 I thought that my ambition to edit a quality Sunday newspaper was gone. Actually, I didn't mind because, by then, I was achieving journalistically through *Magill* what I had wanted to achieve through a Sunday newspaper. However, *The Sunday Tribune* ceased publication in October 1982 and almost by reflex I became involved. I was introduced to Tony Ryan and he agreed to finance a relaunch of the paper and we bought the title via the High Court. I was strongly advised against getting involved by two people. One was John Giles, with whom I was then friendly. He warned that dealing with the number of people I would have to deal with in a newspaper would prove very frustrating. The other person was Eamon McCann. But, in retrospect, I think I was on automatic pilot.

One of the first people I approached in connection with the venture was Barbara Nugent. She was then advertising manager for *Image* magazine. I felt she would bring a drive and professionalism to the advertising operation. The next two people I approached were Paul Tansey and Gerry Barry. Paul was an outstanding economics correspondent for *The Irish Times*. Gerry was RTE's leading current affairs interviewer - there had been nobody better than him in news features in RTE and there has been none better since.

As I mentioned, Tony Ryan appointed my friend John

Kelleher managing director and he appointed two other people central to the operation thereafter, Martin Dobey, who became financial director, and Tina Roche, now the deputy managing director. John played a crucial role in the launch of the paper but had a falling-out with Tony Ryan and left in late 1983. The other six of us: Barbara, Paul, Gerry, Martin, Tina and myself, along with Gordon, became the core editorially and commercially. It was one of my regrets the great solidarity between us broke down under considerable strain in 1991.

Barbara went on from being advertising manager to become marketing director and then managing director. She had great strengths in marketing and in the management of people and great instincts in the editorial area. I regard her departure from the paper in less than pleasant circumstances in May 1991 as one of my major failures in *The Tribune*. Paul Tansey left the staff in 1985 but remained our regular economics correspondent. He brought precisely to the newspaper what I wanted him to bring: authority. By far the most important person has been Gerry Barry - for long stretches he carried the paper editorially. He is the finest journalist I have known, although he will never win a journalist's prize for the simple reason he would not enter for one. Gerry and I are now characterised as the two old codgers in the Muppet Show.

Tina Roche has been one of the pillars of *The Tribune*. She has come through all its vicissitudes, has been the management sweeper (as in Franz Beckenbauer), the last line of defence. She twice had wanted to leave to take up other projects but, happily, was persuaded not to. Martin Dobey was an essential element in the survival of *The Tribune* and I was sorry that he, like Barbara, left in less than happy circumstances.

Tony Ryan and I were destined not to get on together in business - we are too much alike, although he lacks my tact and I his patience. I was given the right to appoint one nominee to the board and I chose Sean MacBride, the former Minister for External Affairs and the winner of both the Nobel and Lenin peace prizes. Tony claims Sean had to intervene between him and me and that, once, we exchanged blows while Sean tried to keep us apart.

Tony withdrew from *The Tribune* in July 1984 and, almost immediately after we resumed a friendship that had waxed briefly when we first met. He has great humour, extraordinary energy and flair. I felt sorry for him during his difficulties with GPA and went so far as to offer him lodgings should the worst come to the worst. But he has the ability to . . .

> Make one heap of all your winnings
> And risk it on one turn of pitch-and-toss,
> And lose, and start again at your beginnings
> And never breathe a word about your loss.

Mainly through the ingenuity of Gordon Colleary, we survived throughout the rest of 1984 and 1985, and in early 1986 we were able to raise money through the Business Expansion Scheme. Declan Collins then of SKC was critical in our raising finance and one of our earliest supporters was Dermot Desmond.

We ran into major difficulties in late 1991, in part over the launch of another newspaper, *The Dublin Tribune*. I had believed for some time that, on its own, *The Sunday Tribune* would be a marginal enterprise because overhead costs for a one-a-week newspaper are difficult to carry. *The Observer* in London ran into similar difficulties. My belief was we should either join or become a larger group. A link-up with *The Irish Times* would have been the ideal partnership but *The Irish Times* was never interested. I thought an involvement by us with The Irish Press Group should be pursued and, in that connection, we had several meetings both with Ralph Ingersoll and Eamon de Valera. I feel a sense of relief this did not work out, given the conflict that has emerged within that company.

Having failed to join a larger group, our minds began to turn towards expanding our own base and it seemed the best opportunity was to launch a free newspaper for the Dublin region. Free newspapers had been successful elsewhere and the Dublin market seemed particularly attractive. This was because the media in Dublin were very fragmented - the newspaper medium with four morning newspapers published here, along with all the daily imports from Britain; the television medium because of the availability of cable; and the radio medium with the licensing of commercial radio. A medium that would provide total market coverage should, in theory, be very successful, giving advertisers a one-hit opportunity to get through to the crucial Dublin market. There were persuasive reasons for us *not* to proceed with this idea at the time: we had only just got *The Sunday Tribune* into profitability and we needed to focus on getting it right and its growth consolidated; our management resources were stretched already; we did not have the capital required for the project.

On the face of it, these reasons would have been compelling but there were countervailing ones. The first was, if we waited, there was a danger, we believed, that the Ingersoll organisation, which at the time had very successful free newspapers in the US notably in St. Louis, would move in and rob us of the chance; there were widespread projections of strong economic growth for years to come and we wanted to avoid starting another project at the beginning of a recession; we seemed to have resolved the management problem through recruitment; and we seemed to have access to adequate capital.

On balance, we decided to go ahead and, in retrospect, it was a mistake. We did not get the amount of capital we required and our expectations regarding management proved too optimistic. But primarily we ran into a recession on the advertising market almost immediately, following the invasion of Kuwait by Iraq. The strains these difficulties caused were intensified greatly by Independent Newspapers grabbing 30 per cent of our shareholding on the stock market - we had joined the Small Companies Market.

As a result of this, I think the company was in disarray for a long time, during which period Barbara Nugent resigned. Two directors from Independent Newspapers came on to our board, Liam Healy and John Meagher, at the same time as Martin Birrane. Martin's brother, John Birrane, had become an investor in the company back in early 1986. His death in 1988 was a loss.

There is a genuine conflict between freedom of speech on the one hand and the right to one's good name on the other - both values are given constitutional recognition. But I think that on matters to do with public affairs, there should be constitutional protection for publications, provided there is no malice involved on the part of the publishers or writers and provided there is adequate redress in the form of a right to reply for persons libelled. In a democratic society, reputation rights should not automatically trump the right of citizens to access to information about the performance of public officials - otherwise democracy is to some degree frustrated. This is all the more so given that there are means whereby public officials, whose reputations have been unfairly impugned, can have their reputations vindicated - the right of reply being one such means.

The constitution itself acknowledges the necessity to remove obstacles to the free flow of democratic debate, obstacles such as libel, by giving members of the Oireachtas *absolute immunity* or, as it is known in legal jargon, absolute privilege, from legal action arising out of what is said in the Oireachtas. Why then should the media, which also plays a crucial role in the democratic process, not have limited immunity, or qualified privilege, when dealing with public issues?

I accept there is no right of intrusion into the private lives of either public or private persons unless there is a genuine public interest, as distinct from public curiosity, or unless the individual in question chooses to make public issues to do with their private lives - for instance if a politician seeks votes, even by implication, on the false pretext of being a faithful married person, it is legitimate for the media to alert the public that this *is* a false pretext.

The widespread public perception of the media as arrogant and exclusionary is understandable. The problem lies in the grossly unequal access to and unequal control of the media.

Just as there is an unfairness at the heart of the political system in allowing private wealth to intrude into the political arena, so too is there an unfairness in the media being controlled by a few people who have at least in part the capacity to control the political agenda. This is not just a question of ownership, it relates also to the unequal control editors and journalists have. I believe the prevailing notions about the rights of private property must not be allowed to extend to the media, given the role the media play in a democratic society. There have got to be extensive controls over concentrations of media ownership, and measures through which as many people as possible can be brought into the media scene, through tax breaks and a nondiscriminatory grants system.

Above all, this requires editors and journalists to behave as surrogates for readers, rather than as representatives of the owners or of advertisers or, perhaps more relevantly, of their own sectional interests - editors and journalists are better paid than is the norm in society; their children go to better schools, they live more comfortably than people do generally.

We have all erred in this and it would be preposterous for me to claim that *The Sunday Tribune* has represented a wide span of views throughout society, but we try to do that and we will try harder.

Concern about media ownership may seem odd coming from me, since I was the one who proposed in 1991 that Independent Newspapers should be allowed take over The Tribune Group. I made this proposal, in conjunction with Gordon Colleary and Gerry Barry, given that Independent Newspapers had already taken a 30 per cent shareholding in *The Tribune* ; that the company was in disarray and was losing money heavily; that jobs in *The Sunday Tribune* and *Dublin Tribune* were at stake; and that Independent Newspapers gave undertakings on editorial independence which I believed would stick. I also believed it was likely we would fall into the lap of Independent Newspapers and that we were more likely to get an acceptable deal if *we* proposed a take-over than if it happened through force of circumstances.

In the event the Competition Authority advised against a

take-over and Desmond O'Malley, as Minister for Industry and Commerce, prohibited it. I was the one who dealt primarily with Des O'Malley on the issue. I went to see him in his offices one afternoon in early November 1991, having asked to see him on his own on a non-journalistic matter. We were both under pressure at that meeting - his wife was waiting for him outside in the state car and my father was waiting in my illegally-parked car. He gave me the clear impression from the first few seconds that he was obdurately opposed.

Initially, when Independent Newspapers took the 30 per cent stake our reaction was one of dismay but we then sought to make the most of it. I was invited around to lunch with John Meagher and Liam Healy at Independent Newspaper headquarters on the following day - this was in November 1991 - there to be regaled by Liam Healy with stories concerning my conduct while I was an employee of the *Independent.* I had known John Meagher for several years and had always enjoyed his company. Liam recalled that when he was financial director, some time in 1976, he was approached by a very agitated accounts manager, who informed him that I had managed to convert a taxi docket into "legal tender" by getting money for it in the Oval Bar the previous Saturday night - this, apparently, was an outrage that had not been exceeded by any other employee up to then and threatened financial ruin on the company unless it was stamped out. I had a vague recollection of somebody making a fuss over the "cashing" of a "blue docket", as the currency was then known, and of not being able to understand what the hullabaloo was about, since I needed the money, presumably for more drink.

After 11 years in *The Sunday Tribune* I have felt it time to move on but I also feel there is unfinished business: we have not yet created the strong newspaper we set out to create. Our aim is a newspaper with broad appeal, that presents a wide range of opinions and entertainment and is also the anvil on which the issues of public life in Ireland are hammered out. Having secured the refinancing of the newspaper, we are in a position now to get on with that project. We have assembled a fine team of journalists: Joe O'Connor, who is a great feature writer and reporter; Ann Marie Hourihan who as features editor can breathe new life into the lifestyles area; Veronica Guerin, emerging as the best news reporter in the country; along with the likes of Paul Kimmage, Rory Godson, David Nally, Susan McKay, Fergal Keane, Diarmuid Doyle and Ursula Halligan. All young talent, many relatively new to journalism, now among the best around. Stephen Ryan, our design editor, in conjunction with our production editor, Paul Hopkins, has just won eight awards for excellence in the annual competition of the American Society of Newspaper Design, having previously won the best designed newspaper award in the British Society. And then there are the mainstays of the paper, Gerry Barry of course, but also Ciaran Carty, the arts editor and Ger Siggins, the books editor, as well as Tom Vavasour, the production manager.

The Sunday Tribune does try to represent values, not just in the journalistic sphere, but in the broader political sphere and these, perhaps inevitably since I am editor, reflect my own views. My views politically hinge around the notion of equality: that there should be a basic equality in the distribution of resources in society, subject only to the operation of those incentives necessary to improve the overall wealth of society and specifically the wealth and welfare of the least well-off group. I believe the inequalities that exist are unjustifiable. There is surely something wrong with a society that spends vast resources on relative trivialities - take, for instance private transport - while ignoring the poverty in which so many people are embedded. I don't think it is enough to talk of the alleviation of this poverty primarily in terms of employment generation, although I acknowledge that poverty is very much linked to unemployment. Given that there are going to be high levels of unemployment for the foreseeable future, we have to start thinking in terms of a basic income that is paid to everyone irrespective of what work they do or even whether they work. There are incentive difficulties with this proposition and it would involve high levels of taxation. It is preferable to deal with problems of that kind than to continue to permit gross disparities of wealth.

6

Michael Brophy
The Star

All news is comment.

The conversation took place on August 16 1993

At the time the conversation took place Michael Brophy was editor and director of *The Star*.[*]

He was born in Dublin on October 22 1949.

His father was William Brophy, a bread salesman.

His mother was Una Andrews, a schoolteacher.

He was fourth in a family of six: Moira, John, Madeleine, Eugene and Una.

He is married to Eileen Noonan, a medical laboratory technician.

Their children are Karl (18) and Fay (15).

He was educated at Drimnagh Castle Primary School; the Marian College, Ballsbridge and Kevin Street College of Technology.

He joined the Irish Press in 1969 as a copy-boy and in October 1969 joined *The Kilkenny People*. 1970 reporter on the *Irish Independent*. 1977 assistant to the editor of *The Evening Herald*. 1980-1985 *Irish Independent* assistant to the editor, features editor and night editor. 1985 editor of *The Evening Herald*. 1989 editor and director of the newly established *Independent Star*.

His hobbies are reading, walking, listening to music and watching all types of sport.

[*] See Epilogue.

When I was in secondary school I did a career guidance test with Fr. Paul Andrews. He advised me to undertake two totally polarised careers: electronics or journalism. There was no opening in journalism, so I joined an electronics course in the College of Technology, Kevin Street. While there, I tried everything to avoid electronics. I sat for a year doing almost nothing and then started a college magazine. I got my first-year exam with no enthusiasm but had awful problems when I went back for my second year. The only parts of the course which interested me were French and economics - I was a totally square peg. I had problems reconciling the logic of maths. One day I was trying to work out a long theorem and about half-way through came to a brick wall where it was necessary to call in another formula. However, you had to know by rote which formula to call in, there was no logic. I had thought that maths was a progressive finding out of truth, but patently this was not the case. I fell out with maths. I just drifted through the last six months - I wanted to work in newspapers.

I went into Ciaran Carty, then in the *Sunday Independent*, now with *The Tribune*, and began reporting from Kevin Street for a page which he ran in the *Sunday Independent* on third-level colleges. I sent reports in to *The Evening Press* and *The Evening Herald* - tiny reports about silly things. Then I started buying specialist medical magazines and writing articles out of them, sending them particularly to the Irish Press Group. In summer 1969, the year all the troubles started in the North, I applied to the *Irish Press* for a job as anything. The late Bill Redmond, who was chief news editor, a classic newspaperman, a big man with great power, interviewed me. He asked me if I would take a job as a copy-boy. I said yes and he cautioned me that under no circumstances would I ever become a journalist. They used to have a scheme in the *Irish Press* under which copy-boys became sub-editors - people like Vinnie Doyle and Ronan Farren, now literary editor of the *Sunday Independent*, were just two of the graduates. But the man who went before me was supposed to be the last in the *Irish Press* scheme. They were now going to set up career copy-boys and recruit their journalists from other sources.

I liked the *Irish Press* and people there were good to me. I remember particularly people like John Garvey, who is now deputy editor of the *Irish Press*, Fintan Faulkner, Jack Jones and Pat Quigley. They could see I wanted to become one of them and they gave me every assistance. After six months learning the ropes in Burgh Quay, I applied to *The Kilkenny People* for a job as a reporter. All my family are from Kilkenny and I have strong links with the region. *The Kilkenny People* goes back to the eighteenth century. It was sold in the mid-1700s for three pence, a handsome price for a newspaper at the time. A former editor, E.T. Keane, was one of the most distinguished journalists in the country. John Kerry Keane, his nephew, interviewed me and gave me my first job as a journalist. E.T. Keane hated a schoolteacher in the town and always referred to him as John Smith, BA (Pass). He was sued over it but won the case.

I moved to Kilkenny in the autumn of 1969. It was a magnificent training ground and Kilkenny is a beautiful city. I lived with my grandmother and two aunts in a house overlooking the river Nore. I joined the cinema club, the arts society and followed every sport the city could offer. It was like being in college all over again except this was a course I enjoyed.

I worked closely with the paper's senior reporter, Peter Houlihan, a wonderful philosopher of life. Peter knew journalism as it was then practised inside-out. He knew what to do at all times and, when others would not listen to him, I would. I learned how to meet people, how to handle difficult situations, how to report on a wide cross-section of issues. He taught me the rudiments of journalism and gave me a great interest in politics. Peter sent me on the most chilling job I've ever done. There was a road accident in Kilkenny in which a three-year old girl was killed. Peter knew the girl. He told me to go up to the house and ask for a picture of the child - normal routine journalism. The way the woman answered the door, smiling, I knew she did not know her daughter had been killed. I stood on the doorstep, looking at this woman, and said, "I am from *The Kilkenny People*. My name is Michael

Brophy." She said, "Yes?" I said quickly, "Are you, eh, Mrs. Doyle?" When she said no, I said, "I am sorry - I must have the wrong house".

When you work as a reporter in a town like Kilkenny, you become something of a celebrity and you quickly find doors are opened to you. You sit down to dinner with people of importance and you are quickly absorbed by the local society.

One of my jobs was to write the obituary of everybody who died in Kilkenny. I checked the death notices every morning and, if a local person had died, I was obliged to go to the house where I would collect details for the obituary. I remember coming home to lunch with my grandmother who had lived in Kilkenny all her life. When I was passing a local hospital I saw a hearse coming out followed by a long line of mourners. I was upset, not about the death, but that I had not heard about it. When I got home I checked the *Irish Independent* - no mention of a death. My grandmother knew everything that happened in Kilkenny and when we were sitting at the table I asked, "Granny, did somebody die in the hospital today?" She replied, "No, not that I know of. Sure, if they did, we'll read it in *The Kilkenny People*". The origin of the news was not important to her, that it was printed in *The Kilkenny People* was.

I covered everything from sport to theatre to local agriculture shows. And I learned about sensitivity. I remember I was sent to see a John B. Keane play in a local hall during the winter. I have loved theatre all my life and here I was getting paid to watch it. I was the Frank Rich of Kilkenny. The show was staged by an amateur company and, to say the least, it didn't come off. I went back to the office and wrote a vicious review. John Kerry Keane called me into his office and told me the report was unusable. These were amateur actors and actresses and we did not want to tear them apart. When I reflected on it, I agreed with him. It wasn't our job to discourage their efforts to develop the theatre in Kilkenny, a city which now has its own theatre.

The Kilkenny People appealed to all levels of society, from the business and city people through the archaeological society to the farmers outside the city and the people involved in sports. It was part of the community. We were constantly getting requests to put things into the newspaper and keep things out. John Keane had a policy that, if anybody made representations about keeping something out of the paper, the item was definitely printed, possibly on page one.

A couple of years ago I was down on the stone in *The Evening Herald*. I don't think journalists give enough examination to the consequences of their actions. Sometimes they just bang stuff into a newspaper and forget about it unaware of the hurt that's going to ripple through. I dumped this court case article into the vacant space on the page - it was about a fellow up for drunken driving. He had been put off the road for six months and it went onto page one of *The Evening Herald*. I will always take phone calls from a reader and that evening I got one: "My name is Joe Soap - why did you put my court case onto the front page of *The Evening Herald*? You have almost destroyed my life." I did not try to argue with him or tell him he should have thought of that before he had his fifteenth pint. I told him exactly what happened. He said, "I did not tell my wife about this case. My children have to go to school tomorrow morning. Did you not think?" We should not see ourselves as judge and jury. Our job is to assess how important a story is, not to add to a person's punishment - that's a matter for the court.

I was in Kilkenny for only a year. The *Irish Independent* was beginning to build up its news team. The Group was going through that great change of the 70s. Aidan Pender had taken over as editor and was beginning to develop it into the product it is today away from its traditional alignments heavily in favour of Church matters. Aidan was a great editor. When asked by a concerned churchman of the time, "Mr. Pender, what are you trying to do with the *Irish Independent*?" he replied, "Sell it, Your Grace."

I applied for a job to Bill Shine, the then chief news editor, a distinguished journalist and a man who played a leading role in changing the face of Irish newspapers. There was no vacancy immediately but I kept plugging away and eventually got signed up to the best news team of the time. I joined the Independent Group in 1970 and have never left it.

When I was in Kilkenny, I was consumed by what I was doing. When I went into the *Independent* I was absolutely consumed. Whether I came home or not did not worry me. I was getting well paid for what I liked doing. My early days in the *Independent* were frenetic. I went into a newsroom full of people all of whom welcomed me and I was at the heart of a busy, active and developing newspaper. I never sensed any major difference between the journalism practised in Kilkenny and on a metropolitan newspaper. It was the same thing to me whether you were writing about an amateur drama society or probing a major international fraud. I approached them in the same way. I had a great desire to find out *exactly* what happened.

As a reporter, you become a silent traveller on the shoulder of society - you're like Long John Silver's parrot. You're a constant observer. Bill Shine, who was a great teacher, always insisted that you would dress in a manner that did not stand out in the crowd. In the 70s there was a news team in the *Independent* which helped journalism evolve. We were constantly on the road. We covered everything - arms trials, sackings of ministers. I uncovered the Erin Foods fraud - I was the first to report on it for *The Evening Herald* and spent a long time investigating it. I had a great contact in the Fraud Squad and worked closely with him for nearly a year. The story had a major impact at the time.

I don't think reporters have to be tough, foot-in-the-door characters. They have to be understanding and have to have the ability to take advantage of situations. If a reporter is distinguished and trustworthy, people will use him as a confessor. Those early days in the *Independent* were ones of great excitement. Charlie Haughey was emerging and the country was developing with great speed. Were there politics before Charlie Haughey?

It appeared to me I was part of a news team on a newspaper that was changing the face of the country. Up to that newspapers were dominated by set pieces, forums like the Corporation and the Dail. The Dail was given two pages in the *Irish Independent*, four in *The Irish Times*. Today there is no Dail coverage for the sake of coverage.

In the 70s in the *Independent*, we had a young news team which was creating the news and a production team led by Vinnie Doyle and the late Niall Hanley, who became editor of *The Herald*. I met Vinnie in my early days in the *Independent* and was lucky to begin a friendship which has lasted to this day. At that time Vinnie was ringing the changes in Irish journalism. He would take a story and say, "Let's do this, this and this" and young active reporters responded to him. Gradually a whole movement of change developed. Pender was the editor who presided over all this and a man who managed to fulfil his ambition of selling the *Irish Independent*. The paper reached record sales levels.

Many of us on the *Irish Independent* were students coming out of the 60s, influenced by the liberalism of that time. I don't think my basic views have changed in any way from 1970 to today. They weren't even revolutionary views - they were just quite open. We did not want the newspaper to be dusty and formal and moribund. We wanted to see our energy translated into writing. We cast our net as broad as we could and we trawled deep. We were asking questions of the national institutions. We found that by asking the right questions we were getting answers. Suddenly, stories that would have passed as insignificant five years before were rippling the waters ever so slightly.

Being a reporter on a national newspaper uses up every ounce of energy and every bit of mental capacity you can muster. You have to have the right motives and to stand back from issues to the degree that you cannot be compromised. You must come to the court with clean hands. Everybody from PR companies to senior Government ministers try to use newspapers for their own ends. They try to manufacture news and manipulate the media and many times the media allow themselves to be manipulated. I'm not saying it's wrong or right, it's just how it operates. Every Government press conference is to some extent manipulation. News is a product which should be handled delicately. When a news reporter comes across a cause which he or she wishes to champion the difficulty begins. Then the bias emerges. There is nothing as bad as a biased reporter.

I am intensely interested in politics but have no political affiliations. I have a passionate disrespect for politics and politicians. It is the nature of their profession to manipulate and mislead. And it is the duty of newspapers to act as their watchdogs and show them to the public for what they are. There is an ethos in Independent Newspapers which is clear and which I share. That ethos is to be absolutely fair, truthful, honest, strong, and intolerant of those who are being less than scrupulous. Did we create the ethos or did it create us?

In newspapers today it is sometimes difficult to uncover the thin dividing line between news and opinion. Take *The Irish Times* - the political correspondent of that newspaper is a former Progressive Democrats TD. Can it really be expected she will not be influenced by the considerable time she spent associated with the PD Party? Will her views on other political parties not be coloured by that association? We are driven by what we see and what we believe. You have asked me to give an example of the blurring of the lines between news and comment. For it I would go back to the last presidential election. At the time Mary Robinson was fighting Brian Lenihan for the presidency. The *Irish Independent* tried to run it right down the middle - The *Irish Press* and *The Star* did much the same. *The Irish Times* set out to get Mary Robinson elected by constantly giving her news opportunities, by over-marking her, by not bothering that much with Brian Lenihan. That's comment.

All news is comment. Look at the front pages of the papers - there are positions being taken up all the time. That is inherent in the headlines. After Dick Spring was made Tanaiste, he commented on the Bosnian crisis and it made the lead story in *The Irish Times*. There was an awful lot happening at that time and that was not really the most important story. That was a statement by *The Irish Times* they believed the most important thing happening that morning was a speech by Dick Spring. That is comment.

When Vinnie Doyle became editor of *The Evening Herald*, he asked me to become assistant editor. Prior to that it was sub-editors who always became editors because it was felt the successful candidate had to know a lot about the production of newspapers. I made the jump to assistant editor from reporter. It was the old *Evening Herald* then and it was going down the tubes. The figures were worse than even Vinnie knew about when he joined it. Being a reporter, you had to wait to see your story published. Being an editor was marvellous. You could take other people's copy, mould it, put headlines on it - you could develop the newspaper as you wanted to develop it. We tried to bring a wider range of interests to it.

One of the most serious errors of judgment we ever made was the time Sir Anthony Blunt was named in the House of Commons - I think by Margaret Thatcher - as the Fourth Man. He was named in the afternoon, too late for any normal edition. Vinnie and I decided to print a special edition of *The Evening Herald* - 25,000, it sold about one! We were interested because both of us were great students of the Cold War but it left the Irish public unmoved.

When Vinnie became editor of the *Irish Independent* I went over with him as his assistant editor. I worked with him from 1977 for about 15 years. We set up a news features department which Jim Farrelly subsequently headed up. Before Jim, I had been responsible for features and it was the hardest job I ever did. You could never take a night off - if you did not do it, nobody else did. In other sections of the newspaper you could work with great intensity then stand back and somebody else would fill it in like quicksand.

I then became night editor of the *Irish Independent*. Night editor is the guy who makes it happen though, of course,

Vinnie would always be there. We started the news analysis page at that time. Bruce Arnold helped significantly to set up that page. Vinnie and I finally decided that we couldn't handle it by ourselves - we were doing the news analysis page in the morning, something else in the afternoon and then editing the paper at night. It was then a news analysis editor was appointed.

Night editing is one of the most perfect jobs in journalism. All the people who want to influence you are gone home by then and, by the time they get up in the morning and see the newspaper you have produced, you're in bed. You have all the power of editing the newspaper without any of the hassle.

When Niall Hanley was killed tragically in the Bordeaux air crash, I took over from him on *The Herald*. Niall had brought it into tabloid and to great heights. It was the kind of newspaper that suited me. I really loved *The Herald*. In the middle of that, Vinnie went into hospital and I edited the *Irish Independent* for him. For six months I carried full responsibility and then went back to *The Herald*.

When I was asked to edit *The Star*, it didn't take me long to make up my mind. The paper was in great difficulties. It had a circulation of less than 40,000 - that figure today is nearer 70,000. I felt here was a paper that could work. When I decided to move from *The Herald* to *The Star*, the opprobrium I took within the industry was serious. People told me I was foolish. *The Star* was seen as a lost cause. I took with me two people for whom I have nothing but the highest respect, Colm McGinty and Paddy Murray. Without these two people the paper would not have got off the ground. McGinty developed the design side of the newspaper and Murray did just about everything. The people we joined on *The Star*, led by a great journalist in news editor John Donlon, threw their weight behind the project and a powerful newspaper team got moving.

Colm has gone back to be deputy editor of the *Sunday Independent* and Paddy is still with me. We were three people with a common cause, developed on *The Herald*. Colm had been features editor on *The Herald* and Paddy was a man who could make things happen.

We joined *The Star* in an old tram-shed in Terenure - we have a new building there now. For two years we worked day and night, seven days a week - ten o'clock in the morning until one o'clock the following morning. We always knew it was going to succeed, that if we did things right, and constantly brought our experience to bear on this new young product, we could make a go of it. We were like a football team down five points at half-time but knowing that, if you really worked hard, you could win. I know Tony O'Reilly has said, there may be a gap in the market but is there a market in the gap? We did not even think about that - it was just blood, sweat and tears, page after page. We felt people would slowly come to understand what we were doing and approve of it. We are all passionately interested in sport and made it our forte. We recruited young people - there is nothing I like better than working with energetic young minds. We put them into the production area where they hadn't a clue but I was happy enough to help them develop their skills. Consequently we have a production crew I would match with anybody.

There is also another aspect of *The Star*, the commercial end. When we were developing I became closely involved in the financial structures of the newspaper and worked at developing our sources of income. We got support from Government departments for advertising programmes and from a range of companies which placed their faith in the paper from the start.

One thing about being the editor of a newspaper is the ability both to reflect and to mould public opinion. *The Star* did a campaign last year about the absence of TDs from the Dail. We kept at it and at it. Of course, the TDs told us most of their work was done outside the Dail. We said if that were so then we had best look at another structure for running the country, something that didn't include the Dail. Perhaps we need an Executive and get rid of the Dail. We were told, oh no, you have to have the Dail. That debate led to the setting up of more parliamentary committees and we would claim partial responsibility - they had to do something.

A tabloid newspaper is a more accentuated form of journalism. The *Irish Independent* and *The Irish Times* have more time and space in which to develop their arguments. A tabloid newspaper has to say things quicker.

In *The Star* we constantly express intolerance. We are intolerant of the structures that exist in this society. We have an experienced team in a young newspaper. Most of our reporters are in their mid-20s but then you have experienced people like myself and my deputy, Paul Drury, who was the former deputy editor of the *Irish Independent**. Sometimes we scream with intolerance and find that many people in this country scream with us. What we are doing is reflecting a *widespread* intolerance. You stop anyone in the street and they will tell you they don't think TDs work enough. The TDs will turn around and tell you that you don't understand, the easiest way to dismiss an argument - it's what you say when you want to get rid of a child: go away and I'll explain to you later. We are saying, explain to us now why you go away on three months' holidays. That's where news and comment are mixed up.

The Star's franchise includes people in our society who are less than privileged. If we can give them a little mouthpiece somewhere along the line, we will try to do it. The last refuge for a person in difficulty or for the victim of bureaucracy is the phone number of the local newspaper. He can't get on to RTE. *The Irish Times* doesn't realise he exists. The last thing he can do is pick up a phone and ring the newspaper and say, the roof is falling off my house - can you do something about it? They are the kind of exposés I like to be involved in - not the exposés of great business scandals, though I do think the newspapers have been magnificent on the business reporting. The people who put things into newspapers are powerful people. The weak man does not get an opportunity to speak. So, when we run a campaign about the Dail being empty most of the time, we are speaking on his behalf.

Intrinsically, people do not expect a lot from a colour tabloid newspaper because they have been influenced over the years by the mindless journalism practised in some British imports. *The*

* See Epilogue.

Star has managed to change that in this country. For too long, many newspapers have been pouring out stuff the editors think people want to hear. That's why you get such a reaction to, say, a tough article by Eamon Dunphy on Dick Spring. But isn't it great that people talk openly about our leaders, whether we agree with them or not? We certainly have to defend their right to say what they think. When P.J. Mara was Government press secretary, he would become angry with a newspaper which had published something he did not like about Charlie Haughey. He was intolerant of any criticism and developed what, I believe, was to become a serious influence on Irish life - the lobby system for political journalists. This resulted in the grouping together of the correspondents under the virtual domination of a Government press secretary. What is wrong with Eamon Dunphy giving his opinion on a major political figure - provided you allow Dick Spring to give his opinion? Politicians won't, of course, write half as entertainingly as Eamon Dunphy. Writers like Shane Ross and Eamon Dunphy are saying things that an awful lot of people believe.

Newspapers must represent people. *The Star* tries to do that as best we can. I tell reporters and writers in the paper they must give people the mental ammunition to carry on in life. If you are working on a production-line in a factory, it is quite important for you to know who won yesterday between Shels and Rovers. If you go to the pub and meet the gang, it's important to have information to trade, to be able to comment on current events. *The Star* supplies people with information. They supply us with opinion. That opinion is translated back into the information which they carry around with them. It's a constant interchange between the reader and ourselves.

I try to travel in taxis around Dublin because taxi-drivers tell me about my paper. They will tell me that the junior soccer results were the reason for them to buy it. People buy newspapers for all sorts of different reasons - we are lucky in *The Star* that we can take those reasons and translate them into sales.

Let me qualify - or flesh out - what I have just said. We let ourselves down badly as newspapers if we permit the indulgence of personal vendettas. It is one thing to have strong and informed criticism of public personages. It is quite another to permit the self-indulgence of less-than-qualified journalists. You can analyse political failings or poor business performance, but to attack people's personal shortcomings is going down the wrong road. Conor Cruise O'Brien and Charlie Haughey were something quite different. Conor is a distinguished politician and a thinker - the Cruiser is one of the few philosophers in Irish life. Bruce Arnold has been an ardent critic of Charlie Haughey but has done it with an intellectualism and a force that are well-founded.

In the 70s, we were able to have stimulating debates about politics because we were getting inside information from John Healy. He was having a cut, Bruce Arnold was having a cut. Charlie Haughey was writing to the papers. Arthur Noonan in the *Independent* and Michael McInerney in *The Times* were writing. You were getting really good pungent comment on politics then. There were Dick Walsh's political profiles on Saturday in *The Irish Times*. Now I turn to the newspapers in the era after the political management of P.J. Mara and I find an awful lot of good comment has been washed out. I feel politicians have forgotten they are answerable to their public and they are being allowed forget it. When was the last time that you read in a newspaper about what went on in a cabinet meeting? The amount of political information which we get through the newspapers in this country is minimal. We get only what politicians want us to get - there are very few inside tracks. That's regrettable.

If newspapers can continue to explore what is going on in the society around them, without exposing themselves to the dreadful oppression of the laws of libel, there is a future for them. They must constantly explore the frontiers and they cannot be prohibited by lack of information, by PRs or information officers who say I am sorry, I cannot give you details. Our attitude, particularly with semi-state companies, is they are being paid by us. We are not being arrogant but we would like the information. If it takes ten days, that's fine.

More and more, we are trying to move out of the strait-jacket of all the different people who want to manipulate newspapers. It's hard to get out of that strait-jacket.

Newspapers lead and follow. They are moulded by many different forces, by the many people who come in contact with them. That is a totally different philosophy from the British tabloid which says we will go out and sell the goddamn newspaper and hit or hurt anybody.

What I am really saying is that everybody should have access to a newspaper. Newspapers are human. They have human frailties. If they are attacked, they may want to get their own back and, in so doing, lose some of their objectivity. We have been attacked many times by RTE and by *The Irish Times*. The only thing I've ever done was to ring *The Irish Times* and force corrections out of them because they always described us as *The* Daily *Star*. Get the title right and you can say anything you want about us - we don't mind.

As a reporter on the *Independent* I was influenced by the kind of journalism practised by Vinnie Doyle. He had great leadership qualities. He and I had a driving ambition, not necessarily to become editors of newspapers, but to influence them as much as we could in the direction that we wanted them to go. In 1978, a significant appointment in the modern history of Irish newspapers was made. Joe Hayes, a former brand manager from the cigarette industry, joined Independent Newspapers. Joe has had an impact on the newspaper industry greater than any other single person. I was lucky to work closely with him from the start and became involved in a number of projects he spearheaded. The relationship has continued - he is chairman of *The Star*.[*] Joe developed the newspaper industry along modern marketing lines and gave the Independent Group its strength throughout the 80s. *The Star* is now a sound commercial proposition. It is second only to the *Irish Independent* in readership. Its birth pangs are behind it.

---

[*] See Epilogue.

7

Hugh Lambert
Irish Press

Papers need much stronger personalities now than they did in the days before television. A paper has to say: this is what we stand for, this is what we believe. Not many papers have succeeded in doing that.

The conversation took place on June 17 1993

Hugh Lambert is the editor of the *Irish Press*.

He was born in Dublin on May 27 1944.

His father was Hubert Lambert, a printer.

His mother was Kathleen Farrelly, housewife.

He is the eldest son in a family of seven: Carol, Brendan, John, Liam, Kathleen and Laura.

He is married to Angela Byrne, housewife and amateur potter.

Their children are Alan (23), Paul (21), John (18), and Sam (8).

He was educated at Scoil Eoin Baiste, Clontarf; O'Connells CBS; Rathmines College of Commerce (Journalism); Goethe Institute (German).

1960 joined the *Evening Press* as a copy-boy. 1961 sub-editor. 1971 transferred to the *Sunday Press* as columnist and diarist. 1980 assistant editor the *Sunday Press*. 1987 appointed editor of the *Irish Press*.

He enjoys languages (French and German), European history and historical novels.

I remember quite well when I first became aware of newspapers - it was 1954, a hot summer and I was ten. My father was working in *The Irish Times*. There was a fire in *The Irish Times* and the *Press* agreed to keep some of the printers on the payroll while the case-room was rebuilt. Around that time in Clontarf - and I suppose elsewhere in the City - there was a big poster campaign: "It's coming, it's coming." I wondered what *it* could be and on a Monday the *Evening Press* arrived. My father brought it home and asked, "What do you think of that?" I have since learned that, in the six months following, the *Evening Press* was nearly closed down - it was not working. Eventually, however, it took off and became the dominant evening paper in Dublin. The *Evening Mail* was the sufferer in that equation. It must have been some years after that the *Mail* closed because I was in the *Evening Press* at the time running the letters page for the editor, Conor O'Brien. He asked me one day, "Any Protestant letters there at all, Hugh?" I said, "What do you mean, Mr. O'Brien?" He said, "Anything to do with The Eye and Ear or St. Patrick's or Christ Church or anything like that?" The *Mail* was going and I was told to dig out anything that might help the *Evening Press* move in on the *Mail's* close relationship with Dublin's Protestant community - and on the *Mail's* letter-writing readers. This was just before television burst upon Ireland - people wrote copiously to the papers. It was *The Irish Times* and the *Mail* that got the letters - the *Mail* had a smashing letters page.

I did the usual things kids do, we got out scout magazines and I wrote stories on my father's Remington. Numbers, in school, were a foreign world to me - I can't do a domestic, let alone a newspaper, budget. Words are what make life worthwhile - the nuances, the origins, the delicate meanings. Every language has its own particular appeal - some are very coarse, some are much more subtle than others. English is an immensely subtle language. It's an eternal joy to play with.

After the Leaving Cert, I had gone to London to work in a supermarket. My father was in the *Irish Press* at this time and he buttonholed Colm Traynor - Colm was the general manager

- and told him he had a lad who was reasonably bright and any chance of a job. I was called rapidly back from London and in I went as a copy-boy and got my first Irish pay-packet: £1.17s.4d. - there's still a photograph of it somewhere at home.

The *Press* offices were bursting with life - the sheer chaos of getting out a paper always impressed me. Conor O'Brien was at the top of the newsroom - the news editor down the far end. They'd be bellowing at each other about what was the latest news and what should be on page one. The Major, Vivion de Valera, would come in occasionally to see what was going on. Another great character in there, of course, was Tim Pat Coogan.

At that time, the *Evening Press* had settled well into its stride - Conor O'Brien was a gifted journalist: he did all the usual things but he always added in that little extra ingredient, that surprise element. He tried to get off-beat, different pieces from people outside the business. It gave the *Evening Press* a special cachet.

Times were simpler then. Television was not a dominant force in Irish life. There was no doubt about what we were doing and where we were going. Our business was disclosure with a modicum of taste and a bow in the direction of our heritage, having sprung from the same set of historical loins as the Fianna Fail party. We were friendly to the Fianna Failers but it never stayed our hand in covering a story.

One of the early upheavals in Fianna Fail was when the Minister for Agriculture, Paddy Smith, resigned. Conor immediately stopped page one. In a flash, the Major was over from O'Connell Street to see what was being done - to make sure the hand was right. Our first loyalty is still to the principles of journalism and, in any event, the link with Fianna Fail is now more tenuous. Fianna Fail does not need a sycophantic paper: it would not be any good for the party, for the paper or for the country. The way we look at things in the *Press* now is that we see ourselves as good friends of Fianna Fail but we will tell them when we think they are putting a foot wrong. Problems may arise and we may get representations but we have to stand our ground. The most important thing is honest, direct disclosure of what's happening in the country. It's a democracy and we have to keep our place by the fireside in that democracy. If we compromise, we are not honouring our particular heritage. The days of intense loyalty to a paper - or to a party - may be gone.

One of the reasons why the *Press* and Fianna Fail did not remain in a symbiotic relationship was Fianna Fail itself was fragmenting. What part of the party were we to relate to? There are seminal organisations in Ireland which have been going through a sea change in the past decade and coping in different ways - the Catholic Church, the GAA, RTE have all had their troubles. They're all questioning what they are at, where they are going and what Ireland means today. At the *Press* we take some comfort from that - we are not alone in the task of redefining purpose and identity.

Conor O'Brien was a great man - in a sense he would be my role model, not that, then, I ever thought I would be editor of the paper. He was from an old cultivated Dun Laoghaire family, a lawyer by profession. He always gave a youngster a chance - myself, Alan Wilkes, Dick O'Riordan, Emmanuel Kehoe, Brian Lynch - we were given responsibility at a young age. That was a feature of the *Press* at the time. The unions often muttered about cheap labour, but it wasn't that - it was Conor's wish to make our lives rewarding and to let us taste the pleasures and the power of journalism.

I spent about a year as a copy-boy running between the subs and the printers. You got to know - you had to know - everybody on the journalistic staff and in the case room. You'd be down in the bowels of the building four or five times a day to bring up the papers fresh off the presses. It was a wonderful way for a young fellow to learn the full process of publishing papers. A deputy news editor did not know who to go to to get an urgent street-poster done and I was able to tell him.

After that I went on the subs' desk. I was delighted when I was given control of the letters page. I moved on to run a strange little department that is now gone from newspapers -

the bush service: the evening paper could appear in Tralee or Sligo with the latest racing results. It worked like this: the paper was printed at about twelve o'clock in Dublin with a quarter of the page blank. While the paper was in transit, it was my job to keep up with the news, do a digest of it and get it down the wire to our ten or 11 local offices; I would transmit some stories to all of them and local ones to where they belonged. The local manager then prepared a stencil of what I sent down, the papers were run through a machine and sold. It was terribly important then to get there first. I don't think now, with television, it's so important. At that time, there were people literally sitting waiting for the paper all over the country.

I did a film column for the *The Sunday Press* for 12 years. I did a bit of everything - working on the stone, the place where the paper was put together. It was a masculine world - a noisy place full of heavy metal and ink and bustle and laughter. It's silent now, just bits of paper moving about. The caseroom was an exciting environment - you felt the power of the medium you were working in. The weight of the material around you emphasised the fact you were a national newspaper - the lead, linotype machines and the great presses thundering away like the engines of a ship.

One of the great stories from those times was the Kennedy assassination. We heard about it at about 6 p.m. - the *Evening Press* staff had all gone home and it would be hours before an edition of the *Irish Press* could be ready. The lads working on the *Irish Press* took matters into their own hands. "Let's get out a late *Evening Press*", they said. The *Evening Press* plates were still on the machines below. They changed the front page and had it selling all over the place that evening.

How times have changed. We did a piece recently in the *Irish Press* on the unsolved murders on the garda files. Back in the 60s, murders were so unusual you would run a story for a month. Now they are ten-a-penny. There is now an immense volume of ponderous news that simply wasn't there in the past - the Beef Tribunal, the courts. I remember, a couple of years ago, there was a run of major national and international stories - Greencore, German reunification, the Soviet collapse - any one of which would in the past have kept papers going for a year. Now you get them in weeks. German reunification was one of the biggest stories of our time but it was just in there amongst the birth of new nations, the rebirth of old nations, the whole Maastricht upheaval.

Most of us in the newspapers were delighted to see Maastricht being stopped in its tracks. You could see this juggernaut that had developed its own momentum, its own raison d'être. It was up there and big and had to keep moving and doing things - we must be thankful to the Danes. We were a bit naive in swallowing the thing. It's something we can't be too proud of. There's something of an inferiority complex in our approach to the European Community - we try too hard to prove ourselves. The Germans or the French or the Dutch don't feel the need to prove that they are good Europeans. They look after themselves. Europe is the best place in the world to live in and that comes from its diversity. I could never see any German giving up the deutschmark or a Frenchman giving up the franc.

In the early 70s I felt the need for something different. Conor O'Brien was going to the *Sunday Independent*, Sean Ward was taking over in the *Evening Press*, so I thought it was an opportunity to look for a change. I asked for a transfer to the *Sunday Press*. My first project was a diary column - a sort of a gossip column without being too nasty. Kevin Marron and I spent about six months setting it up. At that time it was a one-man show. I had a full page to fill - I would get the stories, write them and lay out the page. When Dick Wilkes retired I was appointed assistant editor.

On a Sunday paper, there is a smallish team, very close, and the functions can be mixed. We'd kick off the week with a conference, the reporters would go off and chase their assignments while we were essentially desk-men. You'd work your way through the whole paper from the soft end - features, the book reviews - to the hard end. We would serialise books -

I remember the illustrious Enda O'Coineen, Enda Rabbitte from Galway. We had seen bits and pieces about this strange Irishman who had set off from, I think, Halifax, Nova Scotia, to Ireland in a tiny inflatable boat, had been rescued by the Royal Navy on the high seas and had been picked up by a British vessel off the coast of Ireland. Enda is a delightful fellow - we told him we were interested in his story so off he went to write it himself. You could have built a raft out of the manuscripts he sent in. I boiled it down to three nice episodes.

My great colleague in those days was Willie Collins. For me, he was all things to all men - he was like a father to us in that he stemmed from the old days of the early *Sunday Press*. Set up in 1949, it had an individual view of World War II. It did not quite say it, but it felt the Germans had got a raw deal. The editor was the late Col. Matt Feehan. It did great retrospective spreads on the Battle of Stalingrad and the fall of Berlin. As a young journalist, Willie was weaned on this material. While keeping a foot in the old camp, Willie had a tremendous youthfulness about him. He would try anything. He would egg you on to crazy excesses at times. He was a great reader but he wore his learning lightly. All his sons are in journalism now - Stephen Collins of the *Sunday Press* and Liam Collins in the *Sunday Independent*. No matter how much work was thrown at Willy he would absorb it and march home at the end of the day jaded but happy. At the end of an evening, Col. Feehan would stick his head out of his office door and say, "Wipe your bayonets, lads, you've killed enough today". Willie is retired now.

Matt Feehan was the only editor I have seen who brought his dog into the office. I don't know if Matt had any journalistic background - I suppose people thought a good military mind would be as good as any other mind. He was the first editor of the *Sunday Press* and anybody who sets up a paper and makes it catch - that's an achievement. In the newspaper business, failure is much more commonplace than success. The three papers set up by the Press Group survived. We have troubles now and we are impoverished to a degree but the *Irish Press* was set up in the 30s and, against all the odds, managed to carve out a place for itself. The *Sunday Press* likewise. The *Sunday Press* opened up Sunday journalism in its day - it opened the window on the GAA and on other aspects of Irish life not covered by the *Sunday Independent*. The *Evening Press* was a breath of fresh air in an evening market which was quiet, solid and dull before it arrived. They were pathfinders in many ways. We were the first papers to run wire pictures from abroad.

The Irish newspaper market must be the most competitive in the world. We are comparable to the UK in our consumption of newspapers but way ahead of other European countries. Europe does not have the mass circulation papers we have in Ireland and England. The typical Gascon doesn't want to read what the fellow up in Normandy is reading. It's a question of both history and geography - the countries are bigger and not so unified as Ireland and England are. In Germany, you get immense differences of loyalty and attitude between Bavaria and Schleswig-Holstein. In France, there are vast differences between Alsace and Provence. Proportionately, the *Telegraph, Mail* and *Sun* outsell anything in France or Germany or, indeed, America.

The function of newspapers is always changing and has undergone its greatest change in the past ten years. When I began in journalism, news and sport were what we were about. Features were little added extras not essential to the paper. It was vital to have a good selling story on page one. That's no longer the case - nowadays papers succeed only if they can devise and develop a particular personality, a particular view of the country and its problems. Papers need much stronger personalities now than they did in the days before television. That's the great challenge that faces journalists and publishers. A paper has to say: this is what we stand for, this is what we believe and this is the sort of thing we would say about this or that problem. Not many papers have succeeded in doing that. In Britain, the most successful, I feel, is *The Guardian*. You know exactly how it is going to view something - it's got the most secure and confident identity in the British press. *The Times* is undergoing a metamorphosis - whether it's successful or not I don't know. In the tabloid market, *The Mail* has its particular personality which has a softer female edge to it. *The Express* chases after that and never quite gets it. *The Mail* always hits it on the head while *The Express* often hits it on the thumb.

A difficult question - if the *Irish Press* were a person, what sort of person would it be? It was set up almost as a counterpoint to what then existed, to celebrate plain decent Irish living. The *Irish Independent* was the businessman's paper and the paper of the priests and bishops. It was not seen as a paper of the plain people, of the farm- or factory-worker, the ordinary small person out there involved in the great task of nation building. The *Independent* still had the afflatus of the traitor about it with memories of 1916. *The Irish Times*, of course, was the Protestant paper - the average Irish Catholic probably would not take it. There was a large constituency which was not getting the papers it wanted. They were not getting their sport which was GAA, they were not getting their life which was the little towns of Ireland, the Irish language was not appearing. The *Irish Press* was set up to give a voice to those who were going unheard. That's why it worked. It had a very clear idea of what it was about. There was no side about it, no mystery. As the years passed by, however, that simple identity wasn't enough for a changing Ireland, moving forward, become more circumspect about the old verities.

I think the *Irish Independent* is a massive engine of a paper. In my early days, I remember that, if we started something, the *Independent* was in like a flash. We started a woman's page in the *Evening Press* on a Thursday - within a week the *Herald* had something similar. Anything you did, they came after you. The *Independent* is a good newspaper, it's all things to all men - there's nothing it misses. They are clearly going after *The Irish Times* - the business coverage has dramatically improved. I don't know what the personality of the paper is though. The *Independent* is a successful expression of the callowness of modern Ireland - it's all about acquisition, about how to maximise your money, get your pension right. Maybe that's why it's successful. *The Irish Times* has its particular, polite atmosphere - and I presume always will. However its news approach always puzzled us. In the *Press*, we were baffled by the release of the Brian Lenihan tapes by *The Irish Times* in time for the six o'clock news on television. If we had them in the *Press*, we would have held them and published them exclusively the next morning and I'm sure the *Independent* would have done likewise. The other was the way they held the Bishop Casey story - but I suppose any newspaper would hesitate about that.

In the current constellation of publications in Ireland, I feel the *Irish Press* has a place and a substantial function to perform. It has something to give to Ireland - a view of things which is different from that of the other papers. Of the Irish papers, the *Press* is the nearest to having its finger on the pulse of the ordinary people, not the businessman or doctors or lawyers. It has a natural link with the common people and we want to rebuild and restore that.

The tabloid experience has not worked as we expected. It always takes time for a paper that has changed its shape to re-find its way and to re-connect with its readers. We went tabloid in 1988, five years ago. To a degree, we have had our hands tied behind our backs because of the company's commercial problems which deprived us of vital resources. The difficulties at the top did not help. The first eight weeks of the tabloid format were excellent. The paper was vibrant - people were complimentary. Before that, the paper had been declining slowly through a series of unfortunate events. There were stoppages in the 80s, there was a long stoppage when we went over to computer-setting - we were unable to bring back the morning paper for eight weeks. Many people thought this was a signal to our readers that the *Sunday Press* and the *Evening Press* were more important. It took weeks to get the paper back into the shops all over the country. That did a lot of damage. We never really recovered. Yet it is still a paper with a loyal readership. Unfortunately, our natural rural reading base has been shrinking for many years. The whole lot conspired to set us on a downward path, hard to halt. Once a paper begins to slide it is difficult without massive resources to turn it around. We had a broadsheet - we were unable to give it more than 18 or 20 pages every day. The consensus was it didn't stand comparison with the other broadsheets which often had twice as many pages in them. So, after many long meetings, we thought a viable tabloid could be produced. We did not visualise ourselves in the red market - the market of *The Mirror* or *The Star*. We saw ourselves in the middle market. I am not saying *The Mirror* or *The Star* are not good papers - they are superbly edited and highly successful, but we felt our particular niche was different. One of our problems was our typography was wrong in the early tabloid days - it was too black and coarse. The content of the paper was fine. We had and still have many excellent contributors. We have one of the best political correspondents in the country in Emily O'Reilly. We have writers like Declan Kiberd, Nell McCafferty, and Declan Lynch on television. We have an excellent newsroom, a great sports department. We have regular guest appearances by top political and business figures. But it does not quite come out as we'd like it to come out - we need new presses and that is a massive investment. We thought the partnership with Ingersolls would yield this for us - we were told at the time that one of the gifts of the new partnership would be new plant and new offices. If that had happened, we would be in a much stronger position today.

There are many interesting tabloids in Europe - *El Pais, La Repubblica, Libération, Le Monde*. I am not saying the *Irish Press* is quite that type of tabloid but there is a direction there for us to travel - a paper with a good radical edge to it is sorely needed in Ireland. With resources and a sustained marketing campaign, the *Irish Press* could be such a paper. We are almost victims of our own history because of how and why the paper was set up. These were fine and noble ideas in their day but nowadays they are seen in many ways as millstones - wrongly, I believe, but that is a wide public perception. To transform that is quite an undertaking. It takes resources and courage and conviction and it's not going to happen until we get our problems at the top solved.

There is a difference in kind between being editor and anything else in the paper - in my early days in the job I found that difficult to cope with. I had not aspired to be editor - it came as a complete surprise when I was offered the job. At the time everybody felt that something had to be done with the morning paper. It was simply lying there in the market place, clearly the third paper in the field. It was a fine newspaper but it simply was not connecting with the people. The readership was getting older. It was not where the commercial action of the country was which was in Dublin or along the east coast. The company knew this and there were many sessions in the months before I was involved as editor. I suppose I was selected because basically I had been a production journalist and it was felt that the paper did not look as good as it ought.

Of the three papers in the company, the one to which I related was the *Evening Press*. I grew up on it - it was a Dublin paper. The *Irish Press* was always the other paper in the Group. But, after six years working there, I can tell you the people there are a wonderful team and it's a great paper. It's sad to see it in difficulty. A little success anywhere along the way would have made a difference. We have been with that situation ten years now - we are crisis junkies. It's ten years ago since we were called to a meeting by Colm Traynor and told that the company was losing money. There is an embattled feeling amongst our team. There is great loyalty too. The pressures are immense. Because of our troubles, we're always looking at costs - we now graze meadows of figures instead of talking about Europe or the North or Aer Lingus or the Fianna Fail party. We look at sales figures, budget figures, profit figures, this, that and the other figures. But there is no hinterland - there is nothing happening beyond that at the moment. All you can do is carry on until you learn what the future might hold. But happily we have paper and ink and stories to busy ourselves with every night.

It's been the strangest six years of my life to be editor of the *Irish Press*. There are great pleasures attaching to the job - the staff just keep at it, dig away, get the stories. They give meaning to it all.

What you should be as an editor is unknowable - nobody can tell you beforehand what you should think, how you ought to behave. There is no set rule-book. There are no dilletante editors around. Vinnie Doyle, editor of the *Irish Independent*, and Michael Brophy, editor of *The Star*, have come out of the *Press* - they trudged up through the ranks. They've done all the things. As editor I find myself continually having to stop doing things - I love laying out a page, it's what I enjoy doing most of all: getting a good photograph, laying out your headline nicely - that's my particular pleasure, or devising a really sharp headline for the front page. I have to tell myself I have a whole team of people there to do those things. I am hopeless on sport but I am superbly served by a good team there. John Garvey is our chief leader writer. In devising our leading articles, we ask ourselves what the average intelligent informed person would think. We are concerned with natural justice and fair play. We don't have many preconceived notions about this being right or that being wrong. We don't come down heavily on the side of particular issues in the *Irish Press*. We present the arguments and guide our readers as best we can through a particular question.

On voting day, we would tell people to vote Fianna Fail. That's an old tradition in the house! We would do it on the morning of the election - not too much before that - we close ranks briefly for the day.

Unemployment is a heart-breaking tragedy. The youngsters come into the *Irish Press*, bright-eyed and talented, and we are not able to give them the start they deserve. The other papers can't start them either because contraction is continuing just like any other industry. I think it's going to take about ten years before the thing begins to right itself. Clearly what we have is the tail-end of a spurt of population growth that Ireland went through which has stopped in Europe and is stopping here. Our family sizes are too big. I have four kids - none of the younger people I work with has more than two. Until that becomes the norm, I don't believe we are going to get any balance returning to employment figures. Meanwhile, there is no answer to the vast army of young people who have nowhere to go. England is not the great sponge it was and Europe and America are practically closed. This new generation, unlike the one that went before, is not getting the cars and the foreign holidays, the fancy clothes that people were getting then. The average young person today has a much more abstemious life than I had as a youngster or than the intervening generation had. It's almost like the 30s or the 50s again. I know so many families around Dun Laoghaire whose young people are trying everything and getting nowhere. At the age of 25 I had a car and quite a few holidays under my belt - they are not getting any of that. I do not know whether or not it will embitter them. The great eruption of wealth in Victorian Britain was made possible only by the existence of Australia, a vast empty continent to be filled by people. Those economies worked only because there were plenty of outlets for the excess to be streamed off. That's all closed now right across Europe: there are strict new immigration policies in France and Germany where they have immense problems. Spain is in a bind, Italy is in a state of collapse - so where do they go?

In the newspaper we try and get a flavour of young people's lives without being too negative about it. We try to help them find meaning but the terms are all new - you can't talk about life the way we knew it. It is very difficult to talk to young people who have little opportunity and make sense without coming across as a hypocrite. We are driving around in our motor cars and have our central heating - these young people may not have that. Will they be able to buy houses or rear families? It's an immense tragedy and nobody has an answer to it.

8

Edmund Curran

Belfast Telegraph

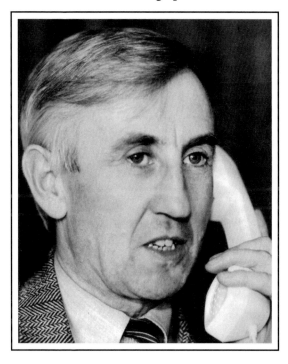

Scratch the surface of us all and, journalists or not, we have our own opinions. The fact that journalists in Northern Ireland have been able to sublimate their views says much for their integrity and I am proud of that.

The conversation took place on July 8 1993

Edmund Curran is editor of the *Belfast Telegraph*.

He was born in Belfast on September 29 1944.

His father was William John Curran, manager of a private bus company in County Tyrone and later on the staff of the Ulster Transport Authority.

His mother was Elizabeth Russell.

He is the youngest in a family of two - one brother Stanley.

He was married to Romaine Carmichael, a physical education teacher, and divorced in 1992.

Their children are Jonathan (20), Cathryn (18), Andrew (17) and Claire (16).

He is engaged to Pauline Hall, an educational psychologist.

He was educated at Derryloran Primary School, Cookstown; Drumglass Primary School, Dungannon; The Royal School, Dungannon; Queens University, Belfast (BSc and Diploma in Education).

1966 joined the Thomson Organisation, which owns *The Belfast Telegraph*, as a trainee journalist. Served first on *The East Antrim Times* in Larne as a trainee reporter. 1968 reporter and features writer on the *Belfast Telegraph*; 1970 leader writer; 1973 assistant editor; 1974 deputy editor; 1988 launch editor of a new Sunday newspaper, *The Sunday Life;* 1991 (for six months) seconded to edit *Wales on Sunday*. *The Sunday Life* won the Regional Newspaper of the Year Award under his editorship, as did *Wales on Sunday*. 1993 editor of the *Belfast Telegraph*.

He has been a contributor to *Time* magazine and a regular broadcaster on Northern Ireland affairs.

He is a member of the board of the *Ulster Gazette*, Armagh, and *The Tyrone Courier*, Dungannon.

1992 Regional Editor of the Year.

1993 played for the Ulster Veterans' Tennis Team - all his family have represented either Ulster or Ireland at tennis or rowing.

His hobbies are reading newspapers, keeping abreast of current affairs, and playing tennis and golf.

I have a 1955 Letts diary from when I was 11 years old and
even then I can see I was interested in current affairs. I
would write in my diary the headlines of the news and sport:
who won the European Cup that year or what Harold
Macmillan or Anthony Eden said. I don't imagine every
schoolboy does that kind of thing. Maybe I had nothing else to
note. My father always listened to the news and would read
newspapers, in particular the one I edit now. I suppose I got
my interest from that. My brother is much older than me - he
played for Cookstown Hockey Club and was the hockey
correspondent for the *Mid-Ulster Mail.* I think he tried to be as
objective as possible. A third influence was at university where
I was interested in student politics and in the university
newspaper, *Gown.* The longer I was at university, the more I
wanted to be a journalist but I was lucky to get in. A lot of
people may feel the same way but only one or two make it.

I did not get in the first time. When I went for interview to
the *Belfast Telegraph,* the editor was John Sayers, an influential
man who had stamped his mark on Northern Ireland by being
a crusading editor and taking an independent line at a time
when it took courage. I got a note from him saying that I was
quite close to getting the job but had not quite made it and
another individual had been chosen. I was deeply disappointed.
Then I got another letter saying that, of the two people he had
chosen, one had decided to pursue a career in law - indeed he
has since become a successful advocate. I got the job and
started in August 1966 as a trainee journalist at a salary of
£800 a year. Having lived on a student wage for the previous
four years, I thought it was manna. I was put on an induction
course and sent around the building to see what other
employees did. One thing stands out in my memory - going
out in a *Telegraph* van delivering the newspaper. They sent me
north up to Ballycastle in County Antrim and the other trainee
went south of Belfast to Newcastle. The circulation manager
went to great trouble - I had bolted into position beside the
driver's seat an old armchair in which I hurtled around the
countryside. As we came to each newsagents or petrol station,

the van-driver would say, "Throw your head back". He would reach round behind him, pick up a parcel, fire it through the open door, and drive on without stopping.

The news editor was hard on us. He did not think graduates could ever become journalists and that we were supernumeraries foisted on him by the editor. He took the view that we might make good magazine writers but never hard news reporters. There were three ways you could get into the newspaper. You might creep in without having much educational qualifications, for example through having been a messenger - as indeed did some of my most distinguished colleagues. Then there were school-leavers - you had to have two A-Levels, one in English. The third was to go in as a graduate as I did. Even to this day it's still restricted - the *Telegraph* will accept one, and occasionally two, each year and there is fierce competition. One year there were 1100 applicants for 11 trainee graduate posts in the Thomson Organisation.

I remember vividly the first time I wrote anything - it was the night John F. Kennedy died. I was still a student at Queens but was at home in Co. Tyrone watching television and saw the news flash. Maybe because of the generation I came from, his death meant an awful lot to me. I sat down and wrote a piece called *In Memoriam* - very pretentiously bylined "By Edmund R. Curran". It was a letter to Mrs. Kennedy in her mourning. When I look back on it now it was a load of drivel, an example of writing in sheer ignorance of the truth, but a lot of people at the time were in that mood. I finished it at midnight, walked a mile into the town of Dungannon and put it through the letterbox of the *Tyrone Courier*. After my weekend at home, I went back to college in Belfast. There was only one shop in Belfast near the university that sold the *Tyrone Courier*. To my surprise, the editor had put my piece in a black border on the front page. I can still see it.

I used to write about all kinds of things for the university newspaper - I wrote a feature on cock-fighting in Co. Tyrone. In 1962 Northern Ireland was a peaceful country - one of the more bizarre and illegal happenings was a cockfight. I never actually went but I talked to the people who owned the birds. There was a sneaking element of illegality about it, a bit like drinking poteen.

At the *Belfast Telegraph* the editor had the fashion of using only our surnames. He called me in and said, "Curran, I've an important duty for you - I want you to be involved in the Aberfan Disaster Fund". You may remember a slag-heap in Wales had moved and killed 120 children. It was a major story but my job was simply to type out every morning the list of readers who had contributed to the *Belfast Telegraph* Aberfan Disaster Fund. When recently I was seconded for six months to edit *Wales on Sunday*, I went down to Aberfan, 25 years to the day. I walked around the scene and managed to find a photographer who had done colour pictures in 1966 for *Time* magazine. We ran an exclusive in the Welsh paper, "The Pictures the World Saw 25 Years Ago". It is a sad and early memory from my career as a journalist.

Back to the 60s. I also volunteered to cover sports fixtures at the weekend, standing in the rain at many a rugby match, doing four paragraphs on the first half, four on the second half, and phoning in the names of the teams before the match started. If you were lucky, the *Sunday Times* would want a report as well and for that you used a different language. Because their Irish edition was printed early, they wanted 400 words for the first half and 50 for the second. That was all very well if the scores were evenly spread across the match - but on one occasion the score was nil-all at half-time and then Mike Gibson ran riot in the second half. His team ended up winning by 33 points to nil. I couldn't get 33 points into 50 words, so I had to get special permission to re-write my report.

One of the earlier assignments I received from Jack Sayers was to go up to Coleraine where the new university had opened. He said, "I want you to behave like a student for a week and to send a column each day to the paper". As I drove to Coleraine on October 6 1968 I remember listening on the car radio to the lunchtime news and hearing Mary Holland reporting on how the police had baton-charged a crowd in Londonderry the day before and how Gerry Fitt had been amongst those attacked. That was the beginning of it all and it was just 20 miles from Coleraine. Tragically the opening week of that university coincided with the opening week of the Ulster troubles and events that dominated my life.

I was sent to my home town one evening to cover an early civil rights meeting. It turned out to be a classic Ulster street confrontation. The rally was primarily Catholic but the Protestant community from which I had sprung (and many of whom I knew) were standing there in opposition. A clash was inevitable. The following morning, the Protestant newspaper, *The News Letter*, said in its report that the Catholic crowd had thrown stones first. *The Irish News* reported the opposite. My report said, "There was an exchange of missiles between two factions". The deputy editor called me in and suggested that I had not reported what I had seen. I felt quite sore because my integrity had been questioned. Because I came from one section of the population of Dungannon, he was suggesting I might be biased in my reporting. However, every journalist from Northern Ireland must inevitably come from one section or the other and that little episode has stuck with me to this day. I was truly not on the spot when the first stone was thrown and I wonder if any of the other reporters had been there either but it did serve to show me how sensitive a reporter's role in Ulster can be.

I had a dual life then. I wanted to be a journalist but I felt that I could also play a role in politics. When I was at college I had been chairman of the Conservative and Unionist Association. It was regarded by many Unionists as being beyond the Pale - indeed all the more so because my successor was a Catholic. Few if any Catholics had ever been the chairman of a Unionist Association. Students called it the Tory Club and cabinet ministers from the old Northern Ireland Government came to speak to us and we would have debates with members of other parties. We were seen as liberal Unionists, which didn't go down too well with the mainstream rank-and-file of the party.

At 24, I was a Unionist candidate in the 1969 general election for the Northern Ireland Parliament. I appeared on Captain Terence O'Neill's election broadcast at that time. He called it his "crossroads" election. It turned out to be the last one to the Northern Ireland Parliament, which was suspended by Edward Heath in 1972. In those days the Conservative Party had a direct link with the Unionist Party in Northern Ireland but subsequently they went their independent ways. When I was a student, I used to go to quarterly meetings in London of the Conservative Students' Association and felt like a duck out of water - the issues they were talking about were irrelevant to Northern Ireland.

My opponent in the election was Austin Currie, who has since been a candidate for the presidency of Ireland. The election was seen as an opportunity for the Protestant community to support either more liberal policies or more conservative ones. It was the Rev. Ian Paisley versus O'Neill. I was standing in East Tyrone, my home area, and Austin Currie and I were products of the same university but of different cultures. Both of us, in our own ways, were trying to break the mould a bit. Austin Currie's politics were more subtle than his predecessors in the Nationalist Party - the Social Democratic and Labour Party had not been founded then. The Nationalists in the area were in the majority and had always won the seat. Austin Currie had a phrase for me which we have often joked about in the years since. He described me as "tip-toeing through the Orange Halls of Co. Tyrone", a reference to my O'Neill liberalism. During the election, the editor, who did not approve of my candidacy, dispatched me to the courts where he felt I could do no harm. Of course I lost the election. Austin Currie has been most helpful to me since in my journalistic career. He has said to me I was a lucky man not to win because it would have changed my life. I know that, in his own case, he made the most enormous sacrifices. He was attacked and abused, his wife was attacked, his life was far from comfortable. I have often thought there but for the grace of God, and the numerical situation in Co. Tyrone, go I. That was the end of my brief political interest. I had been deluding myself that I could be a card-carrying member of a political party and retain any degree of objectivity as a journalist. This may be possible in the Republic and in Britain but the Northern Ireland situation is so divided as to make it impossible here. However, I would say one advantage of my going forward for election was I got to know a lot of people in politics and that has helped me in journalism. Indeed I believe it would be very hard to be a journalist in Ulster and not to be interested in politics. It is central to so much that happens.

After this episode, I became a feature writer and really enjoyed writing profiles and doing "in-depth" interviews with political and military figures. I interviewed the first British army generals who came to Ulster. I would go to the Bogside or the Shankill Road and do mood pieces - trying to find out what the people were really thinking. I enjoyed getting a little bit under the skin - finding out if people were really supporting the IRA, or were they extreme loyalists, or were they moderates or whatever. I had a bit of an ambition that if I did the job well enough, I might become a reporter on the *Sunday Times*. In those days under Harold Evans it was the epitome of good journalism. He had begun really to develop investigative journalism with the *Insight* team. In 1971 I went to an awards ceremony in London - I was a runner-up for the Regional Feature Writer of the Year Award. All the leading figures in British journalism were there. It was in the Cafe Royal and this was my big chance I thought. I managed to speak to Harold Evans in the lift - national editors are sometimes looking around to see who's coming up in the regions. He was complimentary and subsequently wrote to me: "On the *very* next opportunity that arises, I shall have you over for interview". I never heard from him but was told later it wasn't unusual for Harold Evans to promise two people the same job.

When I came back, I told the editor I was getting itchy feet and he responded by offering me the chance to become assistant editor. At that time I had been writing editorials - the paper had a chief leader writer and two others. They would usually write features as well. I remember writing features entitled "How Stormont Fell" and "Inside the Mind of the IRA" - that was the early days when we had the Official IRA. Indeed I recall interviewing Tomás MacGiolla, now Lord Mayor of Dublin. In those days, he was a spokesman for the Official Republican movement and I had a clandestine meeting with him in the Charlemont Hotel in Armagh one evening.

At that time I had no sub-editing experience - my background was in writing and reporting. I was dispatched off to the *Newcastle Journal* and the *Evening Chronicle* - morning and evening papers, to get training as a sub-editor and when I returned I became assistant editor of *The Telegraph* in January 1974. Northern Ireland was on the brink of civil war. Day-to-day life, particularly in Belfast, was near to anarchy. There were 2000 bombs in 1972 alone. 450 people were killed. One of the things that struck me at the time was how important the balance and objectivity of the *Belfast Telegraph* were to the body politic, to the life and soul of Northern Ireland.

The major event of 1974 was the Ulster Workers' Council strike. The entire Province was brought to a standstill for three weeks and the power-sharing Executive was brought down. We lurched from one crisis to another: the downfall of successive Unionist prime ministers, the downfall of Stormont, the strike, the upsurge of the IRA and Republican violence. They were heady days to be a journalist, and Belfast was awash with British and international correspondents. When I saw some of them operating in Belfast, my ambition to become a Fleet Street journalist disappeared. When you saw their stories, you realised they were no better than many of the journalists working here. Indeed some of them were pretty awful.

Belfast was a barren place to live in in the 70s and political events were pervasive.

The *Belfast Telegraph* strongly supported power-sharing. It was seen by extreme Unionists as being somewhat traitorous. As a young journalist, even though I came from a Protestant background, I often felt more comfortable going up the Falls

Road than the Shankill Road because the media were so critical of the Protestant community. On the other hand, the Catholics on the Falls saw the media as highlighting some of their grievances. There were, consequently, pressures on all of us who worked here - including the people on this paper who came from both traditions. It's a tribute to the media in Northern Ireland that they have managed to hold themselves together despite outside influences. Scratch the surface of us all and, journalists or not, we have our own opinions. The fact that journalists in Northern Ireland have been able to sublimate their personal views says much for their integrity and I am proud of that.

We have had ten British Secretaries of State here over the years and some have said they looked to the *Telegraph* as a voice of sanity. We have always tried to step back when people have been speaking loudly. The former editor, Roy Lilley, late in the evening, if we had had a bit of a party, was sometimes persuaded to sing, "A Bridge Over Troubled Waters". I feel that's as good a signature tune as you could possibly get for the *Belfast Telegraph* and a great tribute to his editorship over 20 years.

I was deputy editor under him, probably for far too long, but I enjoyed every moment of it. Northern Ireland was ever-changing, on and off the boil, unpredictable, not the kind of place that journalists from outside could readily understand. You don't have a lot of mobility with journalists here - because of the violence, people would not move to Belfast from other Thomson newspapers.

Another big difference between now and the 70s in the newspaper industry centred on industrial relations problems. A month would not pass without a dispute - the industry was destroying itself. You had the NUJ, SOGAT, the NGA. It was inhibiting because, as a journalist, you had loyalty to the newspaper and to a union. At times it was impossible to hold a balance. In those days, as deputy editor, I had to be a member of the NUJ. There was a six weeks' strike and the NUJ insisted I and the other senior executives totally support it. The management told me to abide by the union's instructions and go home because it wasn't worth having a great hassle over my behaviour once the strike was settled. The watershed in all of this was Rupert Murdoch and Wapping in the 1980s. Since then, the atmosphere in the newspaper industry in Northern Ireland has changed tremendously: not in the Republic where it is still hoist with a lot of these old practices. In the old days, you could have a dispute over the thickness of a piece of string tying up the bundles of newspapers. You had dreadful demarcation disputes. There was overmanning. You name it, it was all there. At times, it would make you despair - here we were in the middle of this great story, the story of Northern Ireland, and an industrial relations row would take precedence. There was great virtue however in the fact that the *Telegraph* was not owned by people who lived in Northern Ireland. When Lord Thomson bought the *Belfast Telegraph* in the early 1960s, there was a lot of opposition. It had been in the Baird family since 1870 and was seen as traditional Unionist. The Thomson Organisation brought to the *Telegraph* their commercial instincts and have turned it into a successful business. Secondly, and important in the Northern Ireland context, they had no political axe to grind. The editors have been independent. I can never recall political interference despite all the crises this country faced.

The *Telegraph* has argued over the years in its editorial policy that there cannot be a united Ireland, if there is ever going to be one, before there is a united Northern Ireland. The policy is threefold. One, the newspaper supports the fact that Northern Ireland is part of the United Kingdom, but not for any narrow, political motive. We believe the best interests of all the people of Northern Ireland are served by the union - certainly no one has come up with a viable economic alternative. Secondly, the newspaper has consistently supported any means through which the two communities could be encouraged to work closely together politically and to share resources and power within the context of Northern Ireland. That has not made us very popular with certain sections at times. Third, we believe there should be a close relationship with the Republic - we support measures of cooperation but we think a constitutional link not accepted by the majority in Ulster would simply cause trouble and be counterproductive.

I think it is possible for us in Ireland, North and South, to come closer together in the context of the European Community. John Hume has pointed out that Britain and Ireland are no longer enemies - they are partners in Europe - and the Republican tradition has failed to recognise that. And there is much more cooperation between people North and South than meets the eye.

The *Telegraph*, in the last paragraph of a leading article in 1985, said of the Anglo-Irish Agreement: "This will not work". We felt that there should be some relationship with the Republic but the one put in place was counterproductive. It was done without the consent of the Protestant community and would, therefore, always be flawed. No agreement will work unless you can get the vast majority of people to support it - you will never get everybody to support everything but in this instance you are talking about the majority community in Northern Ireland. Almost to a man they were opposed to the Anglo-Irish Agreement. It was a recipe for the unrest and violence which we warned at the time would happen. No one can say in 1993 the Pact has been a stirring success. It has not been a failure but it has caused a lot of anguish - its imperfection lies in the inability of the Governments in London and Dublin to get the support of the majority. Despite that, and despite this paper's opposition, I do believe that the Agreement is not going to go away - it's cast in stone. Neither side could break it. If the British Government were to say we're doing away with this because the Unionists don't like it, the Irish Government would cause an international stir and the Nationalist community would rebel - that would also be counterproductive. So it's there and the Unionist community will have to come to accept it. They have, in a sense, even though their political leaders will not publicly admit to it. They drew 250,000 people outside the City Hall in 1985. I doubt if they would draw a tenth of that crowd in 1993.

The Anglo-Irish process has contributed to more equanimity for the Catholic community but the Protestants see no one standing up for them. The Nationalist community has a guarantor in the Irish Government but the British Government is not seen as a guarantor for the Unionists, even though people in Dublin may think differently. The British Government is increasingly neutral - the guarantor of all the people of Northern Ireland.

It's very hard to see any "solution" to the "problem" in the immediate future. I have been looking at it for 25 years - the more you look at it, the more complex it becomes. The people closest to the problem have the most difficulty in seeing a solution because we can see so many nuances, so many sensitivities. In the early years, people from outside would come up with simplistic answers. There are intractable problems around the world and maybe this is one of them.

After the Anglo-Irish Pact was signed I remember talking over dinner in Dublin with the then Irish Prime Minister, Dr. Garret FitzGerald. He believed the Agreement he had signed gave the Irish Government more than a consultative position in Northern Ireland affairs. It was put about in Dublin that it had given the Irish Government almost a shared sovereignty. Nationalist leaders in the North conveyed that impression too, whether it was deliberate or whether they just got it wrong. That did not do anything to help the Unionists over their difficulties. It confirmed their worst fears. As the years passed, the Agreement has been whittled down and Irish Government ministers will now say that what they have is consultation only, but it remains a blurred area. The extent of Dublin's say in Northern Ireland affairs seems to go up and down depending on who is Secretary of State for Northern Ireland and how the wind is blowing.

Our editorial view now is that the Anglo-Irish Pact was a bridge too far. That's a view held by the former head of the Northern Ireland Civil Service, Sir Kenneth Bloomfield, who also used that phrase. Both Governments have got to work on the Unionist community quite a bit to get them to accept even the present arrangement before they can talk about shared sovereignty, as Dick Spring or Kevin McNamara have recently done. All you do with that kind of talk is raise another era of unrest.

There is an inevitable path, one that must lead to a closer relationship between the peoples of North and South. That is the way Europe is going. It is the way Ireland is going. Electronic communications or better roads will inevitably lead us closer together. Business and commerce and the European Community will lead us together. But it is doubtful if the sovereignty of the United Kingdom needs to be breached. Yes, you can say you are on a road leading to greater cooperation between the Republic and Northern Ireland but who is to say that relationship will ever lead to a united Ireland in the simplistic form the founding fathers of the Irish State believed in or the Irish Constitution holds it to be? Economically it seems crazy. The New Ireland Forum, which was probably the forerunner of the Anglo-Irish Pact, produced economic studies few people have read. The studies concluded that the possibility of the Republic's looking after Northern Ireland, divorced from Britain, was remote. I don't see the United States or the European Community or anybody queueing up to pour into Northern Ireland the billions of pounds the United Kingdom Government has.

In that respect, I think the greatest Unionists in Northern Ireland may eventually turn out to be members of the Catholic community because they have the most to lose. If the British decided tomorrow morning to withdraw economically from Northern Ireland, the people most severely damaged in their pocket would be the deprived section of the community, and in many unfortunate cases that means the poorer section of the Catholic community as well as many Protestants too.

Leaving sectarianism aside, which in any event I abhor, Northern Ireland is attached to one of the top 12 countries in the world in terms of economic power. It's a peculiar situation that people want to get away from one of the world's most affluent nations to join one of the poorest in Europe, a country with a population a third the size of London, but with all the panoply of Government. The Republic has nothing like the UK's economic or political clout. When the chips are down, I wonder if the people of Northern Ireland would really wish to be part of a tiny republic. Add us all together and we have the population of Greater Manchester. Sometimes when I see a line of Government ministers waiting at Dublin Airport for the President to return with the red carpet rolled out and the chauffeur-driven Government limousines waiting, I think to myself, is this the real world at all? Are they leading a population of 3.5 million people or playing a game? They are not really any more than a great county council. Are they doing anything other than the Unionists used to do in Northern Ireland? When I began in journalism, the Unionist Government ran a population of l.6 million. It was a law unto itself, master in its own house. It had all the array of a Cabinet, a magnificent parliament at Stormont. It had a Governor and Prime Minister - Acts of Parliament, the lot. There is not that much difference between that and the Republic. A jaundiced Northern view of the Republic is that those who are running the Dail are no better than the people who were in the Stormont Parliament. It was said about Northern Ireland that, among the 52 members of the Stormont Parliament, possibly only one or two of them, if that, would have made cabinet rank in Britain. How many members of the Irish Cabinet and Dail are of that calibre? Yet they are given equal status in the corridors of power in Europe. On numerical terms there is probably a better chance the chairman of Greater London Council would be of a calibre higher than a member of the Irish Cabinet.

Looking at the media in the Republic, I sometimes feel the Irish have an ability to contemplate their political navels. I watch RTE quite a bit. In both the newspapers and on television, to put it bluntly, two-bit political figures are elevated almost to the stature of international statesmen. There is a gross exaggeration of the importance of Irish politics and the media are a party to that. It would be exactly the same if I were to represent to the people of Northern Ireland the 17 Westminster MPs in this fashion but I don't think we do.

One argument for Irish unity is it is the only way you will get stability in Northern Ireland. There might be a plus point in the fact that a new dynamism would be created because we were all working together. But, if the population genuinely believed the IRA was winning, you would have a civil war. The Protestant community does not think the IRA is either winning or losing. It has come to accept violence in the same way it accepts road accidents. If violence does not impinge on them personally, people get on with their lives. If a property is destroyed, it will be rebuilt eventually. There is not a feeling the IRA will eventually win.

I think the Nationalist community has suddenly found itself in Northern Ireland. One of the reasons it favours Irish unity may relate to the way in which it has been treated by the Protestant majority and by the British. I happen to have gone to university when the Catholic community was coming to the fore - my Catholic counterparts were the people who became the leaders of the civil rights movement. If you look around Northern Ireland today, the place is being transformed. The leaders of the civil service, of industry and commerce, are coming increasingly from the Catholic community. It has a dynamism the Protestants do not realise is there. It is throwing up entrepreneurs left, right and centre. The bastion of well-to-do Ulster Protestantism was South Belfast - the Malone Road, the Ballsbridge of Dublin. Who is inhabiting it now? The Catholic church, St. Brigid's, was founded in the 1850s for the servants of the big houses. If you go to that church this weekend you'll see the lines of Mercs and BMWs. The big houses are now occupied by Catholics. There's been a remarkable transformation. It is not complete but it is not stoppable. The most important civil right given to the population in general in Northern Ireland and which affected the Catholic population particularly was the Education Reform Act in the 1940s. It gave to a very large number of people the opportunity for a university education. I come from a poor background and I went to university through that. People from the Catholic community would certainly not have been there without it - Austin Currie and Bernadette McAliskey. Increasingly, I see affluent Catholics taking their place in Northern Ireland, and as they do, they do not want to be dominated by Dublin any more than the Unionists do.

The SDLP is described simplistically as a Nationalist party but in reality it is much more subtle than that. It's a party which has said for the last 20 years it is prepared to play its part in the British Parliament and in the political process in Northern Ireland. It is prepared to take whatever benefits are coming from the British way of life at the same time retaining the aspiration to Irish unity. That is a lot less blunt than the old-fashioned Nationalist position. It's a half-way house. It is by no means the old Fianna Fail or de Valera position. It's more the old Fine Gael position - we will sign a treaty, make a deal. The SDLP does not have its roots in the working-class Catholic community: it represents the emerging and more affluent Catholic society.

It's a delusion that the Irish Republic is an independent State. After all, it recently negotiated £7.6b or so from Europe. The Republic could not exist without subsidies from Brussels. Where does the money come from - Germany, Britain and France. The reality is neither North nor South is independent. That's where the Republican tradition does not face reality.

There is a distinction between the Republican "tradition" and the Loyalist "cause". Obviously I don't come from the Republican tradition but it has always seemed to me that it has had more principle about it, it has not been as corrupted as extreme Loyalism. I'm not for a moment suggesting the IRA and those associated with them are lily-white but some of them seem prepared to make greater personal sacrifices than the Loyalists. Dying on hunger-strike is an example of the sacrifices the Republicans have made. It is difficult to see the same kind of exercise carried through with the same strength of will on the Loyalist side.

The problem in Northern Ireland is that now, after 20 years, it has a base of militancy/gangsterism. That will take a very long time to erase, even if you had a settlement tomorrow. There is an anarchic element in both communities. It is most manifest in protection money and the fact that small men have built themselves into positions of muscle. They are not going to give way readily.

The *Belfast Telegraph* is the main newspaper in Northern Ireland. That means we must not propagandise - we are in a privileged position. It is important, first, that we are seen not to abuse that privilege. We must not be seen to exclude one or other part of the community from expressing their view. We must never be seen to twist that view. We draw a very firm dividing line between the one small column of opinion and the rest of the paper. I don't believe our reporters should be influenced in any respect by the paper's editorial policy in terms of how they actually report the news. If they were, we could not possibly be reflecting life in Northern Ireland objectively and accurately. It's an accident of fate that I am the editor of the paper - I can't use my position to express my personal views. The views of the paper have been developed over 20 years. That established view is greater than that of any editor or any other member of its staff. We might be critical editorially of the Rev. Ian Paisley or of Gerry Adams or indeed of any of the political leaders but they get coverage in the pages of the *Belfast Telegraph* and rightly so.

Life has moved on in Northern Ireland. In the 70s and 80s politics and violence dominated everything. These are the issues people worry about deep down - but there's a lot more to the place than that and a newspaper has a duty to reflect it. There's more going on than the headlines you see in the international press. Aside from being a newspaper, we are part of the community. We are, for example, playing a part in a campaign, "Positively Belfast". The community contributes to the lifeblood of the *Telegraph* and we must do the same for the community.

The nature of newspapers has changed. The old cliché

trotted out pretentiously by editors was that their aim was "to inform, educate and entertain" in that order. I do think we can inform and I believe we should entertain a bit, given the darkness at times. A bit of froth and fun goes a long way - things unrelated to politics and violence. But nowadays newspapers are no longer the main medium through which people get the news - television does that - so we have to widen our brief. We have to do more than television does - we have to give people more information than the electronic media can give them and we have to analyse it. For instance, television and radio ignore completely the births, marriages and deaths columns - the most important days in a person's life. There will always be newspapers so long as the electronic media generalises so much and overlooks so much that is important to people.

The most noticeable impact of television was the decline in the evening newspaper market in the 60s, 70s and early 80s. We believe there has been a levelling out of the downward curve. Perhaps people are becoming more sophisticated about what they watch - television has become fragmented and this newspaper remains the principal advertising medium in Northern Ireland. We are one newspaper channel beaming out to the Northern Ireland public every evening. The more television channels there are, the more that will help us. People are also buying newspapers for different reasons. If all they want the newspaper for is to sell a second-hand car, so be it. British newspapers have come into Ireland, North and South, and have eaten up the morning newspaper market. It's a sorry fact of life that a newspaper like *The Sun* is the second best-selling newspaper in Northern Ireland and, despite the fact that it wraps the Union Jack around practically every page, it seems to be a paper people in the Republic also enjoy.

For a small country, *The Irish Times* is an exceptionally fine newspaper. I think, in general, Ireland is well-served by its newspapers. But Dublin has a lot of daily and Sunday newspapers and I find it difficult to see how they can all survive.

Over the last 20 years, newspapers here have had to change just as the community changed - and it's been a bit painful. When I look back, the media in general would not have reflected the minority culture in the way it does today. Now you will find extensive coverage of GAA on the BBC - and rightly so. A difficulty we face, in both newspapers and television, is understanding the entire community. I may claim I can understand both communities but, if truth were told, I probably cannot - no more than, deep down, Catholics can understand the community I come from. Therefore you have to have people in the newspaper who come from across the spectrum of opinion and background - and to listen to them.

The *Belfast Telegraph* is one of the biggest and strongest regional newspapers in these islands and it has to have the best and most professional staff we can get. The two Belfast morning newspapers, *The News Letter* and *The Irish News*, have improved but they are prisoners of their past. While they are broader than they were, it will be difficult for them to break out of the unfortunate sectarian mould in which they have been cast for generations.

Some people will say life on a small island like Ireland is better than being part of the great rat-race. It has always struck me life is a bit more relaxed in the South but it's a pity that is disappearing as the South becomes more like Britain and Europe. One of the great things about going South was the people of the Republic moved at their own pace - now they are starting to run, like so many other places.

The Northern Ireland psyche is difficult to understand at times. I was sitting at dinner last week with a Northern Ireland Office Minister and he asked each of us at the table were we British or Irish. Even among that little group, there was tremendous divergence. I answered that I was British - however, when it comes to certain aspects of life, people like me can be confusing. At Windsor Park or Lansdowne Road, I am as strongly Irish and as fiercely anti-English as anyone could imagine. Perhaps I am a hybrid. The two most emotional moments I can think of are standing in Windsor

Park for God Save the Queen when Northern Ireland are about
to play a soccer international and, before a rugby international
in Lansdowne Road, standing to attention for the Irish
national anthem.

9

Fergus O'Callaghan

The Cork Examiner

I would be described as a hands-on editor.   My sub-editors sit just two feet away from me. But the two feet in the move to being editor made an unbelievable difference.

The conversation took place on June 9 1993

Fergus O'Callaghan is the editor of The Cork Examiner.

He was born in Cork on September 27 1937.

His father was James O'Callaghan, a plasterer.

His mother was Augusta MacCarthy, a nurse.

He is the youngest of a family of five, two brothers, James and Cormac, two sisters, Irene and Catherine.

He is married to Ita Crowley.

Their children are Mary (30), Jim (28), Desmond (25), Fergus Cormac (22) and Colin (20).

He was educated at St. Mary's Convent School, Cork; St. Nessan's Christian Brothers and Sullivan's Quay Secondary School.

He joined The Cork Examiner on December 4 1955 in the reading room. He went to the night editorial in 1958. Early 70s appointed chief sub-editor. 1976 appointed editor.

Won a city and county hurling medal with Nemo Rangers, junior championship and league medals with Lough Rovers.

Hobbies are trout and sea fishing, golf and walking.

I remember the war years and the sawdust buckets in the yard, the porridge being put in a Barry's tea-chest with straw to keep it hot for the morning. My father used to send me down for the evening paper, the *Echo* - it then cost a penny. I remember a woman saying that there were oranges and bananas in a shop at the end of Green Street. I'd never seen an orange or a banana. My father used to smoke. There was a little huckster's shop at the end of Green Street, near Barrack Street, and you'd have to go there dead on half-past nine at night, knock on the door and a little old lady, Mrs. Dwyer, would hand you five Gold Flake. You'd bring them back up and the old man would smoke one as if he'd never smoked before.

My brothers had it rougher than I had - they were there when the war started. I came in at the tail-end of it. I had a brother started in the railway - he was what you would call a real swot. He got Junior Ex, spent a few years in London at the Embassy and then came back to Dublin. The second lad went to Dublin when he was 16. He did the civil service exam and got third place. There were two vacancies. The second fellow didn't take it. I was close to the sister who was next to me in age - the other one could be bossy to a young fellow. I have fond memories of being young. Times were tough but not that tough. You got to the pictures about once a fortnight - they cost four pence: the Palace and the Assems (the Assembly Rooms). The Palace at night-time was a shilling and the Savoy was nine pence if you got in before five o'clock up to the gods, but you could stay in and see the film twice. There was a Lido cinema in Blackpool that I never went to - you could get into the matinee with four jam jars. Cork was small then. Even where we live now was all farm land. There was no television. You made your own entertainment. You played football on the road every Sunday, you played cards around the corner - halfpenny poker or pontoon, that's all you had. Then times got better. Cork started to expand when industry came in: Verolme, Fords and Dunlop. In the 50s there were plenty of jobs available.

I was good at English and Irish at school, maths were OK. I had the option to go to college but I did not want to. I was missing for three weeks before the Leaving Cert exam - "mitching" you'd call it, here we call it "on the lang". However I turned up on the day of the exam and sat it. When the results came out, one of the Brothers came and shook my hand and said, "Fergie, I don't know how you did it". I wanted to work all right, but I did not know what I wanted. I had not liked school but I am grateful to the Christian Brothers for what they did for me. To be honest, I did not like their methods.

It's a funny thing how I got into *The Examiner*. I had no interest in journalism - I had no interest in anything except enjoying myself. Some time before the Leaving, three of us were playing poker in a friend's house one night. One of them happened to be in *The Examiner* in the reading room. At ten o'clock, our host's father came downstairs to ask us if we had no homes to go to and one lad told us he had handed in his notice, he had got the County Council. I went home and told Ma that Noel Dillon was leaving *The Examiner*. Ma said, "Sit down there now, boy, and write out an application and we'll send it in tomorrow". I was called for an interview. The fact that I had still to do my Leaving militated against me. I was told to go away and do it and they would keep the application on file. I forgot all about the application and, after the Leaving, I was doing economics in the School of Commerce, bored to tears, when I was called. I was interviewed by John Leland, Mary Leland's father, and asked if I could start on Monday. I said sure. Noel Dillon, who left *The Examiner* when I went in, is now the County Manager in Cork.

I was on day work for a month. You started at £2 2s 6d. I will never forget it - the reading room in *The Examiner* was the greatest place I've ever been in. A reading room is where the proofs come from the printing floor and are read and corrected by readers. There's a copy holder, a junior, somebody like me at that stage. The reader reads out the proof and the copy holder holds the original copy. If the reader calls out something the copy holder does not have in the original text, you stop him. In the reading room I learned about life. They say that if you haven't been in the reading room, you have not lived in *The Examiner*. I won't say they were the greatest collection of rogues you could assemble in any one place but you can't really describe them - each one of them was a character. There was one old gentleman who used to do the night shift starting at ten o'clock and finishing at half-four in the morning. He was a hunchback. His father was a Fenian. He was a mad Irishian. He used to nod off occasionally and one night somebody draped a Union Jack over him. He went spare.

A close colleague's wife died. There was a collection for a wreath. It was a Wednesday, the middle of the week, and nobody had any money, so they drank the money for the wreath. Then they were in a terrible state. They went to one of the local cemeteries and got one of those glass-topped wreaths. It was full of condensation. They took off the glass and cleaned it. They turned up the following morning with the wreath and a new card in it. When the grave was filled in, they put the wreath back in its original place. Nothing was beyond them but they had hearts of gold.

One of my sub-editors, he died young, was on the desk one night. There was only one phone in the place. I picked it up and it was the Guards to say somebody had phoned to tell them that cyanide had been thrown into the reservoirs at Shanakiel and they were checking it out. When I got off the phone, the sub-editor, in a typical Cork accent, said, "Who da-at?" I told him what had happened. He said, "Jesus, I'd better ring home". The conversation went something like: "Is that you, son? Dad here. Listen, son, some lout has thrown cyanide into the reservoirs above in Shanakiel. For God sake, boy, tonight when you're going to bed, don't brush your teeth, don't wash yourself - just go to bed and you can do all that in the morning. All right, son? I'll be home later - and son, don't tell your mother!"

Another night he came in from his break at midnight with maybe one too many. The phone rang and it was one of the Crosbies, the proprietors of the paper, who asked, "Who's that?" He gave his name. The Crosbie identified himself and was answered with, "Yes, and I'm genuflecting".

The place was full of characters - and they have sadly gone. Work has taken over. The reading room as I knew it is gone.

Now everybody has become litigation-conscious. It is ambulance-chasing in the States, here it is paper-chasing. We were caught badly some years ago. We were joined with the IFA in an action and damages were awarded against us. The case was dropped against the IFA. It was the High Court costs that really mounted up in the end.

Tim Pat Coogan, editor of the *Irish Press*, was good to me in my early days. He would have from eight to 16 libel actions always pending. I could never understand that - we had never anything like it. If there was one libel action, there was pandemonium in our place. Now it's different - you could have up to 20 claims against you and some of them will have to be paid.

I would be described as a hands-on editor. My sub-editors sit just two feet away from me. My night news editor sits two feet on the other side of them. I sit in the middle of the place and, if there's work to be done, you just row in with everybody. Everything passes through your hands. The sports editor is over there, he has a problem with a particular columnist, it ends up on your desk. But the two feet in the move to being editor made an unbelievable difference.

I was actually out of the country when I was appointed. I was told in October I would probably be taking over in March and I said that I did not want it. I was happy where I was. I had a system worked out. Nothing would ruffle me. You went into work at seven, finished at half-two or three in the morning and then you forgot about the paper. It was a lot smaller in those days. We did not have the constant bombardment of the news every hour. If a thing did not get in today, it got in tomorrow. The dog-cards would come from Kilkenny, Thurles and Tralee on telegraphic paper, you re-wrote them on ordinary paper. The printers ruled the roost at that stage - they were the king-pins, they were the people who were paid most, they got overtime while we were on a set wage. We were the "salaried" people but it was the printers who made the money. Times have totally changed. It's the journalists who make the money. I am not saying the printers are badly paid - of course they are well paid - but there are few of them there, their craft has nearly gone. Within five years, everything will be electronically transmittable. We'll see different papers. We introduced colour in 1976 - we were the first. We finished the last hot-metal on a Friday night and I remember there was a bottle of stout up on the last page - a traditional printer's way of saying goodbye. We came in that Sunday and we had computer-setting. We had an off-set press and people would gather at night to see this new monster with the papers coming out so clean they would jump at you. The thing we noticed most was the silence after 18 machines clattering. You could hear people talk. Things have changed so much: you can get a picture from anywhere in the world now in colour.

When you're the editor you're responsible for everything that goes into your paper whether you see it or not. You are part of a team you depend on. I am lucky - I have a great team. They are loyal and conscientious - and I am not saying that to butter them up - I would stand on my head for them and they for me. The difference those two feet make is that you are in a situation where you are deciding every night on what to put in or leave out. You have phone calls from people who are up for drunken driving and whose mother or father is dying from cancer. You are told that if the case goes in the paper they will lose their job and they have a family. You weigh it up - sometimes they're genuine, sometimes they're not. You would normally go by what the judge says. If it is going to destroy somebody's life, I may record the fact but without the evidence. I would be sympathetic. If somebody takes a bottle of wine from the local supermarket and it's their first offence - I would be slow to publish that. Drunken driving, however, is a serious matter and I always publish that. I figure that if I abide by the law - and coming up to Christmas with so many receptions I leave my car at home - I don't see why someone else can't do the same. If I am sober coming home and a drunken driver knocks me off the road and kills me, it's my family who are going to suffer.

I think I am humane - I am a family man and I live in a place surrounded by great neighbours. This end of the estate is called, would you believe, Millionaires' Row, I suppose because we might cut the grass more often than others do. The fact that I am the editor of the daily paper doesn't signify anything when they see me up on a ladder painting the windows. My friends, who know me, talk to me quite openly. I am not one for snooping or listening to private conversations. I will never, in any event, go with a one-sided story - if you run with it, you are bound to get into trouble. You've got to check. We were caught out during the last election. We sat on a story for a month and eventually decided to go with it, having once again asked the reporter if it had been checked out. But the TD in question had not been checked with and he denied the story. We settled with him for an undisclosed sum. Sometimes you get a leak and it turns out not to be a leak at all - somebody is telling you something for their own advantage or to do damage to somebody else. You have to be careful - and the greater the truth, the greater the libel. Ivor, journalism at the moment is a minefield.

A few years ago, we had Britain's Ten Most-Wanted Men which included a guy from Kerry. This was something we took from the Press Association who sent it out because they got it from Scotland Yard and we printed it because it was outside the jurisdiction but the guy was living in Kerry and that brought it within our jurisdiction.

The Cork Examiner sees itself as the voice outside Dublin, outside the Pale. While we carry national news, we are a regional paper. We cover, for example, Clare and send a lot of papers up to Galway city, also to Portlaoise because of so many Guards there, all of Tipp, South Kilkenny and Carlow, back into Wexford and Waterford and then again East Cork and, of course, Kerry is good to us, especially Killarney and South Kerry. North Kerry would be classed as *Independent* country as would Limerick. Funnily enough, the Dublins are pulling permanent people out of the regions and making do with stringers. The *Indo* has a man in Cork, Dick Cross, but the *Press* has not.

Newspapers have got dear because there is a massive cost involved. You could spend six hours of a night chasing a story and you might end up with five lines. Then, if you get a good story, by the time you have run it past your solicitor, you may not have a story at all.

We had a great exclusive a few years ago - when the Pope was coming I got a tip. We sat on it for nearly ten days - it was a good tip, it came from my brother via Rome. This is the first time that story is told. We dug and dug. The Papal Nuncio refused to say anything - maybe he's coming, maybe he's not. I was off at the time. I had a deputy, Liam Moher, and I opened *The Examiner* on a Monday to find Scoop: The Pope Was Coming. He had run it because there was nothing else there. An awful bad reason but it had checked out.

The other major story was Whiddy, the *Betelgeuse* blast. Jack Lynch was Taoiseach at the time and had made a major speech in one of the local hotels. The paper was set up at one o'clock in the morning and I decided to go home. I got home and had a cup of tea with Ita - I did not see her that much with my hours. My mother was sick at the time and the phone went and I thought to myself that's Mum for sure. I asked Ita to go down and answer it. She came back up and said that it was Tom Hickey in the office, there'd been a massive explosion in Bantry and there were bodies everywhere. I got up, pants on over the pyjamas, put a sweater on over the top and headed in. I phoned Donal Crosbie, the editorial director, and told him we were holding the first edition. He was in in five minutes. There were only three of us there: Liam Moher, Tom Hickey and the man in the wire-room - Michael Marley. We had a foreman printer, Dan Linehan, we had an assistant and there was one stone-man. The phones were hopping. We got in touch with our own man in West Cork at the time, Jim Cluskey, and the photographer, Mickey Minihane. People were ringing us up to tell us what was happening, giving us eye-witness accounts. Jim Cluskey got there at 3.30 by which time we had missed all our connections for the delivery of the paper. We had only about six paragraphs of the story so we blew it up, got a stock picture of the Whiddy oil tanks and we went finally at half-past three: we got off a first edition of about 20,000 copies. There were calls coming in from all around the world looking for news of the explosion. We decided we'd keep it to ourselves - we'd have an exclusive. The final edition went out at 5.15 when we had quite a good story. We were the only paper to have it. *The Irish Times* had a special edition but it did not have much in it.

There was a funny side too to that tragic story. My daughter Mary had graduated and there were two pictures on the back page, one of her and one of a friend. I said to Donal Crosbie that we'd have to pull Mary. He said, "Indeed you won't, we'll pull the other one!"

That story went on for three days, bed to work, there was a great buzz. We were on top of it which was great.

I remember the first front page I was given to do. It was President Kennedy's inauguration. I also remember the greatest cock-up I made. The print went backwards onto the page and the printer was the only person who could read it like that. We were short of copy for the back page - there is always something you can slot in, pictures of weddings or whatever. To fill the space we put in a picture of a wedding and a picture of an English visitor fishing on the Blackwater. The printer transposed the captions so what we had under the wedding picture was, "Mr. Henry Jones of Kent displaying his fine catch". About 8,000 copies of that went out before we could stop the press. It's a collector's item.

Working for a family-owned concern, like *The Cork Examiner*, is totally different from working for a board. I can honestly say that in all my years there they have stood 100 per cent behind me - they have never interfered. I have had a totally free hand. When times were tough during the recession, everybody had to tighten their belts. We had to pull back on pages but you still got out the same amount of news. It was edited more carefully. I would consider the *Irish Press* the best subbed paper. Everything is rewritten and rewritten - it's a subs' paper. We have taken a lot of people from the printing floor, they have been retrained as sub-editors. The success rate has been excellent. Subs are the forgotten people of newspapers - the reporters are the glamour people with the big by-lines. The subs lay out the stories, they put the headline on them - if the headline is not attractive, people won't read it - it's an art in itself. And there's an art in cutting stuff without losing the thread of the story.

Being based in Cork might seem as if we were a long way from the action but with technology we are not. Our photographer in Dublin puts the images into a machine and they appear on screen in Cork.

In Cork, if you ask for the editor you're put through. In Dublin you would not get near him. There would be several filters. I remember trying to get through to Tim Pat Coogan and I was told he was busy and could I leave a message and they would have him ring me back. While I know Conor Brady, I don't have a personal relationship with him such as I have with Vinnie Doyle and with Michael Brophy. Maybe it is because we were all together on a trip to Portugal once - it all helps. I know Michael because we judge the Young Journalist of the Year together. We exchange pictures - if he's stuck we supply him and vice versa. We don't do that with the *Indo* because we consider it as the opposition but we would actually buy pictures from the *Independent* and from *The Irish Times*. There is a bit of cooperation between us but not a lot.

There is no editors' club. Ben Bradlee, editor of the *Washington Post* at the time, came over in the 70s. The Shannon Free Airport Development Company used to sponsor a weekend for us and bring in somebody big. It went on for five years and all the editors used to go, the dailies and many of the provincials. It was a fabulous weekend. All newspaper people talk about is newspapers.

Newspaper people are different - I wouldn't want it any

other way now that I've been through it. It's been rewarding in lots of ways - I've been to the States about five times, across Europe, I spent a night on an aircraft carrier, the *Saratoga*. I was catapulted off the deck - they're the sort of things you remember. People think it's a glamorous job - and there is a lot of glamour attached to it: the invitations that come in are unbelievable. You could be in Dublin seven days of the week. It's a novelty until you start meeting the same people. It is nice to meet them now and again but not every day. I just ignore a lot of invitations.

I have four lads and a daughter and we have a great family relationship, we talk openly about almost anything. Even Mary when she was 13 or 14 could talk to me about boyfriends and there was no hassle. I have always listened to them, I've grown up with them. We've even discussed drugs. I have always kept an open mind - I am a good listener. I am a Libran - I don't rush into things. I try and balance everything I do. I have not been known to make rash decisions - that is probably why I have survived in the job when everybody else has changed. I know what can happen in families. I am in touch with people. They matter to me. The friends I have I hold dear. It's a combination of all of those that gives you your sense of values. It's the reactions to some of the stories. Let me give you an illustration - it's a good few years ago now. We got a new lens for one of the cameras -I don't know whether it was 200 or 2000 yards. One of our photographers went out with it and took a picture of nuns paddling on the beach. One of them had her skirts over her knees showing a little more than she should. What she showed was miniscule and we used the picture on the front page. I did not see any harm in it. Letters and phone calls from convents and elsewhere tore us apart for an invasion of privacy. You learn a lot about your readers.

You are not producing a paper for your personal satisfaction. You are producing it for people who want to buy it. You have got to give them what they want. I am not talking about giving them page three *Sun* girls - we are not into that. When we first changed the technology, the reproduction was so sharp that one of the directors said from here on you've got to be careful: young girls breasting tapes at sports meetings or brides who wear see-through blouses, everything was coming out in the photographs. And then we had a hurler running for a ball who bared all and 12,000 copies went out before we spotted it. It was hanging up in a lot of the pubs around town. Someone said you could not get better advertising. But your own values are what come across and you have to be in touch with what's happening. Common sense is the key to everything you do.

We believe divorce should be made available. There is more marital breakdown than there ever was before. We are not saying that, if your marriage is in danger of breaking down, you should immediately go away and get a divorce. A person goes to church and makes a commitment and that's a commitment for life. But, take a person who goes to a registry office or whatever and eventually decides that things are not working out - the facility should be there for them. We are not urging people to get divorced. You ask me if *The Cork Examiner* will take a stand on issues. You have to be careful here. The answer is, not always. But we would, for example, be against abortion on demand. Totally. That stand would emerge from a discussion and agreement between the two editors, morning and evening, the news editors, the chief executive, Alan Crosbie, the executive chairman, the editorial director and the solicitor. They would meet at what we call a policy meeting, ad hoc, when something comes up. Most of the time you fly by the seat of your pants.

We don't take sides in elections. Most of the parties criticise us which means we've done a good job. We have been told we have been bashing Fianna Fail, Fine Gael and Labour - they all come back at us. Yet, at the end of a campaign, if you measure the column inches, you'll find they nearly come out the same for every party. We would never have an eve-of-poll leader suggesting to people they vote one way or the other. Looking at what happened in the past, we might maintain that strong single-party government is better than coalitions, maybe better than a coalition of Fine Gael, PDs and Labour where you'd have three tails trying to wag the dog. We believe our approach to be objective, not partisan. Our job is to put the facts before people. It's up to them to decide. It's not our business to tell people how to vote.

For myself, I don't have politics. The minute I entered *The Examiner* I forgot about them. My interest is simply from the newspaper's point of view, not personal.

Talking about going into the office - one evening I was met there by a fellow who handed me a letter. When I took it from him, he said, "I won't be needing this", and he took out a flick-knife. He said, "Read the letter - I'll call back later". I got behind the counter, he went out the door and I went upstairs and rang the Guards. I gave a description of the guy and they sent a squad car over, but they missed him. I opened the letter: this guy intended to stab me inside my office and then stab himself. He actually came back at twenty-past ten. I was called downstairs not knowing it would be him. I said, "Look, I've read your letter. Everything is fine. Good luck, I'll talk to you again." The girl on the switch rang the Guards. He ran out and I never saw him again. About four months later I was asking if there was any news of him. He had been picked up in Youghal for molesting some young kid. He was sent to a psychiatric hospital. Things are all changed now. There is high security.

I was telling you about how I had been appointed editor and I digressed. I was in Brussels at the time at a conference with Jack Fagan. They were slating editors, really slating them about their commitment to the EC. We were very committed to the EC when it started. Jack Fagan and I had a bit of a ball while we were there and, when we were coming back on the plane, he turned to me and said, "You're a right so-and-so". On the front page of *The Irish Times*, which he was reading, was a story: "Editorial Changes in The Cork Examiner". I said, "Show me". He said, "You are the so-and-so editor". I told you earlier I did not want it and that was true. When I got home the phone was hopping with people congratulating me. A lot of the joy of it came from friends whom I grew up with and played hurling with calling me and saying, "Isn't it great, boy, you made it!" At Mass on Sunday morning, people came up to me and said, "We're delighted, one of our own". The ordinary people.

Starting from scratch, I suppose I had a great relationship with all the people in the paper. Nobody called me Mr. O'Callaghan - just Fergie and that's it. The result is I can go anywhere in the building at night, get things done. I've had occasions where the staffing would be down and I wanted colour and they would say, "For you, Fergie, no problem". If they wanted a wedding picture in colour the following week, if it was possible, I'd do it for them. We have a machine room golf outing next Saturday - I'm asked and it's an honour.

The power is the thing you can't think about. As I said to you, you could spend your days at receptions and the like, but you would neglect the job and the job is paramount. You ask me if the editor of *The Cork Examiner* is an important personage in Cork because there isn't any other daily paper here. That's something I never like to think about but I would imagine, yes. If you wanted to lead a high social life, you could easily do it. Being editor of *The Examiner* can open an awful lot of doors. You can pick up the phone and ring anybody.

Jack Lynch and I are good friends. My father lived in Shandon Street under Shandon Bells where he was born. Jack lived in Dominick Street just behind. My father fought in the troubles. He was called at that time an intelligence officer. He was offered a post in the Army and would not take it. He never had a medal and when he died my elder brother said he should have got one. We got on to Jack and the medal came. It's nice to have it. It's put away upstairs in a drawer. My dad's brother was a good pianist. One night he turned round from the piano and said to me, "You know, I was nearly your father." "How come, Uncle Gussie?" "The night they were blowing up Ballincollig Barracks, your father was out there and he had a date with your mother and I had to go up and tell her that he wouldn't be arriving that night. I nearly went off with her."

Yes, the editor of *The Examiner* would have clout - if you needed it. It depends on the type of person you are whether you use it or not. I am basically a backroom person. I even dreaded talking to you today. I have never craved the limelight. I have vouchers for meals I've never taken up. I am not somebody to take advantage of the position I'm in. It's a job I do to the best of my ability. 17 years is a long time. They say now you're only good for three. If you move somebody after three years, you destroy the continuity. I remember one of the lads saying to me, "Gosh, Fergie, you've been there a long time - you've survived". I have seen five different editors on the evening paper since I took over. *The Examiner* and the evening paper are, incidentally, quite separate.

The circulation of *The Cork Examiner* is 56,000 and *The Evening Echo* around 31,000. *The Examiner* did go up to 71,000 in the early 70s, the boom period. Fords had an awful effect on us and Dunlops - 500 *Examiners* a day down the Swanee, six days a week.

I was in Florida a couple of years ago and was looking at the technology of the local paper. It would frighten you what they could do. It was the local version of *Today*. They had the option of taking 20 pages by satellite. They had a circulation of 50,000. I asked if I could sit in at the news conference. The editor was a lawyer, 38, greyer than myself, a small little man with a briefcase. I was made welcome. There was an eight-page schedule for a 24-page paper - it was meticulous: the name of the reporter would be there, the time his copy would be in, the time black and white pictures would arrive and then colour. Everything was listed across those eight pages and then you had the option of the pages by satellite if you wanted them. He turned to the production man who said that there was a local election on and the results would be expected at 12 o'clock. They would have the results printed with a picture by 12.25. The editor said, "We print at 11.20", and walked out the door. I could not believe it.

Advertising is our bread and butter. The cover price does not cover costs which are astronomical. We're all on budgets now - I find it strange to have a budget. I try to ignore the fact that I have one. The news is paramount - if you are going after a story, you have to get the best story you can, no matter what it costs. If the budget goes over, well, you're not going to hear about it for a month anyway, until the accountants step in. Then, if you're over, somebody else could be down - it's swings and roundabouts. I don't have any responsibility for advertising but it does encroach on the news space which can be a problem. Being realistic, nobody fires out ads. If you are selling a one-page feature, you may throw in a colour photo as an incentive. That means one page of colour gone from the news because you can do only so many colour pages. There is supposed to be a limit on the size of the ads we carry in the front page but, when times are bad, you might extend that.

Cork is slowly picking itself up - there is a bit of a buzz there at the moment, a small one. While the big factories are gone, you have an awful lot of small industry, little places where there are six or seven people working. They are quite viable. The northside is a black spot. The quays are idle and many of the dockers came from the northside. A lot of business is going into the lower harbour - that's where the ferries pull in now.

Yes, we do have crusades - we have a small one going at the moment - it's to get the new Bord Bia, the food board, to Cork. The Minister, Joe Walsh, is from West Cork. We've generated enough interest to get the local Chamber of Commerce in on it. We've had a few calls from the IFA. We were instrumental in getting the airport here. There was the issue of multi-channel television. We were discriminated against - while you had BBC in Dublin, we were stuck with RTE 1. We were front-runners in that campaign, even though television does affect us.

News has changed totally. I listen to an awful lot of news bulletins from the time I get up because you have to be au fait with what is happening. While you may not lead with the top story on Sky Television, my job is to anticipate tomorrow's stories. If you watch the television news at one, you will see pictures of the destruction caused by a car bomb. That picture may be offered to us by an agency in Belfast at six o'clock that evening. By the time you've paid 90 quid for it, it's an old picture. Eventually, you get wise and you don't take them. You look for something else. It's tomorrow's stories you're talking about, not today's. Today is gone - if we don't come out with something different from the Dublin papers, we may as well not come out at all because we are addressing a different audience.

There is no immediacy in television. Television news is the news they have pictures for. Television will give the main news story of the day, all right, possibly without film. The rest of the news can be coloured by what they have had cameras on.

When we have our news conference, we seldom disagree with one another - the only person might be the night news editor who would be pushing a local Cork story for page one. We might fob it off but then we might go back to it later if we wanted it. Take last night: we were doing a preview of the Latvia v Ireland match. Our reporter, Jim Beglin, had had an incident with a drunken militia man. We said yes to the report but that it was not a preview of the match, perhaps we'll run the match under it. Then everything changed because some Irish fans witnessed a bank raid in which three people were shot dead. Beglin, instead of topping up the story, went down further. It helped that we had a man out there - we had our own story. All news is relative. With the electronic system we have, it's easy to change things about. All our regional reporters type their stuff directly into the main computer. Then they phone in and tell us what the catch word is and we just call it up on the screen. You edit on the screen.

We don't have the resources to do the deep investigative stuff. We do highlight things occasionally, like the local authority flats that were slapped up in the 70s to get people out of the inner city. We do dig, but we are careful. It's not that we don't want to ruffle any feathers. In Dublin you have three papers and you have to fight for circulation. Probably our biggest threat is the cheap English tabloids and then the *Independent - The Irish Times* is big in College but then it is heavily subsidised. It's fashionable for students to be seen with it. People don't buy the *Press* much now - they used to. It's sad to see it in its present state. No, we do not have the luxury of somebody sitting on a story for a fortnight. I suppose it's a question of balance - finally it comes down to people like me who sit in chairs and say we can do without this, there is more immediate stuff to be done. The first thing you say to anybody who joins *The Examiner* is that they deal in fact and must have a balanced story. Even if you ring a person with an allegation and they say, "No comment", at least you've tried.

We were slagging Charlie Haughey at one stage, slagging him hard. He was down at a Siamsa concert and Donal Crosbie was there. Charlie said, "Donal, I'd like to write one of your leading articles some morning". Donal said, "Any time, Charlie - so long as I can sub it". I don't write the leading articles but they do end up on my desk.

We have one leader-writer with us at the moment who is excellent - he's been with me for eight years. He's on every night and we have a discussion about what we're going to do. The leading article is the paper talking. Of course we wag the finger occasionally - we would take on the Government or ministers or the health authority. We take on anybody who needs to be taken on. Years ago we had a leader writer who, in 20 minutes, could bash off two columns. He had a gift, like some politicians do, of saying nothing - it's a high art and it means that you never get into trouble.

But times have changed in the *Examiner*. We took the GAA head-on recently, something that would never have happened before. A few years ago, we probably would have brought them in, had a lunch with them and sorted things out. Some years ago, compromise would have been the way out and compromise does not always work. You can't let your staff down.

Younger staff have totally different values. They talk about you being past your sell-by date in your middle-50s - that comes across to me more and more because my staff are quite young. They don't remember the Niemba ambush when nine Irish soldiers were killed in the Congo on a UN peacekeeping mission. Somebody in the city dies, they don't know who he is, ask Fergie - he will know. We have a lot of outsiders on the staff, reporters from Galway who worked on the *Connacht Tribune*, guys from *The Tipperary Star, The Kerryman*. They would not know the situation in the greater Cork area as much as we Corkonians would. If you evaluate stories on their news-content rather than on the area they are from, things can be totally different. Take our regional man - Johnny Murphy, a very good man, covers all of West Waterford. He will come on and say to the news editor, "Donal, there's a great case on today, not only does it involve Dungarvan, but there are relations 40 miles around - this is worth splashing in the morning." He's on the ground so we would take his advice. I have built up a great network of contacts: meetings can be held behind closed doors and within half-an-hour I know what's happened. That's trust. More often than not, the person who rings me is not looking for anything in the paper.

It's a funny business - I don't know how you describe it. My mother once said that you must be mad to work in a newspaper. Maybe she was right, because you do get crazy days. You have enough to fill 48 pages and you must still get it into 24. What do you leave out? A guy has spent two days at the courts in West Cork, gets nothing in and two days later that news is dead. If you publish after three days you could be accused of malice, maybe. Journalists live in a twilight world.

In the RTE morning programme, *It Says In The Papers,* you are at the mercy of one person. Whatever crack of the whip *The Cork Examiner* gets depends on who's on, but the programme tends to concentrate on the three Dublin papers with glancing references to the Belfast ones.

You ask me if the *Cork* in the title of the paper is in any way inhibiting. We have talked about that, about dropping the *Cork* and simply calling it *The Examiner* but, if we did that, a lot of tradition would go down with it. We are still looking at it - *The Examiner* would be a lovely title, but really what we're looking at is editionising for various areas because that can be done with the equipment we have. At the moment, we do West and North Cork supplements. With modern technology, you can change your front page photograph very quickly and, say, put in one from Limerick or from Waterford or from North Cork. You can give the regions something that they won't get in any other paper except their local weekly.

I would never like to write. I suppose my forte, if you were to sum it up, is I know what news is and I create an atmosphere inside where people can work, are allowed to work. How can I explain that to you? It's not like school - if you get up and are gone from your desk for 20 minutes, I am not going to ask you where you were when you come back. I trust my staff because I know they are not going to abuse what they have. I worked myself under a hard taskmaster, Paddy Dorgan. You could send nine stories down for print and he would change the nine headings on them. You saw the paper in the morning with your nine headings changed and he would never say anything to you. Much of what he had done you'd ask yourself why you had not thought of that, but with other stuff you could not understand the reason for the change. What happened is that you changed yourself. When you had a story the following night you would ask yourself what did he want. You began to think like him. In fact, he was a fabulous editor. While he was tough, he lived at a time when there was no pressure on news. He was a good sub, rare things these days. He used to be able to cut copy without losing any of the story - he cut out the bull, the red tape, and got to the heart of the matter. He maintained that five lines of a story is better than no story at all. I learned from him.

There's no point in having a full-length photograph of a group of priests because they're black from the knees down - so you crop and you show them from up. You don't like cutting off ladies' legs because they're attractive to look at and they add life to a page.

We were sitting down at the end of work one night having a game of 45 of all things. It was around Christmas time. This lad was on the wire and he came in and handed over a sheet of copy off the Creed machine. It was a PA snap - "De Valera Dead". Pandemonium. What were we going to do at five-to-two in the morning? Everybody was gone out of the library so we went upstairs and got out the obits. We were running around like red-assed bees. We were trying to dig up old photographs. And then the guy said, "Relax, lads. I just typed it up myself". Having called him all the names under the sun, we went back in to our cards, to find there was a note from the Press Association on the machine: "Can you confirm please? Is de Valera dead?" He had forgotten to pull out the plug to PA.

10

Aengus Fanning

Sunday Independent

*It doesn't do the Sunday Independent any good to have the editor
personalised - the title is bigger than any individual and it's certainly
bigger than the editor.   All editors have feet of clay.   I shouldn't be
talking to you at all.*

The conversation took place on June 1 1993

Aengus Fanning is editor of the *Sunday Independent.*

He was born in Tralee, Co. Kerry on April 22 1944.

His father was Arnold P. Fanning, a school teacher.

His mother is Clara Connell.

He was fourth in a family of six, four brothers and one sister: Rio, Betty, Brian, Patrick and Connell.

He is married to Mary O'Brien, director of a small company.

Their children are Dion (21), Evan (14), and Stephen (7).

He was educated at the Christian Brothers, Tralee, and University College Cork (B. Comm.).

1964-1969 reporter in the Midland Tribune. 1969 joined Independent Newspapers as a reporter. 1973 Group agriculture correspondent. 1982 news analysis editor of Irish Independent. 1984 appointed editor of the Sunday Independent.

Played football for Kerry Minors and Seniors.

Played rugby for UCC, Tralee and Birr.

Hobbies include playing the clarinet, cricket, jazz, classical music, swimming, theatre and reading.

We can all make sense of things retrospectively, find the thread. My great-grandfather, John Powell, was the first manager of a paper called *The Midland Tribune*. It was started in Birr, Co. Offaly, about 1882. It was a Land League paper, the funds of £1,000 were raised by three curates. Subsequently my great-grandfather became owner of it and it passed on to my grandmother, a lady I remember well. Then to my uncle in Birr, James I. Fanning. My father, Arnold P. Fanning, sold out his half-share in the paper and went down to Tralee to be a school teacher where he led a pleasant and active life. He was an honours science graduate, a mathematician and a botanist, but also a highly literate man. He produced and wrote plays, including *Vigil*, Cyril Cusack's first Abbey Theatre part, directed by Lennox Robinson in 1932.

My mother came from solid Presbyterian stock in Northern Ireland. In fact, her great-grandfather, Charles Connell, built the first passenger steamship in Belfast, the S.S. *Aurora*, in the mid-nineteenth century. She became a convert to Catholicism and has lived all her adult life in Tralee.

When I was a kid I spent three or four months a year in Birr. We all came up to Birr to my grandmother's home for the summer and at Christmas and Easter. I hung around the newspaper, went out in the vans with the reporters, pestering them with questions. I went to the County Council meetings and sat beside the reporter, J.F. "Bud" Burke. I went to the courts and would sit there quietly and listen all day.

As soon as I could read, I read proofs with my grandmother - she would correct them while I would read the copy. I was what would have been called a copy-holder. I absorbed an awful lot, Ivor, without being conscious of it. I absorbed things through the pores of my skin that now seem second-nature. My uncle Jimmy, who was a father-figure to me in many ways, always felt I should go into journalism. So, when I left college, coincidentally he had a vacancy in *The Midland Tribune*. That's how I started.

While Jimmy was absolutely convinced I should be a journalist, my father thought I should be an accountant - a

more specialised qualification. My father foresaw accurately
that, with the development of the economy, accountancy
would become a more vigorous corporate profession than
merely the auditing of a local firm's books. Journalism was
badly paid - my first salary was £7 15s 0d a week. That was in
1964. You rarely get well paid by your own family.

Much of the job in those early days was boring. On Sundays
you might have to cover three matches - I covered North
Tipperary and Offaly. The Linotype machines had to have
copy first thing on Monday morning. You wrote up the
matches on Sunday night. The imperative was often length
rather than quality - the main thing was to keep the machines
clanking away producing the hot metal. If you had six columns
of copy, great - that would keep two of the three machines busy
for most of Monday morning.

I spent a day in Roscrea every week to get material for the
Roscrea Notes. You called on everybody under the sun:
politicians, clubs, badminton, golf, Macra na Feirme, ICA, the
meat and bacon factories - Donal Ward, the Antigen factory -
George Fasenfeld. It was a great way to get to know the texture
of a small community. I knew Roscrea as well as any politician.
People were glad to see you - they wanted their publicity. You
were always getting little messages to call on this or that
person: people dying, weddings, people back from America.
Nobody ever came back from America who wasn't a huge
success over there. Apart from the odd court case, it was all
benign. You learned some things, like getting the name,
address and age right. If you got it wrong, they'd be into the
office or you'd meet them the next day - everything was close at
hand. The most contentious area was hurling matches. The
rivalries between parishes were pretty fierce. You could be in
hot water for criticising a team for rough play. You went to two
or more courts a week - Portumna, Kilcormac, Tullamore, Birr,
Clara, Roscrea. My very first court case was in Kilcormac -
Donagh McDonagh was the judge, he wrote *God's Gentry*. I
learned some diplomatic skills - Jimmy, my editor and
proprietor, was a member of the Urban Council and when I

had written a report of a meeting, he would come in and say, "I didn't say that, or, if I did, it's not what I meant!" I really liked him.

I applied for a job in the *Independent*. My wages at that stage were £15 a week, I wanted to get married, I had met my wife who lived five miles from Birr, and the wages offered in the *Independent* were, so far as I remember, £25 a week. That was the difference between getting married and not getting married. Jimmy was able to offer me pleasant vistas but only a little more money. If I had stayed at that time, I suppose I would still be down there and Birr is a pleasant place. It lulls you in a stable and secure way. It was seductive, probably not good in the long term. If you go back you find that people are saying and doing the same things they did 20 years ago. When I go back now I'm one of the Fannings of Birr and that's that, for better or worse. I feel my ancestral roots are there. But I'm proud of my Kerry background and upbringing. Is that confusing?

My first day in Middle Abbey Street I was in awe. I thought that everybody there must be good. I was sitting in Brian Barrett's office - he was the Group news editor. A well-known columnist passed the open door and Brian said, in a loud voice, "There are no geniuses out there!" The columnist looked startled before continuing on his stately way.

I couldn't believe the small amount of work I had to do compared with the local paper where you were working seven days a week and wrote an awful lot of the content. It took me a while to get used to being given a couple of short pieces a day. In those days you had to have about 20 years experience under your belt before you'd be trusted with an important story. Bill Shine was news editor of *The Evening Herald* and changed a lot of that, he wanted young people. Bill, with Aidan Pender as his editor, broke a lot of the moulds. It was probably needed. He gave young people a chance to make mistakes and to do good things. In 1970 he became news editor of the Group and Aidan became editor of the *Irish Independent* with journalists of great flair such as Vinnie Doyle and the late Niall Hanley at his side. The circulation of the *Irish Independent* peaked at over 190,000 in the late 1970s. That was by far the highest circulation of any daily newspaper in Ireland.

We joined the EEC in 1973 and agriculture was important. Bill Shine appointed me agriculture correspondent. The EEC was like an oil-well in the middle of Europe - all you had to do was to go over there and get the money and bring it back. I spent a lot of time in Brussels and Luxembourg and Strasbourg. When I look back now, I had a great deal of autonomy in that job - I brought in my own stories, met the people I wanted to meet. I probably was not as wise as people thought I was, but nobody knew any better. I was continually being asked to explain the Green Pound so I devised my own plain man's guide. The EEC was mysterious to most people - I set out to make it intelligible. Maybe that's a strand in my career - trying to make things accessible. And I made no apologies for explaining things to the consumer - food prices were contentious and a big factor in the Consumer Price Index. Farm-gate prices and food prices were bounding ahead. We tend to forget they were a huge thing in the inflation rate. Every time farmers got five pence a gallon on milk, butter prices went up substantially. Mark Clinton was Minister for Agriculture at the time and we got on fine but he was absolutely opposed to explaining to the consumer how much increases in farm prices were going to cost them. To work out what milk on the doorstep or a pound of sirloin steak would cost was not regarded by the Department of Agriculture as the patriotic thing to do. But we had a newspaper whose aspiration was to have a broad appeal in urban areas. Quite often we would change the story between the country and the city editions. It was not a perfect technique because a lot of our country editions went to urban areas in rural Ireland. I believe urban Ireland is not that much different wherever you go, in Dublin or the provinces. Many people in Cork or Tullamore know very little about farming. People might have been born on a farm but, after 20 years working in a city, they have a different outlook.

The next step for me was news analysis editor of the *Irish Independent* under Vinnie Doyle. I was responsible for one page and with a fairly small budget. had to get three topical features a day for that page, and that was six days a week. I used often have to write the main 1,500-word piece or the shorter piece for the bottom of the page because I couldn't get anyone else - 1,500 words at eight o'clock at night. It was a pretty tough job because you started off each day with a clean sheet. I did that for two years before I was appointed editor of the *Sunday Independent* in January 1984.

I hate pontificating or preaching, but, frankly, Ivor, I have a lot of stuff worked out about marketing a newspaper that is significantly different from what is done here or even in Britain. All it takes is one or two people out there to think the same way and get their hands on the resources to do it, so I'll speak only in the most general terms. That might sound like paranoia - or quackery, that I've got a secret recipe.

Most newspapers are wrong - if we're talking about the market. They might see journalism as a higher calling and the market may be incidental, it may not be their driving motivation at all, but I think we live or die by the market, it will always win through. And I don't for one moment believe that serving the market conflicts with good journalism - the opposite, in fact. The conventional wisdom is that, long-term, newspapers are in slow decline. This is caused by the proliferation of other media: electronic, niche publications, specialised newspapers - all that. The future will give us computer- and TV-based home entertainment and information. And if you go back over the Irish market for 15 years, you will find morning, evening and Sunday newspapers in decline. Since I became editor of the *Sunday Independent*, over 100,000 newspapers in aggregate have gone out of the Irish Sunday market, and there are two new titles. The *Sunday Independent* over that period has put on 27,000 in net sales.

I believe if most people continue to produce the sort of newspapers they are now producing, it will fulfil the prophecy of slow decline. What's lacking is the courage and the nerve and the instinct and the honest straight thinking - not wishful thinking - to do something slightly different. What's needed is a chemistry which makes a newspaper compulsive, that you can't ignore it, you've got to buy the bloody thing. All sorts of pressure groups will tell you what they want - or what they think they want, but to get somebody in the broad market to pay their money every Sunday, when nobody is watching them, you have to give them a good reason. That requires doing things differently from the consensus. The consensus, in my view, is producing pretty boring newspapers. In the long term, this means nemesis.

The greatest strength newspapers have is what Rupert Murdoch called "the habit factor", but the fact that people are in the habit of buying newspapers is a weak basis on which to go into the future. The habit factor declines with each generation.

When I became editor of the *Sunday Independent* I found it a bit staid and stale. On Tuesday morning, if there was a teachers' conference in Bundoran, somebody would say let's do a 1,500-word feature on teachers' outrage at class sizes. Then, of course, all during the week the teachers would have had their say in the daily papers and on radio and television. By the time we published our piece, we would seem to be writing about something that happened a fortnight ago. A week is a long time. The *Sunday Independent* was also a male-dominated newspaper, there were no women journalists on it.

The first critical appointment I made was Anne Harris as features editor in 1985. A brilliant all-round journalist with an instinctive sense of the market, she brought to the paper a remarkable flair for creative commissioning, for identifying, encouraging, inspiring and developing journalists of talent and unrealised potential. As well as possessing outstanding writing flair herself on serious issues, her commitment to people-based journalism is a constant reminder a paper will not prosper on opinion and think pieces alone. Few enough people, you know, are interested in concepts or the logical thread of an argument. They are interested in people.

I think women are better than I am at understanding and interpreting human behaviour. I also think, by and large, they have a better intuitive intelligence than men. I may be wrong extrapolating from myself to all men. I suppose I expect all people to be fairly rational which is a bit silly of me. Ideas and theories are fine but they reach probably 20 per cent of the readers. I love good stimulating think-pieces - and they are genuinely needed in causing people to think and understand *why* things happen, not just *what* happens, but they do address a minority of readers.

I think I have an instinct for a journalist who is both good and marketable. What I am always looking for is flair, that rarest of qualities in a human being, which Charles Wintour, former editor of *The Evening Standard*, called the divine spark. There is an idea you must be pompous and boring and correct, pseudo-intellectual - that's fine, let them get on with it and bore people. I went for Eamon Dunphy as soon as he left *The Tribune* in 1986. He was writing sports only at the time. I met him in the Goat Grill and asked him if he would write across a broad canvas, "Dunphy at Large", and he said he wasn't ready for it. He's now doing it brilliantly. The one real writing asset I inherited was Hugh Leonard. Then, bit by bit, we recruited people at different levels of experience - some of them were unknowns. As well as Eamon Dunphy and Hugh Leonard, we now have writers like Colm Toibin, Anthony Cronin, Gene Kerrigan, Anne Harris, Shane Ross, Terry Keane, Sam Smyth, Patricia Redlich, Mark Smith, Liam Collins, Trevor Danker, Kevin Moore, Stephen Dodd, Stan Gebler Davies, Joseph O'Malley and, in sport, David Walsh, Mick Doyle, Kevin Cashman and Raymond Smith. Then there are younger people like Eilis O'Hanlon, Declan Lynch, Brighid McLaughlin, Molly McAnailly Burke - and Barry Egan, who infuriates a lot of people. Yet if I ask my sons who their friends read in the *Sunday Independent*, they will remember Dunphy and Keane, and they certainly read Barry Egan. They may not always like him but he reaches them. But these names are only the tip of the iceberg. Without good layout, news editing, reporting and production, we would be nothing. We have people of the calibre of Colm McGinty, Campbell Spray, Willie Kealy, Adhamhnan O'Sullivan, John Kearney, Ronan Farren, Martin Fitzpatrick, Madeleine Keane, Pat Comyn, Sean Ryan, Mary Hallissey, Kevin O'Connor, Lise Hand, Eamonn Butler, Frank Byrne, and so on. They have contributed more to the success of the paper than I can ever acknowledge adequately.

Some of our educated younger people would amaze you. Some years ago a young man came into the house having just got 22 points in his Leaving. Gemma Hussey's book was lying on the table and he asked, "Who's she?" I mean, she was the Minister for Education just a few years previously and this chap had just got a good Leaving Certificate. Can you understand that? You'd begin to wonder about literacy, about how you are to reach some of these people at all.

I put my faith in good journalism and try to span the market. I don't believe Eamon Dunphy or Terry Keane can be put into any niche. Their readership covers the entire market. Since we have to maintain our dominance of the ABs and the ABC1s, over which we have a stranglehold, that kind of journalism is fantastic.

I like the word chemistry when I'm thinking about newspapers. It means a mixture, a potency, it means the paper is alive. If some of this sounds mystical to you, it's probably rubbish, but I can pick up a paper and flick through it and know when it is living or dead. I think there is a chemistry about the *Sunday Independent.*

I regard myself as a liberal but it all depends what you mean by liberal. I hope I use it in the classical sense. And of course I am liberal with people who agree with me: they are highly intelligent. We use specialised commentators such as Ronan Fanning, Michael McDowell, John A. Murphy, Colm McCarthy, John Dillon, Sean Barrett and Anthony Clare. I have absolutely no party political allegiances. The party faithful can like it or lump it.

For example, I think Shane Ross is an excellent commentator, pungent, critical and informed - and most important, accessible. For a guy who writes mainly about business matters, he reaches a broad readership. The fact he is also a Fine Gael Senator is relevant, but it doesn't necessarily undermine the merits of his arguments. It is his arguments I am interested in, not his politics.

What we have done could not have been done without the sort of management we have. It could not have been done without Joe Hayes, the managing director*, or a proprietor like Tony O'Reilly, people who understand what ultimately drives us. My best guarantor is success in the market, success when it hits the bottom line. Our circulation at this point is 252,000 - going on for 1m readers in all. If the public relish what you do - and the public are intelligent people - you are giving them value for money. Public opinion has developed far more than our politicians realise or act on. People may not always agree with Eamon Dunphy but they will invariably say they admire the fact he has taken a particular position. People may not like what the paper says but they like the fact we have the guts to publish opinions that sometimes go against the stream.

I am conscious of the fact that the market is all over the country. It is not this little incestuous coterie of media people who meet each other at dinner parties and in pubs, fortifying their own illusions and delusions. Add them all up, they hardly amount to 1,000 people. I certainly couldn't serve the market on the basis of their approval. I have rarely sought peer approval. I have, to a great extent, ignored the media consensus. I think I have done my best to keep focusing on value for money. You're asking people to spend their money on your paper every Sunday when they have a choice of 15 papers. They have complete free will.

There's a lot of envy and begrudgery about. If three or four papers out of 15 are successful and the others are not, they may say they're not driven by the market, they have some higher vocation: to serve the public interest or some pompous stuff like that. That's how they feel good about themselves. Fair enough, if that's how they want to explain the world. It's a grand excuse for relative failure.

* See Epilogue.

I was reading recently a piece about the regional press in England where they were criticising other media for stealing their readers. What they were doing was criticising their readers, blaming them for their own paper's shortcomings. That's probably an extreme statement of an attitude, but it's fatal. What they're saying is what we're doing is right and good and, if the market does not respond, there is something wrong with the market.

Newspapers generally, due in part to the shaky financial predicament of most of them, and partly because of often absurd and excessive libel awards, have become cautious to the point of timorousness. This can express itself in a reluctance to take on the important job of questioning, challenging, and sometimes dissenting from the official line, whether on the economy, the North, or even the arts. For instance, the *Sunday Independent* was considered unpatriotic in official quarters for calling for a devaluation from an early stage of the currency crisis in autumn, 1992. *The Irish Times* and other newspapers promoted the official line, the main political parties in opposition couldn't make their minds up, a strong currency became a symbol of our nationhood. It is now acknowledged we devalued too late. In any event the ERM has practically broken up since then. But most media during the crisis did not, in my opinion, cover themselves in glory in terms of independent thinking and in challenging the official dogma.

You ask me where the boundaries are, particularly in relation to sexual matters. I believe sex is a normal healthy human activity. I don't like these sex abuse or incest cases. Often the socially-correct way of dealing with sex consists of giving two pages of some awful, gruesome story - that's far more nauseating than normal healthy sex. Sure, sex helps to sell newspapers. Normal healthy sex is part of life and what's wrong with that? Sport, politics, economics, business, entertainment, they're all part of life and should be dealt with in newspapers. I would draw the line absolutely at sick sex. We like to think we handle sex as we handle a lot of other things - like, for example, being completely up-front about market economics. We have no ambivalence about that - we really espouse the market in a way no other newspaper in this country does because they're afraid of alienating pretty powerful interest groups in the public sector, the unions, and in some political quarters. I don't make any moral case for the market, but I believe deeply that, while, like democracy, it is a far from perfect mechanism, it's the better way of achieving higher standards of living and employment - if that's what we want. If it's not what we want, fine. That to me would be quite a sophisticated decision to take but we have not decided that, in common with most people all over the world. I don't know whether or not more consumer goods ultimately make people any happier. Perhaps they don't. The avoidance of poverty or hardship certainly reduces unhappiness.

Against that background, the economic policies we have pursued for 20 years have been wrong. They have reduced our disposable income and our freedom of choice - I don't like half my income being confiscated without any say in how politicians spend it in pursuit of votes. Of course, there is no Utopia - the word in Greek actually means "no place". There is neither a capitalist nor a socialist Utopia. There will be victims of society under any system and most of all under the former totalitarian regimes of Eastern Europe. I can't see why the free enterprises of capitalism or of the market, whatever you like to call it, can be blamed for people who fall victim to the sometimes brutal forces operating in society. I believe it's a matter of proportion. I believe people should have the right to exercise their free will within the law. If people have more money in their pockets they can provide for contingencies, for illness, for their old age, and so on. We've gone a different route altogether - the way of dependence. The market way is not Utopian, but I believe it would enable the average boat to ride a little higher in the water.

The *Sunday Independent* is utterly implacable in its opposition to terrorism. The IRA and its Loyalist counterparts have behaved like barbarians and put themselves outside the Pale of civilised society. I don't believe they should be entitled to the freedom or benefits of constitutional democracy.

I don't get every decision right but my definition of competence is if you get four out of every five decisions right, you are basically competent. If you get three-and-a-half decisions wrong out of five, you're incompetent.

The difference between a Sunday paper and a weekday paper is Sunday is a leisure day. What has come up many times in our research is that Sunday is boring for many people. That surprised me but the research is amazingly consistent. People traipse around the place visiting, they have lunch, they fall asleep in the afternoon, the kids are about . . . look, I would not be unhappy to have a Sunday newspaper described as show business as distinct from the self-importance and pomposity of "The Fourth Estate". What I market is a mixture and indeed I confront some of the serious issues more directly than other newspapers do. What we have is entertainment, information, analysis, opinion, provocative pieces, gossip - the whole lot - it goes out as a cocktail. And an occasional laugh is worth 2,000 words.

There is no staple diet of news on a Saturday. What the *Sunday Independent* is is a magazine wrapped up in a newspaper. News still has a place in the scheme of things on a Sunday but what I have consciously gone for is more of a magazine. If people are as bored on Sunday as they say they are, they need entertainment, they need a talking point, something to provoke and stimulate. To me it was meat and drink when we ran Mick Doyle's remarkable life story. Everywhere I went there were heated arguments around the table for and against Mick Doyle, probably breaking down on the gender divide: men were mostly for him and women were against him. Some of the people I saw did not even know I worked in the *Sunday Independent* and there they were, talking about Mick Doyle.

One does make errors of judgment. The Bishop Casey story was a case in point. It brought out a bit of righteousness on the part of the other papers. I think it ill becomes us to get moralistic and righteous in this business. The *Sunday*

Independent admitted the error of judgment and we apologised to our readers. On the other hand, I believe it was justifiable to seek Bishop Casey, to put some questions to him, and to photograph him.

Joe Hayes is a brilliant businessman and I believe good businessmen are creative. Creativity is not something confined to the arts, which we seem to see in mystical terms, some druidic thing where you have to be out in the mists of Galway or somewhere, looking for a grant from Michael D. Higgins. Tony O'Reilly is as creative as any of our artists. O'Reilly and Hayes are contrasting people, but they are one-off, there isn't a mould like any of them anywhere. Then you have Liam Healy as Group chief executive, a newspaper man to his fingertips, he's been in it all his life, it's in his blood albeit from a different perspective - he's fond of the bottom line.

Pressure from outside? You know something, Ivor, I ignore it. If you start thinking about it, if you start pulling back a bit, you're done for, because then they will hound you to hell. I happen to have deep convictions about the economy and how I see society - I would like to see a liberal, pluralist and confident society, based on civilised, intelligent democracy and market economics. I would like to see us without any hangups, without any desire to congregate into these self-protective groups whether they are trade unions or something else where you feel safe in the middle of that big herd.

The younger generation, if they are given a chance, could be a lot different. I have a son of 21 and most of his friends are just marking time. They all left school at 18, three years later they are all together - in my time we scattered. Now they're being supported by their parents while they hope for something to turn up. Yet, they are more confident and independent than my generation.

I like Sean Barrett's idea of the drawbridge. The way the politicians have encouraged us to organise our affairs is that the haves inside the fortress pull up the drawbridge to make sure that the have-nots don't get in. The so-called social contract is, in essence, insidiously anti-market and anti-competition and is perpetuating an under-performing economy with the result many of our best young people have to leave. Those who can't get into the system here have to emigrate and that's a terrible failure on our part. In personal terms, it might not be the end of the world for the young people - they might do quite well abroad - but it's not much credit to us who are left behind.

I don't know why economics is not taught in schools. It's not a science - it's midway between a science and an art because it rests ultimately on human behaviour which does not always obey rational rules. But public understanding of the rudiments of economics is dismal. That leads to a lot of confusion and an inability in the public mind to understand what's really going on in politics and public affairs. We try to do this in our paper - it's a kind of hobby-horse of mine. I couldn't honestly say it's a great help in selling newspapers but I think it's an important thing in the mix.

Rupert Murdoch said, if you were to believe market research, there would be a boom in literary supplements. I am not led by the nose by research but it's useful, it can give you insights and ideas, but to follow it slavishly would be dangerous because people are self-conscious about what they tell you they like. You have to sift what they *tell* you they like, what they *think* they like, what they *really* like and what they will spend their money every Sunday actually buying. And no matter how skilled the psychologist is on qualitative research, it still takes a lot of judgment to make good decisions in the light of that research. I was down in Cork on a market research exercise, sitting in with a group of women who did not know who I was. When it came to our Living and Leisure supplement, they purred over it. They saw Terry Keane as a send-up, a far more sophisticated reaction than some of the dinner party people around Dublin with something up their noses. With Eamon Dunphy they said they often did not agree with him but they were glad he was there. So, there's your mixture, some of which may provoke you to outrage. Ultimately, you're making an act of faith in people's intelligence. One should not underestimate the public's ability to tease things out in their own heads. They don't, deep down, accept hook, line and sinker the bland platitudes dished out to them by public figures.

When Eamon Dunphy called the present Tanaiste, quoting Brendan Behan, "the highest bollocks in Ireland", I felt we were breaking new ground. It was expressing something in the vernacular, in language in daily use. I instinctively went with it. I knew what he was doing: it was giving the paper that chemistry I talked about earlier. And it transpired that Dick Spring had, in public, used the same word about Brendan Halligan.

So, there are a number of people who hate us and invent all sorts of conspiracy theories - there's nothing new in that. Some people have a limited ability to deal with things other than in an absolutist, dogmatic way. They believe you are either entirely for them or entirely against them. To some of them, business and profit are synonymous with corruption - I don't know how they think people are going to get jobs or who's going to pay for them. In the *Sunday Independent* we use the word profit unashamedly. I believe that subliminally it's a word that people in Ireland shy away from - they use that awful word profitability, what does that mean? They say, "The company returned to profitability last year". Why not just say "profit"? There are important clues in the way we use words.

Making money is a good thing. It is not the most harmful of human activities. We need to be healthy about these things and you strike a chord with people when you tell the truth. They know that the more timorous politicians have failed us. They have done so through a mixture of cynicism and cravenness.

Politicians could be a lot more courageous about policies that don't seem immediately popular. They are lagging 15 years behind public opinion. They're afraid. They continue with this pattern of cynicism, which is the pursuit of their self-interest and their spinelessness in failing to pursue unpopular policies. They think their cautious, catch-all rhetoric wins more votes but in the long run I think they are wrong.

There is a very clear distinction between being an editor and being a journalist. In Dublin alone, there are dozens of people who are far better journalists than I am. David Ogilvy said something like: (I am paraphrasing here) if you employ pygmies you become a pygmy yourself, if you employ giants, you might just become a giant. Ego is something I dispense with as far as I can - I am quite happy to employ people who are better than me, who have strong egos, strong drives. What I have to do is to arbitrate constantly between all sorts of advice. A lot of it is well-meaning, some of it not so well-meaning, some of it may be devious. I can get from experienced, intelligent journalists, diametrically opposite advice on the policy of the paper. You can't please them all. I believe the best journalists don't make the best editors. When it comes to the point where you must subsume your own ability and ego into what you see as the overall picture, the best journalists are not good at that. I think people don't see that distinction.

I would like to be invisible. It doesn't do the *Sunday Independent* any good to have the editor personalised - the title is bigger than any individual and it's certainly bigger than the editor. All editors have feet of clay. I shouldn't be talking to you at all

11

Kieran Walsh

The Munster Express

You are not really dead until your name is in the deaths column of The Munster Express.

The conversation took place on September 9 1993

225

Kieran Walsh is editor of .

He was born in Waterford on May 9 1957.

His father was Joseph James Walsh, newspaper proprietor, chairman and managing director.

His mother was Josephine Phyllis Higgins, a nurse.

He is fifth in a family of five, two brothers and two sisters: Edward, Myriam, Nicholas and Priscilla.

He is married to Roswitha Hertrich, a German teacher and translator.

Their children are Christoph and Kilian, twins aged 4.

He was educated at Waterpark Junior and Senior Schools; South Bank Polytechnic, London (BA Hons in Business Studies); Institute of Marketing Diploma, London; Diploma in Legal Studies, Rathmines College of Commerce; post-graduate diploma in printing and publishing, London College of Printing.

1978, market researcher with Harrisons Printers, West London; 1980 financial reporter with Business and Finance magazine; 1981 business editor of The Sunday Journal; 1982 freelance for the Irish Press; since 1984 with The Munster Express in various capacities; 1985 advertising manager; 1992 editor and joint managing director.

He is vice-president of Iverk Show, the oldest agricultural show in Ireland.

His hobbies are golf, football, theatre and travel.

You are doing three provincial papers. They are all different. *The Kerryman* is owned by a large group, the *Connacht Tribune* is a private company, and we are a family company. It's a good mixture.

Growing up in Waterford in the 1960s I was keen on soccer. Waterford Football Club was the rage. I was asked by my Dad to go to the World Cup in Mexico but felt I was too young and it was too far from home. I had just turned 13 but at that age I wrote an article on international soccer for our Christmas supplement. I did not write anything else for the newspaper until I was at college when I used to help out during the summer holidays, writing obituaries, doing travel articles, writing up little happenings in the area. I did not really want to work in the business at all. There were enough family members involved. I took business studies for my degree because it was broad and opened the door to many disciplines. I was offered a job as a media buyer for an advertising agency but ended up instead working on *Business and Finance*. I was put through the hoops by Jim Dunne, the then editor, and Bill Ambrose, the managing editor. I had to write a few trial articles - I did an interview with Ken Rohan of Rohan Construction, which they published. The job I had really wanted was to do market research in France. I had spent some time there and speak reasonably good French but there was a recession on and it was not to be. I was keen to establish myself in my own right on my return to Ireland rather than go into the family business where my father would have overshadowed me.

We had had a comfortable upbringing, we did not want for anything, but there was a certain pressure being the son of one of the best-known men in Waterford. There was power there - there were things you could not do in other businesses, influence people, write about them. As a consequence, people were cagey with you and there could be an element of jealousy but a lot depended on yourself and I certainly was down to earth. Aengus Fanning would appreciate my feelings following his stint on *The Midland Tribune*. It's like being a politician's son - you are watched a lot. Teachers will expect more of you.

When I went away from home - to London and to Paris - it was frowned on a little, most people went to Dublin: you could get all sorts of influences outside of Ireland. I found the experience stimulating. You had access to world-class concerts and art galleries but, most of all, you met people from backgrounds totally different to your own. I'll never regret it. It gave one a more worldly rather than an insular view of life and people.

Business and Finance was interesting. Ronnie Hoffman was the deputy editor, Aileen O'Toole was news editor and Gerald Luke was on the staff. I learned a great deal from Aileen. She is now deputy editor of *The Sunday Business Post*. Frank Fitzgibbon was there - he became editor of *Irish Business* and was subsequently involved also with *The Sunday Business Post*. It was a good team. I stayed there for about seven months. I was interviewing people on incomes much higher than my own and wondered if I should get out into business and make money for myself. There was also increasing pressure on me to go home to the family business.

Jim Aughney left *Business and Finance* to join *The Sunday Journal*. He then left it to go to the *Irish Independent*. That left no one in *The Sunday Journal* to write on finance and economics. Willy Kealy approached me in Dublin at the time, there was a salary increase and the prospect of getting involved in general news, so I said yes. I became business editor. Willie is now with the *Sunday Independent*. That continued for 17 months until *The Sunday Journal* ceased publication. It was founded originally with capital from England. When the PMPA took it over it should have changed the title - the Dubs reckoned it was the same as *The Irish Farmers' Journal*. *The Sunday Journal* was particularly well laid out by John Paul Thompson who had been recruited from the *Belfast Telegraph* but this was the time the *Sunday World* was going ahead by leaps and bounds in both the Republic and in Northern Ireland. Being owned by the late Joe Moore of the PMPA, *The Sunday Journal* leant towards Fianna Fail. Joe was a great friend of Charles Haughey. Tony Fitzpatrick, the editor, subsequently became Charlie Haughey's press officer prior to P.J. Mara. Joe Moore was puritanical and did not go along with sex and nudity and page-three girls. Today *The Sunday Journal* would be more like *The Star* than the *Sunday World.* Liam Nolan was the sports editor, John Saunders used to do the soccer - there was good talent there, good people to learn from. It was a shame it did not get the circulation to make it attractive to the advertisers - maybe it was before its time. There was a bit of quality mixed with colour. At that time, colour was associated only with the red-tops such as the English tabloids. It never targeted its niche.

While I worked in *The Sunday Journal,* I kept in touch with home, particularly in the summer - Waterford is lovely in the summer.In Dublin I shared a house with my sister Myriam who lectured in French in TCD. Priscilla, my sister, was news editor and I saw her frequently in Dublin with our Dad. It was a bad time in Ireland - Dad was complaining about costs inflating and advertising revenue plummeting. The country was badly-led politically and *The Munster Express* complained a great deal about that. It took seven years for the country to wake up. We had editorials about the solutions to our problems but nobody was listening. It was only in England, when they began to speak about the country being taken over by the International Monetary Fund back in the 1970s, that people began to hear. After the 1987 election, when Ray McSharry went to Finance, things began to come right again. Being married to a German, I can see how they think medium- and long-term, not like us thinking short-term and just drifting.

I would not admit it but I suppose all the time it was in the back of my mind that I would come back to work on the family newspaper. Priscilla was doing a great job but I don't think she wanted to take it all on on her own. Newspaper life is tough.

There were 50 years between my father and me - I would have preferred if he were ten years younger or I was ten years older. It might have been better if I had spent five years getting experience elsewhere. In 1983/84, he was over 70 and wanted to play a bit more golf in the mornings and take more breaks.

When *The Sunday Journal* went bust, I stayed in Dublin to finish a law course at the Rathmines College of Commerce. I got a call from Brian O'Connor, business editor of the *Irish Press* - he subsequently became editor of *Business and Finance* and is now city editor of the *Daily Mail*. He asked me to do a regular Monday slot. That kept my hand in. There were not that many opportunities in Dublin at the time and it became a toss-up whether I'd go home or go back to London - I still had no ties. I plumped for London and some more education but the pressure was still on from home. Dad wanted me to learn about the family business while he was still around.

In 1984, he and Priscilla went off to the Los Angeles Olympics and I went back to edit the paper. I subsequently got involved in all manner of things - canvassing adverts, doing the accounts, writing. Then I succeeded the retiring advertising manager which took me into the commercial end of the newspaper - the most important end because it keeps everybody in a job. I was in touch with the advertising agencies and the big local advertisers - the supermarkets, builders, auctioneers, ringing up garages for their ads. While I was doing that, Davey Daniels, our main ad canvasser, was, and still is, out selling advertising. Davey is an Alderman and a former Mayor of Waterford, very well-known. I took on much of the news editing - I was covering two or three jobs from 1987. It did me no harm to get a baptism of fire.

There are nearly 30 people employed by the paper - covering editorial, printers, accounts, sales and maintenance. We do job-printing, but not as much as *The Kerryman* or *Kilkenny People*. We are installing direct-input systems and have agreed lower manning levels with the printers through natural wastage. It is only now, when we are beginning to get over the trauma of my Dad's death, that new initiatives are emerging. Our circulation is now steady at 19,000. The provincial press tends to have a great loyalty - it neither grows nor declines very much. We have over 71 per cent readership in our area according to an independent survey carried out this year - it is hard to go above that. You can go only so far in a provincial area unless there is population growth, not the case in Ireland. The troubles in Waterford Crystal did not affect our circulation to any major extent. There are comings and goings in Waterford, new houses being built - Bausch & Lomb are taking on 400 workers. Even people who are out of work might have a read of the paper to see if there are any jobs going. We did a survey of an area in Waterford where 50 per cent of the people are on welfare and over two-thirds of the homes were still getting the paper - but they were not buying a daily newspaper. Farmers are also great loyal readers.

A provincial paper is much closer to its readers than a daily paper is. Through your network of correspondents in both rural and urban areas you get a feel for what is happening. A small community is more intimate than a large urban one where people commute to work every day. With us, the stories come from the ground up. We rarely feed off the other news media, as daily papers often do. We find our own news. Our readers also provide us with interesting news items, as they know they can trust us.

The Munster Express was the first provincial paper to change over from hot metal to Web Offset. We did it in one week, in 1975, around the same time as *The Cork Examiner*. My father had seen the technology in, of all places, Nairobi, in a paper owned by the Aga Khan. My brother Nicholas had studied printing, production and management in the London College of Printing. He helped instal the new technology. It went smoothly enough - there was a guarantee of no redundancies. My father always thought that massive payments for redundancy were an absurd waste of money.

You, Ivor, point out the constraints in a family business where family members always want to occupy the top positions. I think that is changing and the best family businesses will bring in professional people to manage alongside them. Provincial papers will always be limited by the size of their market unless they choose to go outside that

231

market either geographically or into different products and that's a new game altogether. On the other hand, provided they are well-managed and costs controlled, they are a steady business.

The paper is important to Waterford - "I read it in the *Munster*". Once it's in the paper, it's fact. It is the authoritative voice of the area. You are not really dead until your name is in the deaths column of *The Munster Express*. And people know, because of the intimacy of our relationship with our readers, that, if they don't get a fair crack of the whip, we will always listen to them, make it up to people, straighten it out. You can always put a paragraph in the following week - "It was brought to our attention . . ." You might leave out certain relatives' names in an obituary or part of the person's life story and you could put an addendum in a subsequent publication. It may be a bit boring for the general reader but you would like to give that satisfaction to the people involved.

Jobs are the biggest issue today. We are lucky that we have had a few recent developments in Waterford such as the timber processing mill, the new port, the shopping centre and the hospital. With the troubles in Waterford Crystal, people have been in a negative mood. Although there have been 550 job losses there in the last 12 months, the outlook is now brighter. There is hope but there will never be full employment again - witness the latest National Plan which admits this. We see it as part of our job to encourage business, to encourage Government to be economically logical, not doing things simply for short-term political gain. Waterford has the lowest percentage of Fianna Fail first-preference votes in the whole of Ireland, so we don't get the patronage the West of Ireland gets even though, for 700 years, Waterford has been the most logical port through which to trade with Britain and continental ports.

My grandfather was Mayor of Waterford for two years - he was part of the Home Rule crusade before the First World War. He was offered a knighthood and turned it down. He thought it would have been against Ireland to accept it. During the War of Independence, Waterford was quiet. There was a great deal of trade and it benefitted economically from having a number of army barracks. There was commercial advantage in supporting Britain - the city had a substantial food industry on which many depended: in the county it was Republican. There is still that mixture in our readership. Fianna Fail are weak in the city, there is a strong working-class vote which goes to Labour, the Workers Party or Democratic Left. Fine Gael were strong but are now weak. The PDs have a Dail seat here. My grandfather was a member of the Redmondite Party, the National League, which merged with Cumann na nGaedheal to form Fine Gael. The paper was constitutional and against the Civil War, it was in favour of neutrality and would have been against de Valera's isolationism - in the Economic War the area suffered heavily. The paper would have been pro-Lemass because he was positive and progressive and willing to learn from other countries. My father was friendly with him and was in Boston with him in the late 1950s. He invited him to the centenary dinner of the paper in 1959.

There was a much-reported incident in 1986 with Garret FitzGerald. It happened like this. When Garret FitzGerald was Taoiseach, my father wrote an editorial criticising him for pushing his wife around in a wheelchair while he was on a visit to the USA for St. Patrick's Day. My father felt that Dr. FitzGerald should have been engaged in higher things and have given to somebody else the responsibility for escorting his wife. It was controversial at the time and made the front pages of the daily papers. We felt the whole matter had been blown out of proportion by the Fine Gael handlers - Garret FitzGerald avoided having a press conference when he was here to open the Waterford Crystal Gallery.

Two days after the controversy, my father went away and I was left to man the barricades. I went to a conference of the Marketing Institute held in the Royal Hospital, Kilmainham, and met Brendan McCabe, the advertising manager of the *Independent*. He told me that I was a brave man to show my face in public after what we had been through. I did not go out after that for about ten days - everywhere you'd look, people would be talking about you. My wife and I went to Wicklow to get away from the pressure - it was enormous. My mother was watching the *Late Late Show* and there was mention of my father and Joan FitzGerald and my mother got about five irate phone calls. She was on her own at home. She was upset that strangers should ring up and abuse her when she was not directly concerned. However, her neighbours and friends in Tramore were nice to her. It gives you a perspective on the news - you might be a bit more sensitive to how other people think and feel, having been under the spotlight yourself.

We now like to feel that we are independent, free to criticise any party. People say that, in my father's time, we were not pro-Republican, but I would not agree with that. The columns were open to people of Republican disposition if they wanted them. When we went for a radio franchise and did not get it - one of my big disappointments - it was suggested to me that perhaps we were not favoured. We were the only bidder with a public company backing us - Waterford Foods - to get refused a county licence. It was a bit of a blow at the time - we felt we had the right package - but you put these things behind you and get on with it and now we co-exist with the local radio station. The franchise was secured by the former pirate station who gave the people what they wanted. *The Limerick Leader* also had substantial financial backing but did not get the franchise.

Local radio stations are a new competitive element for provincial newspapers, both for news and for advertising. They cover the same stories we do, so we have to do rather better than mere sound bites.

What is news for a provincial paper? It could be tourism, industry, farming, political intrigue. It could be about a pop concert in Tramore or lack of Government interest in the area, lack of Government spending on infrastructure, insufficient political clout at the cabinet table. The road from Dublin to Kilkenny is pretty awful, isn't it? I met the Taoiseach last week at the opening of Waterford Port and asked him about it. He smiled. He usually comes in by helicopter, except during an election campaign, when he drives in. News? News is like a great competition. You try not to have the same story every week - you could write about Waterford Glass for years. With so many highly-paid jobs there is an awful lot at stake. Very few factories will come in now and pay the kind of wages that Waterford Glass employees got.

The Waterford Glass dispute was a major test for the paper. Though I was working at the news end, my father was editor at the time. Logic would suggest that management were right - they won out in the end but you also have to take account of the fact that the workers are your readers. You have got to give them both a bit of a show, not take sides. During the strike, management would not talk to the unions and the unions would not talk to management until they paid the bonanza money. The only way they discussed things was through press statements. It got a bit rough at times - one week you would be accused by one side and one week by the other. When you're accused by both, you feel you are all right. Our reporters, Tom Young and John O'Connor, had excellent sources both in management and in the unions. I also wrote on the issue. We were able to check things and be sure we were not being fed a wrong story. The workers felt that the *The Munster Express* knew what was going on. We often held back on stories that other papers ran with if we felt they were not fully true. We had to be absolutely sure. This gave the paper great credibility. The editor of one of the big Dublin dailies is not stopped in the street if he gets things wrong. Because our sources were so good, the newspaper got TV or radio exposure, other times our stories were lifted by other newspapers without any attribution. The provincial public are tough task-masters. It is only when you are deeply involved that you realise how discerning they are. The political columnists are continually saying the public are smarter than the politicians - I think they are right.

Journalists are egotistical. Brian Patterson of Waterford Glass recently wrote a letter to *The Irish Times* in response to something a columnist, John Waters, had written. You don't start a row with someone who has ink by the bucket. They can keep the pot stirred and they always have the last word. We don't do that - you have to be thick-skinned in our business. There was a critical article about us in a trade magazine and people said we should respond - we did not bother. There are people out there who will have a go at you anyway - let them be. On the other hand, when you are in a position of responsibility in a paper, people do tend to court you. You have to see through the plamas as to what material is readable and interesting.

There are times during the silly season when it is hard to make an interesting front-page but we always seem to manage it, there will always be some new material and information to bring to the public. By saying that, I do not mean that news is manipulated. But, week after week, we have to come up with a top story. You tell me that we can't come out one week and say to our readers, "There is no news this week". In fact, someone did that once - Vincent Gill, editor of *The Longford News* in the 1950s! He used also say he had heard certain people left town and he was delighted - that was good news! He would not get away with it today.

You ask me what we stand for and what we are against. We are against corruption. We are against people getting away with wrongdoing. But you are restricted by the libel laws - there are many issues you would like to raise and can't because of this limitation. My grandfather used to say the greater the truth, the greater the libel and there have been times when we have felt the wiser choice was not to publish a story. It does mean, I am afraid, there are bad things happening which, because of the libel laws, have to go unreported. I would believe if, for example, a person is defrauding his creditors, the public have a right to know so that they too are not misled. You can be quite critical of public companies - as I know from my financial journalism background - but it is often difficult to get information about the smaller private companies.

However, we were talking about what we stood for. We should promote the interests of the region, harmony in the community, respect for law and order and family values. We should promote respect for authority, for parents, for property. There is a general decline in morality. I was at the recent ordination of the Most Rev. Dr. William Lee, Bishop of Waterford and Lismore, and Cardinal Cahal Daly said the church was in its most difficult period since the Penal Laws. It is under attack from the media and from outside influences, from TV and cinema and from changes in attitudes to contraception. So far as crime is concerned, we have what John Bruton calls the revolving-door syndrome where convicted persons are imprisoned and quickly released to make room for others. Look back through the files of the paper at the depression of the 30s. The judges would come in wearing white gloves to signify that there would be no court that day because there were no cases to be heard. There was far more deprivation then than there is today, so deprivation is not the excuse for the crime level we have. I have been to Third World countries where there is, of course, some thievery but there is also a genuine neighbourly helpfulness. They would not have much but they would share their dinner with you. Ireland today is materialistic and is adopting the worst of the American influences. People envy what other people have and go and take it. The *Irish Independent* did a survey of teenage values and it was quite disturbing. One in every three teenagers in the survey had been involved in shop-lifting, 15 per cent had been involved in burglary or car-theft. In Germany, which I know, or in Third World countries, there is respect for people, especially for parents. We have, I suppose, family values but there is something going wrong and it is getting worse. My father went to school with children in bare feet and all they robbed were apples in an orchard. No one would dare break into a house.

Waterford is the fifth city in the country. We were the eighth lowest in terms of indictable offences per thousand with, of course, Dublin at the top. The media have a large role to play in keeping a situation like that under control. Our job is to encourage a law-abiding community willing to cooperate with the police and with respect for the judiciary. We have to encourage people to be willing to go forward as witnesses in court. People in Waterford are pretty good at that and there is not a serious drug problem here. Waterford has a history of respect for law and order, partly because it was a garrison town. We are still fortunate to have a good quality of life here.

We would be a little different from our counterparts in the regions in that we have had progressive editorials supporting pluralism, saying that the majority did not have the right to dictate to the minority. We would not fit into the conservative mould of many of the provincial newspapers. The pattern of urban voting on moral issues is now quite fluid. This is in contrast to the rural community which tends to be conservative. We have to cater for both of those publics - both opinions have to get a fair run. But, if there are 50,000 people in Ireland wanting divorce, I would not see it as my editorial duty to try to stop them

I distinguish between the rising crime rate and issues of private morality. Private morality is something to be sorted out within the family. Political leaders do not get as high a respect as they used to, especially among younger voters. In the last election, they were apathetic because they saw little progress on the jobs crisis, the most important issue. Their heroes come from the sporting and entertainment world rather than from politics, a change from other decades. A move towards more personal responsibility, less dependence, which is probably linked to our colonial past, could make Ireland a more mature society, able to stand up as equals with other European countries who have had political independence longer than us. A mature society is needed to cope with what lies ahead.

When things are difficult, one of the more important functions of the paper is to entertain people. *The Munster Express* was one of the first provincial papers to carry a theatre column. Waterford has a great history of theatre and there is a discerning audience - middle-class, working-class and rural. High standards are attained every year in the Waterford International Festival of Light Opera with societies from all

238

over Ireland and Britain participating. We encourage music - there is a symphony club in Waterford. We encourage rock 'n' roll, if you can give it a generic term. A rock column has appeared in the paper for 20 years while the daily papers have only begun to do it in a serious way in the last five years. We have three musicians on the staff - that helps.

We carry three or four pages of GAA a week, we have a page of soccer, a page of golf and another page covering rugby, basketball, athletics, rowing, hockey, cricket, tennis and camogie. We are there to remind people who have retired early or who just do not have a job that there are things in life other than TV. This will grow as we move towards a leisured society. The manufacturing base will shrink as Eastern countries join the EC and labour costs become the primary competitive point. We shall probably lose more multinationals. In those circumstances, we should be trying to optimise leisure time and use it constructively and positively. We should invest more in sport and culture, such as music and the visual arts where Government resources are woefully poor compared with other countries. There is no proper planning at the moment - it's only ad hoc. The consequences are there to see in the American inner cities - we would want to act before we head in that direction. We need to offer more hope to the coming generation.

12

Joe Mulholland

Radio Telefis Eireann

You change your mind over the years. If you are a thinking person at all, you will not hold absolute, certain views on a lot of things because you know you may not be right. The more one lives, the more one sees fewer certainties around.

The conversation took place on June 22 1993

Joe Mulholland is Director of News in Radio Telefís Eireann.

He was born on October 24 1940 in Stranorlar, Co. Donegal.

His father is Joe Mulholland, who was a lorry driver.

His mother is Mary Byrne, a housewife.

He is the eldest in a family of five, two brothers and two sisters: Raymond, Celine, Daniel and Elizabeth.

He is married to Annie Vuillemin, a teacher.

Their children are Fiona (24), Sylvain (22), Julien (20).

He was educated at Stranorlar Boys' National School; Finn College, Ballybofey; De la Salle Teachers' Training College, Manchester; London University (External) and the University of Nancy, France. He holds an honours degree in French and Spanish from the University of London, an honours degree in French literature from Nancy (L ès L), and a doctorate in French literature on mediaeval theatre. He studied the Spanish language in the University of Barcelona. He took the examination of the Institute of Linguists.

1959/61 worked in London as a clerk. 1961-64 college in Manchester. 1964-69 while studying in France also taught English. 1969 trainee producer course in RTE. 1970 producer/director RTE. 1980 head of current affairs RTE and editor of *Today Tonight*. 1986 controller of television productions. 1990 director of news.

Has written for *Le Monde* since 1972.

Director of the MacGill Summer School for 11 years.

He has won two Jacobs awards as a producer of documentaries.

Let's start at the beginning. I was a child of the Twin Towns: Stranorlar and Ballybofey. They are on each side of the River Finn. People from Stranorlar would consider me from Stranorlar and people from Ballybofey would consider me from Ballybofey. I was born in Stranorlar but at age 11 we moved to Ballybofey where there was good public housing which got us out of the dreadful conditions we had lived in. I grew up in the Donegal of the 40s and 50s, saw some of the war years. My father was an emigrant: he journeyed back and forth to Britain, worked on the hydro-electric schemes in Scotland. It really was a difficult time for families because the man-of-the-house had to go, there was no work of any kind. The women-folk were left to bring up the families. I am of that generation and I do feel really strongly about emigration. My father would come home twice a year, summer and Christmas, just that. Don't forget, Ivor, that transport was both difficult and expensive. And then you couldn't leave the job - if you had a good job over there you were determined to stay in it. There were plenty more waiting for it. I don't think I realised it at the time but, looking back now, of course it had an effect on me. Ultimately, I left as well, but in slightly different circumstances.

I managed to get a scholarship to the local secondary school, the Finn College. It was unique, in the main street of Ballybofey in the old market hall. It was set up by a Mr. and Mrs. Logue and, unusually for the time, was not clerically run. It was co-ed and multi-denominational long before that became fashionable. In East Donegal, Protestants came to it as well as Catholics. There were practically no facilities - we would go down for games once a week to the local GAA grounds. It had no science which I regretted. Yet it gave people like myself, who could not afford to go to boarding school, the chance to get a secondary education. Throughout my life I have been passionate about education - I was determined to educate myself. For me, the alternatives to Finn College were St. Eunan's in Letterkenny or St. Columb's in Derry - they were totally beyond our reach. Going to boarding school was just not in the psyche. Boys and girls when they reached the age of 15 or 16 went to work.

When I was 11, I was all ready to go to the Marist Brothers in Athlone, destined to become a Marist Brother. Interestingly, my parents stopped me. Taking a decision like that at 11 years of age was normal in those days. A brother came around to the schools, it was a time for films like *Father Damien* and *St. Bernadette* - it was an environment of religion and religious-serving, serving God, serving man. It hit me again when I was about to take the Leaving - one or two of my friends were going to the Sacred Heart Fathers. I was interested, but my parents were never keen because I was the eldest.

I suppose I was a serious child - I was far better read then than I am now! I was not a sporting type at all. It was only in later life, when I went to college in England, that I took up cross-country running. I taught myself to swim when I was working in Spain - back at school in Donegal the river was out of bounds.

When I did the Leaving Cert there were two scholarships to university offered by the County Council. I did the exam for them but did not get one. University was closed off to me. There was just no way somebody coming from my modest background could go to Galway or Dublin and pay fees and boarding. I did various office jobs locally - I worked for Paddy McGowan, the present Senator, who had a fruit-importing business. I was only biding my time because I wanted to get third-level education. I realised I would have to go and live in England in order to qualify to get into teacher-training college there.

I left home when I was 19, went by boat, landed in the middle of London - and got the shock of my life. That was 1959. It was a horrifying day - I have always looked back on it with utter dread. I was coming from a rural environment, a small town, to the heart of one of the biggest bustling cities in the world. I had no relatives or friends in London, so there was nobody to meet me. I stood in Oxford Circus with my suitcases in my hands - I must have appeared like an emigrant - and watched all those people. I could not believe that nobody so much as looked at you. I had come from an environment where everybody saluted you. I had been to Dublin, by the way, once - but Dublin for us was quite remote. We were orientated towards the North, Belfast, Scotland. You went to Dublin only for a football match or for the Eucharistic Congress.

That first day in London, I desperately wanted to go home but realised it was not really an alternative. I checked my bags into a hotel in the West End - it was probably today's equivalent of £100 a night. I think it was a fiver in fact but that was astronomical. I just had to get rid of the bags. I had out of the *Irish Independent* an address for digs, but even before I went there I got a newspaper and started looking for a job. I got one - stacking textiles in the John Lewis store which was nearby. I couldn't go far because I didn't know where to go. I was to start the job on the following Monday. I rang the digs and they had a room, way out in Finsbury Park. I had not the slightest idea how to get there. I got my bags from the hotel, telling them I was sorry, I had changed my mind. A policeman gave me directions for the Underground - I would have to change at Holborn, all of which was Greek to me. I asked a woman who saw how distraught I was and she said follow me. After a dreadul journey, that seemed like the Long Walk, I reached the digs. I was physically and emotionally exhausted. But I got my job and I got my digs - and indeed I was to stay in those digs for all my time in London. I had a good cry that night.

This whole business of emigration has left an indelible mark on me. It has its good sides obviously - you have to get out of a small island but going in the circumstances we had to go in was not good. To get further education and experience is fine but so much emigration has been forced. I have always felt strongly about families being split up - it is not normal. Later, when I lived in France, it surprised me that nobody seemed to emigrate whereas, in Ireland, it was a terrible trauma, particularly for wives, who first saw their husbands leave and then their children. That was what led me to Patrick MacGill who wrote at the beginning of the century about emigration. I remember the bitterness - people who left, left in a resigned fashion, they knew there was no other way out. The bitterness was not expressed in a political way nor was it focused: it was individual. There was a scene in a film that Taviani made where these young boys have to leave the south of Italy, a place like Donegal, and, as an expression of their disgust, they pissed out of the back of the truck onto the olives. There was a pent-up anger in the people who emigrated from Donegal or Mayo. It has left a pervasive sense of failure. Some people think we over-emphasise the sense of failure - for example, I have heard people criticise Joe Lee's book, *Ireland 1912-1985,* because it is too negative. I am talking now about people in Government circles who think that Lee does not emphasise enough the achievements of this country - the education system we have built up, the standard of housing, the political stability of a State established in difficult circumstances. These are a lot of achievements in a small country in a short space of time but, underlying all that, is the fact that we have not been able to build a country that affords its children work and opportunity. That has sapped the morale of the nation whereas, in France, it goes without saying that the French will work in France - unless they choose to go to Quebec.

The French have no self-doubt. They don't have this navel-gazing. We did a series on television, *We The Irish* - it's this constant looking to see who we are and what we are. Of course that is influenced by other factors - we do have a colonial past and we still have the question of the North sapping morale. You have, on the one hand, an economy that has not been able to support its population since independence and then you have murder and mayhem in the North. How could we have the confidence of the French? Until we get our economy right and, hopefully, some settlement on this island which will allow people to live in peace and harmony, we shall never be sure of ourselves. We're never sure of tomorrow.

The youth have a lot more confidence than we had at the same age - that's probably to the credit of our education system but, at the same time, my daughter tells me most of her friends have gone now and she will ultimately go. Many parents in

Ireland have never had the joy of having their children grow
up, get jobs, and live within striking distance. That is failure,
whatever the reasons are. There just has not been an
entrepreneurial spirit in this country. When I was growing up
it was unthinkable that people would invest in manufacturing -
it would have been far too high a risk. In the Lemass era, it was
seen we were not going to achieve much depending only on
indigenous enterprise and capital. We had to look elsewhere.
That was an admirable - perhaps the only - thing to do.

My father worked with Poles, people from Eastern Europe,
Turks - we have been like the North Africans. We have been in
the category of the *Gastarbeiter* - we have not been attacked,
but at times it was difficult for our people abroad. The saga of
our emigrants has not been sufficiently documented. They
lived in the most dreadful conditions. Because of loneliness and
deprivation some sank into alcoholism and ended up in mental
institutions. Nowadays, one is glad to see the agencies that are
there: people like Father Bobby Gilmore in London, the
Camden Town Centre and so on. At least there's an effort to
meet people and offer some shelter, but yet many of our young
people are living on the streets, going into prostitution.

It's easy to blame the politicians. I have worked closely with
politicians over the last 12 years. They work terribly hard - I
have great admiration for some of them, they have a lot of
integrity, contrary to the usual things you hear about them.
But the system, Ivor, encourages, for example, opposition for
opposition's sake. If you depart from that, like Alan Dukes did
with the Tallaght strategy, then you're not going to make it. On
top of that, you have the clientilist system where all you want
from your local TD is that he or she gets a job for your son or
daughter or that they get you planning permission. They are
caught in a dreadful system in which, if anybody is courageous,
they quickly fall foul of it.

Yes, we have incredible energy in some parts of our society.
You say you see it among young executives. I see it in the arts.
My daughter has just qualified from the College of Art. The
standard of design and craftsmanship has come up. In music as

well - fantastic dynamism and energy. Then, some great people in industry - our management has improved terrifically: people like Martin Naughton, Lochlann Quinn, Denis Brosnan.

It would be wrong to get bogged down in doom and gloom but the political system is not geared to giving leadership and you need leadership in any society. It may be a tribal thing but we all need to look up to somebody or something - what we need is *political* leadership. Look at Northern Ireland - there is nobody there to say, "Let's forget all of this, let's recognise reality and let's plan something new". Politicians are afraid to go too far and propose something new, whether it's Articles 2 or 3 or the economy. They are afraid for their seats - they look over their shoulders, not so much at their rivals in other parties but at rivals in their own parties. We are edging towards reform of the Oireachtas - the committee system is hopefully a good development and will give a greater role in legislation to back-benchers. But we need a lot more. We are a small country with a lot of potential but the only thing that can tap that potential is political will, political leadership, political determination. We are not alone - you have the same problem in other countries, Britain for example, where the political system has fallen into disrepute. This is dangerous - all you have to do is look at European history.

Contrary to the snide remarks, there are a lot of intelligent politicians in Dail Eireann. They have plenty of ideas among them but the system does not encourage their expression. Politicians are afraid to go ahead of the posse. It will be their constituency colleagues who will sit back, let them go out in front and get their heads chopped off at the next election. Politics is a tough and can be a dirty game. It's about getting advantage. I believe it is appalling the way President Mary Robinson's recent visit to West Belfast was treated by some politicians. She would have been seen as sympathetic to Unionism and yet she chose to go to this deprived, abandoned part of Belfast, labelled as Provo territory. She showed courtesy to Gerry Adams, who, whether we like it or not, is a leader of his community. I don't accept at all that what she did gave any legitimacy to him. Mary Robinson was civilised when she was in Belfast.

But back to London. I got another job after John Lewis working as a clerk with an American company that was erecting oil refineries. All the time I was applying for admission to teacher training colleges. I did not have the background to enjoy London - I was treating it as a transitional place. I succeeded in getting a place in a training college for men outside Manchester, a little placed called Middleton, run by the De La Salle Brothers. The following three years were the most wonderful of my life. I lived in college. I was always into organising things in the arts and I founded the French Society. I had, unusually for a boy, got honours in French in the Leaving - it was French that opened up another world to me. I took it in training college as my main subject with minors in geography and the principles of education. I had a generous grant from the British Government and I have never forgotten that it was in Britain I was able to get a third-level education. There was great camaraderie between the students and with the Brothers and lay-teachers. It was a small community on its own. Most of the students were from the north of England, Manchester, Liverpool, Salford - Catholics of Irish descent though they might have been of third or fourth generation. Some of them had no consciousness of Ireland at all or no interest. Going across the fields at night to the pub - I look back on it as quite an idyllic period.

I tried not to feel Irish - I wanted to integrate myself into college life as one of the community. Most of my friends were English, even though there were quite a number there from Northern Ireland. Later when I worked and studied in France, I became totally integrated in French society. People coming to France at first could not believe I was Irish. I think that is partly because the education system at the time did not foster a feeling for our own culture. As a result, I had adapted to French society in my dress, in my appearance and, of course, at that time my French was very good. I had cut myself off from Ireland. In college in England, I made no effort at all to assert my Irishness.

At the end of my second year, I was sent on a six-month scholarship to the University of Caen in Normandy - that was a time when the British Government had money to burn on education. Caen opened up another world. There I studied French, history and geography and *civilisation*, as the French call it. I went back to Manchester, completed my teachers' certificate and was faced with the prospect of teaching in Salford or Liverpool. I think, though I am not sure, that I did want to be a teacher but my main purpose in going to teacher-training college was to get third-level education.

The De La Salle Order is French and one of our teachers had been a brother over from France. He got me a job teaching English in a *lycée* in Nancy. It was ideal because, as well as being a day school, it was a boarding school and I was able to live-in and go to university. I started my studies for a *licence* and, simultaneously, enrolled as an external student in London - it had always been in my mind to get a degree. Because I was still terribly interested in the arts, I put on plays with my students. We did two Synge plays including *The Playboy of the Western World* and O'Casey's *The Plough and the Stars*. I met Annie, my wife, in Nancy. She was going to university there. She went to the north of England for a year as part of her English studies. When she came back, she was in one of the plays I did. We came to Donegal to get married in 1968. I was coming back to my own place. I was conscious I was the eldest, I had been away for a long time. We had our wedding breakfast in a most beautiful place, Fintragh House just outside Killybegs. It was a lovely sunny day - a small reception, a few of my friends, a lot of them had gone away. Then we went back to France.

The idea of going back to Ireland was sown in my mind by Irish students who came to Nancy - with them I organised an Irish Week. We introduced Ireland to a lot of people who had never heard of it. They certainly did not know about any Irish products - we brought over Irish whiskey and sweaters from Gaeltarra and had Irish coffee receptions. We did not get a lot of help from the Irish Embassy in Paris.

My thesis was on mediaeval theatre - France was a continuously intellectual and cultural environment. In the college, I was living in a Catholic environment but it was an intellectual Catholicism. We studied writers like François Mauriac and Georges Bernanos. If you are a Catholic in France you certainly are a convinced Catholic, not a practising Catholic, but a convinced one. It was an exciting time of my life that went terribly quickly but the longer it went, the more interested I became in Ireland. One day one of the Irish students showed me an ad in *The Irish Times* for trainee producer directors in RTE. I applied, came over to Dublin twice, then did not hear for months from RTE - which I now know is fairly typical! - finally had to ring and at last heard from them that I was offered a place. Simultaneously, I had been to London for an interview for a lecturership in French at the University of Khartoum in the Sudan. We now had Fiona, a year old, and the idea of going to that disturbed place was not appealing.

It was the first trainee producer course RTE itself had run. It was tough and selective. RTE was nine years old at the time and had gone through a period of bringing in foreign producers - it now wanted to grow its own. About half the people on the course failed. I had come from teaching and was now in a technological environment. I found myself dealing with cameramen, with telecine, with video recording machines - you were dealing with a different world. In fact, I felt that the training in technology left a lot to be desired. I was glad to be still in a creative environment. I had to do a project at the end of the course and I did mine on the French writer, Albert Camus.

My first assignment was to the Irish language programme, *Féach*. The editor at the time was Eoghan Harris. That was a shock to the system. Eoghan is an extraordinary person - the programme made no bones about the fact it was left-wing. You would not get away with that today. My job as producer was mainly to do film work and to get across to best advantage the story that had already been decided on. I was neutral. The programme had as its main presenters Breandán O hEithir and Proinsias MacAonghusa. I was completely at sea for quite a long time. My Irish had practically gone and my political knowledge of the country was zilch. I had grown up in the atmosphere of de Valera and James Dillon - I remember Dev coming to Ballybofey. I had been gone since 1959 - it was now 1970. I had missed an exciting decade and a lot of change. It was no longer the depressed Ireland I had left - new confidence was building. RTE played its part in that. But, so far as *Féach* was concerned, these were the most politically cute and aware people in the country. For me it was a crash course. When it came to the referendum on entry to the European Community, I was determined to vote yes but in that environment I was the odd man out. Harris brought me over to the canteen to ask me why I wanted to vote in that way. I told him I believed Ireland had no future outside Europe and I was a European through and through but, in the environment of that time, the trendy thing was to vote no. *Féach* got me quickly into the political environment and into the gaeltachtai and back into the Irish language - into the country as a whole. Being in Galway with Breandán O hEithir - God be good to him - was like being at school. I was very fond of him - I can't believe he's dead.

At that stage, I was not finding enough creativity in RTE. I managed to get into documentaries, into the *Report* series with Patrick Gallagher as the reporter and Eithne Viney as the researcher. You took great care about the subjects you chose. The programme was researched properly, then filmed and you had time to edit it. I made a documentary called *Belfast 72.* That was my first introduction to the North - at that stage it was extraordinary: the Citizens' Defence Committee on the Falls Road, Magilligan and Long Kesh, the men behind the wire. It was the period of the car bomb - if you walked past an isolated car in the street, you never knew whether or not the bloody thing was going to explode. We were filming in the Markets area of Belfast the night people had escaped from a prison ship in the harbour and there was a search for them.

Stupidly we went over to a barricade where there were British soldiers. We switched on a light. A young soldier suddenly turned round and how he did not shoot us I don't know. The tension was palpable. The British Army were reacting to the Provos, beating down doors in Catholic areas, going in searching - it was the whole result of internment which had been a disaster. We captured a lot of that on film. It got a Jacobs Award - not for me but for the man who edited it, Rory O'Farrell, who is now living in the States. I got the name of being an undisciplined producer because I had shot thousands of feet. It was an unpredictable subject - there was no story line. It was capturing in an impressionistic way life in Belfast at the time. It was an important documentary, unfortunately now destroyed. People were allowed to go into the library in RTE, borrow it, and cut it up. There may be half of it left with the sound gone. I remember filming one night a hall full of women, no men - a kind of shebeen. They were singing "The Men Behind the Wire". We did an amazing panning shot around the whole room going wild. That film is vandalised now. We are nowadays looking after the archives in RTE - apart from what was vandalised, a lot was deteriorating because of the type of film it was shot on.

Little by little, I got into the political climate North and South. I did quite a lot of work in the North and developed a sense of the complexities. I went into Protestant areas, East Belfast, and discovered interesting sides of life. You would have people in East Belfast who had worked in the shipyards but who were not fanatical at all and who would explain to you why they were not interested in an Irish republic. It was in their economic interest not to leave Britain. They felt an Irish republic was mad and could not sustain itself.

The 70s were for me a period of education. I had been in France for the de Gaulle period. De Gaulle had done so much for France which was developing into a modern state. When I went there first, the phone and the road systems were in bits. France is to me the example of a country that can, with planning and determination, transform itself. In the college where I lived and taught, the devil incarnate was Mitterand - the socialists were not in favour of religious-run schools. That was a huge issue in France. Now I think they have reached a modus vivendi. But my political consciousness was formed in RTE working in television. I worked on *Seven Days* in its dying days, worked on education and agriculture programmes, did most things. I did not do light entertainment. Looking back, I would have liked to, but at the time would have considered myself not of that ilk. I had still got the stamp of France and my academic background. I moved in and out of *Féach* because they did not have a lot of producers who had any Irish.

The old *Seven Days* was Muiris MacConghail and people like David Thornley, Brian Farrell and John Feeney - it was a strong team but it had been dissipated and the programme was unsatisfactory. Programmes depend on a strong editor. Current Affairs was not a satisfactory place to work - it did not work for me and I suppose I did not work for *Seven Days*. So I moved around the shop and one my most pleasant experiences was the making of *Folio*, the book programme, with Patrick Gallagher. One of my best achievements - Tony Cronin commented on it to me several years later - was to do a full books programme on Einstein. I struggled long over the Theory of Relativity. I did not make a great fist of the Theory but I enjoyed making the programme.

Current Affairs was in disarray and I was asked in 1980 to set up a new programme and run it. Documentary was my real love - it is the most satisfying area of television for many people because you are in control and you can be creative. *Belfast 72* had been a good documentary - it spoke for itself, very little script, the kind of documentary I like. I had made *Dark City*, a documentary on Dublin at night, no script at all, just impressionistic. I had also done a three-and-a-half-hour documentary on Frank Ryan, *Let My Tombstone Be of Granite*. He was an enigmatic figure who had been in the IRA, had gone to fight in Spain on the Republican side, was captured, imprisoned, then released from prison in Burgos, exchanged for someone in Germany - whether or not he subsequently worked for the Germans was a subject of controversy. He died in Dresden in 1944. I got great help on that programme from the late Michael McInerney of *The Irish Times*. Ryan was claimed by the Left who always denied he was disposed favourably to the Nazis. When I was asked to go to Current Affairs, I realised I had to give up the creative part of my life. I went in with the intention of being there for only a couple of years and ended up the longest-serving editor of Current Affairs, 1980 to 1986. I put all the hours that God made into *Today Tonight*. At first the programme was on five days a week but that was too much, then it was four and finally three. Because it was necessary for us to restore Current Affairs to its former status, we were able to get our pick of staff. Things have phases, troughs and summits, and that is how it has been in RTE. It was challenging, satisfying - and wearing. You were living and breathing the programme and I totally neglected my family at a crucial stage of their upbringing - my eldest daughter was 11 and the other two children were nine and seven. I was hardly ever at home. It was done at great sacrifice. I am one of those people who gives myself totally to things but my wife and the children felt it.

We were in the thick of politics. It was a period of instability - three elections in two years. There were several heaves against the leader of Fianna Fail. Some nights the studio was like a theatre, Greek drama - on one side you had those in favour of Mr. Haughey, on the other those in favour of Mr. O'Malley. We had a good investigative edge to us. We wanted to be the best and we were top of the TAMS - in fact sometimes the whole five programmes of the week were top of the TAMS. The audience for the programme had an insatiable appetite, largely because of the political goings on. We wanted the programme to have a lot of integrity. We lived through the hunger strikes in the North, a difficult period. Section 31 was in place, prohibiting interviews primarily with Sinn Fein.[*] It was difficult in terms of the human drama in the North and the effect it was having down here on the political system, on the social fabric, on everything. We have forgotten the height

[*] See Epilogue.

of these passions, the intimidation, the black flags. The programme tried to do its best in all of that. It got the name, unfairly I feel, of being left wing and close to the Workers Party. Vincent Browne did articles on the Workers Party in *Magill,* how they had infiltrated several unions and State boards - and RTE. In 1983 or 1984, Vincent asked me if he could come in and look at the records of the programme and of course I said yes. I did not even realise this was the perception of the programme. Whatever Vincent Browne's interpretation was, whether he based it on the records or whatever, he mentioned Worker Party influence in his article and this went into the consciousness of people. I have always felt that *Today Tonight* was fair to political parties, straight and probing and was not biased in favour of any party. I suppose we were on the side of the underdog - if that is left wing, then so be it. It was certainly not influenced by any one political party's thinking. In its philosophy, it was anti the violence in the North and, I suppose, was anti-Provisional IRA and that was interpreted perhaps by some as being pro-Workers Party.

The hunger strikes created a dilemma. We did not want to be manipulated or blackmailed by people letting themselves starve to death, yet we had to recognise the effect that had on the Nationalist community, especially on young people. I have gone on record as saying we probably did not represent strongly enough the effect on the Nationalist community and on the growth of Provisional IRA and Provisional Sinn Fein. The very fact we were prevented from interviewing people from Sinn Fein and the IRA perhaps put us off covering sufficiently the Nationalist community but I would not like to be simplistic about this - I think we were also put off more by the belief that this awful tragedy was being used in the most cynical way. Of course there were politicians in the North and South who felt that also and who, particularly in the North, were courageous. It was a time when they had to look under their cars. We were trying, as the main current affairs programme in this State, to steer a careful road through what was a minefield. It was a period even more emotional than the early 70s with Bloody Sunday. We were conscious of intimidation that was going unnoticed even in areas of Dublin. The programme lived through all of that and was successful and, I think, respected - respected certainly by the public and, I believe, by the politicians. We never had any problems getting politicians to come on it, whether it was the Fianna Fail Government or the Coalition. Whatever name it got subsequently, or whatever motives were attributed to it, it was professionally-run. I believed in discussing frequently with all of the staff where we were going, what we were doing, having post-mortems, saying a programme was rubbish or was biased or whatever - it was a programme of open debate, with a professional group of people working on it.

Broadcasting styles have changed particularly in interviewing techniques. Interviewing used to be two protagonists, a fight, put on for the benefit of the spectators. Whilst obviously one of the motives was to find out the truth, or to find out what politicians did not want found out, there was a touch of the arena. Politicians have changed - they have been trained for the media, and interviewers have changed. It is not by being antagonistic you find something out, it is by being kind and nice and accommodating, but the audience wanted to see their politicians grilled. We have always been influenced by the British channels - Robin Day was the guru of interviewers. I set about strengthening the studio end of the programme - not just having reporters coming in and out. I coaxed Barry Cowan from the North. That was a new face and a new technique - Barry is an excellent interviewer. I got Olivia O'Leary back from *The Irish Times*. And, of course, there was the old veteran, Brian Farrell. We had a strong front-of-house team. Behind that, our reporters and producers were doing the investigative documentaries - we had a good mix. Interviewing was tough but it was of a style which has now changed everywhere.

The editor has power to influence the documentary, the filmed bit of a programme, a power which frequently he does not exercise enough. There are a number of things in broadcasting that are sent out without any real supervision or editorial input. A lot of things which appear biased are, but through negligence or sheer ignorance. The informed viewer will not know that. Months after I had sent out a programme I might meet somebody at a party who would berate me for its bias. Looking back, you could see that, but, quite honestly, at the time you could not see it - enough attention had not been paid to it, nor enough thoughtt put into it. I do believe that most broadcasters set out to be fair and even-handed. The product may not end up as that. It may be too difficult to get out of your own subjectivity and be completely objective. So things do go out that are one-sided to some - of course these things depend on the eye of the beholder.

News is much easier than current affairs - it's reporting, not comment, and the reports are short. Our main duty is to report accurately and fairly and we do that. RTE has an excellent news service built up over the years. Current affairs is more difficult because it's comment and analysis and what is one person's analysis may not be another's. No matter how hard you try, you may not achieve balance. You are depending on presenters and reporters and producers. They often think they are being fair when they are not. They are influenced by their own background and thinking processes, otherwise they would not be intelligent human beings. They have to strive all the time to see the points of view of others. They have to understand and accept, for example, that people who are anti-divorce, anti-abortion, have valid points of view held in good faith.

You change your mind over the years. If you are a thinking person at all, you will not hold absolute, certain views on a lot of things because you know you may not be right. On issues like freedom to divorce there is a downside which you can see in other countries. The more one lives, the more one sees fewer certainties around. Nothing has replaced the certainties we had growing up. Societies everywhere need some kind of poles in the sand to guide them. While I would be seen by most people as a liberal, I now question a whole lot of things. I have strong beliefs - on social justice, for example. I believe in intellectual honesty. But on some things I would have mixed views, not certain at all, like divorce and abortion. You just wonder if societies everywhere are going towards a period where there will be no values and no rules. Religion, even in Ireland, has no longer much relevance for young people, although humanitarian values do seem to play quite a part. They are concerned about social justice, about the third world - that probably is a result of religious beliefs.

In all this, I believe the importance of television in changing society is exaggerated, but it does *reflect* change. By reflecting the change, it shows it to a greater number of people and brings them more into it.

Television makes it more difficult to have the kind of leadership we had in the past. Icons are not a great idea but, as I said earlier, people do need people of whom they are proud, in whose integrity and capacity and vision they believe. You have this in our present President. People have found in her somebody they respect, who is young, intelligent, honest and attractive and, of course, who does not have to involve herself in the hurly-burly of politics. Societies everywhere need this and have difficulty finding it, be it in France where they have got totally tired of their regime, or in Germany where Helmut Kohl was seen as a bungler and then became a leader and now things are beginning to go wrong. A lot of this is due to television because it is showing people as they were never shown before. It has been good for democracy - the balance sheet is in favour of it in terms of questioning, of acting on behalf of the citizen, in terms of making people answerable. On the other hand, it is very hard on politicians - it shows their eyes in close-up. If they *appear* to be dishonest or unsure or struggling for words or not to know, then one television appearance can be ruinous - and that's frightening. Had television been there, would Churchill have been the figure he was in World War II? De Gaulle, on the other hand, used television but it was cruel to him in the end. Nowadays, politicians realise a bad performance can be a disaster so they train for it and prepare their answers. Is it now self-defeating?

The best thing on television is to tell the truth, to say, if necessary, "I don't know. I am sorry but you have taken me unawares." The electorate are not stupid. They will know when somebody is refusing to tell the truth only because they are afraid of losing votes.

Working in a state-sponsored body is a double-edged sword. On the one hand, it is an environment not motivated by profit, by gain - so far as home broadcasting is concerned, we have a monopoly. That frees us, at least for the moment, from the pressures that are on broadcasters in Britain. On the other hand, it has disadvantages. Perhaps the edge is not always there, it is more difficult to manage, it is sometimes more difficult to get change - technological change or change of work practices - than it would be in a private concern where you have, to put it bluntly, the possibility to hire and fire. It is lacking in the need to survive. But increasingly we are not, for example, like a state-sponsored transport monopoly - we are getting the competition in from the sky, 20 channels, soon 40, soon 100. We are going to have to be very good to survive - and we depend on advertising. The licence fee has not moved since 1986. If we do not get our audiences, we don't get our advertising. At the moment we are getting 50 per cent of the audience. But for how long? Unless we serve our audience, we won't retain that - they will be zapping between the multitude of channels: sports channels, which you already have, arts, culture, ballet, education - all of this is just around the corner. We are a small exposed organisation in a rapidly changing environment and we may not be changing fast enough. To get change in a state-sponsored body, you have to go through a mating dance of negotiations, for ages. You end up in the Labour Court and maybe the Court's recommendation is rejected. You end up with a strike and you're back to square one. That must change. There has to be a new recognition by the trade unions and by management that it is a new age. One, the customer must come first and two, we have to do things in the most effective way possible. I suppose I can't be objective on this, but I do believe that RTE is a good state-sponsored organisation but it could be better and there are things that are irksome. The state-sponsored environment does not always favour the development of talent and creativity.

I don't believe this country can support a third television channel. The resources are not there and it is not necessary in view of the choice that the viewer already has. However, I do believe you need competition and the new independent sector will provide for a creative environment outside RTE and will enable people in RTE to go outside where their talents might flourish better. Then they will be judged on what they produce. It will serve management better - in that way we shall be able to create a spirit of competition and creativity.

We are as free as, if not freer than, most broadcasting organisations. In my whole time in News and Current Affairs, I could count on one hand the number of times that anybody has tried to interfere. Of course, you get complaints - particularly about *not* covering things but there is an incredible realisation that broadcasting must be free in this State. It is to the credit of our political system that it has been. I know that Lemass's phrase is sometimes held up, that RTE is "an arm of Government policy", but I've always thought that has been misinterpreted. It has certainly not been the case.

13

Conor Brady

The Irish Times

There is a tremendous difference, a difference in kind,
between being editor and being anything else in a newspaper. There is
no comparison between any other newspaper job and the commitment
of 24-hour, seven-day-a-week, 52 weeks a year responsibility which
you have mentally, intellectually, emotionally with the paper
when you're the last man down the line.

The conversation took place on May 28 1993

Conor Brady is editor of *The Irish Times*.

He was born in Dublin on April 24 1949.

His father was Conor Brady, a Garda Superintendent at the Force's foundation.

His mother was Amy MacCarthy, who trained as a pharmacist.

He is one of a family of three with two older sisters, Morna and Geraldine.

He is married to Ann Byron, a teacher.

Their children are Neil (12) and Conor (7).

He was educated at St. Columba's CBS, Tullamore; Mount St. Joseph's, Roscrea; and at UCD where he took a BA in history and politics and an MA in politics.

He joined *The Irish Times* as a trainee reporter in 1969. From 1969 to 1973 he was a reporter in, respectively, London, Belfast and Dublin. From 1973 to 1974 he was editor of *The Garda Review*. 1974 to 1976 reporter/presenter RTE. 1976 features writer in *The Irish Times*. 1977 features editor. 1979 assistant editor of *The Irish Times*. 1980 night editor. 1980-82 editor of *The Sunday Tribune*. 1983 assistant editor *The Irish Times*. 1985 deputy editor *The Irish Times* and appointed to the board. December 1986, editor of *The Irish Times*.

Member of the Board of Counsellors of The European Journalism Centre, Maastricht. Governor of *The Irish Times* Literary Awards. A.T. Cross Award for Outstanding Work in Irish Journalism, 1978.

For me it happened by accident. I was never particularly numerate. At an early stage I learned that I was much stronger in languages and particularly English than I ever was going to be in the sciences or maths. When I went to boarding school in Roscrea, I found there was a terrific environment there for the development of one's language or literary skills. There was a great library, active debating societies and a tradition of the boys running their own newspaper, *The Vexillum*. By the standards of the time, it was liberal. It was financed, handily enough, by the school branch of the Legion of Mary whose involvement, however, was peripheral. A number of boys would get together annually: the editor and the manager emerged by consensus. There was no censorship - it was left entirely to ourselves what we put into it. I got heavily involved in it, I loved it - I had little interest in sport.

I did my Leaving Cert in the summer of 1966 and was back in Dublin. I remember well the first time I got paid for writing anything. I was asked by one of the young monks, Father Cathal, to write something for *The Roscrea Review*. I got a ten-bob note in the post by return. This opened up a whole new world of possibilities. You could actually get paid for doing what you liked.

In UCD there was a newspaper called *Campus*. It was fairly serious and was funded by a group of students, in particular John Crimmins, who, I think, had some private money. It was the time when Lord Thompson of Fleet was going around buying up newspapers and we referred to John Crimmins as Lord Crimmins of Hatch - he had a flat over in Hatch Street. Christina Murphy, who now works with me in *The Irish Times*, was the chairman of *Campus*. My first year I was allowed to sell *Campus* on the street outside Earlsfort Terrace - the second year I was editor. Students were news at the time - the Gentle Revolution - and newspapers began to discover the students' constituency. I got a call, unsolicited, from the features editor of the *Sunday Independent*, Ciaran Carty, wanting to know if I would do a weekly column of student news. He was offering me five guineas - a prince's ransom. Student rent in a flat in

Rathmines was probably about two quid. I produced copy for Ciaran every Friday and began to write longer features for the *Sunday Independent* and for other newspapers. I found the most responsive place was *The Irish Times*. They were interested in considered, researched, serious journalism. Donal O'Donovan was the features editor of *The Irish Times* then. He was succeeded by Brian Fallon. It was the time when UCD was moving to Belfield which was only a hole in the ground with some science undergraduates. There had, of course, been arguments for staying in Earlsfort Terrace and expanding around that area. Even looking back on them now, I wrote what I think were two quite rounded pieces on Belfield. Brian presented them marvellously. I can remember my enormous pride in seeing, while I was still an undergraduate, two half-pages on successive days with my by-line. I said to myself this was for me.

I got to know Donal Foley, the news editor in *The Irish Times*. I was in my final year in UCD. One or two college friends who were a bit ahead of me had gone into *The Irish Times* - Henry Kelly and Renagh Holohan. One day Donal Foley asked me, "Do you know anything about anything that nobody else is writing about?" The only thing I knew about apart from my academic experience in UCD was the Gardai because my father had been a founding member in 1922. He had died when I was quite young and in finding out about the man I had found out a lot about the institution. I knew some senior people in the Guards, contemporaries of my father. By an extraordinary coincidence, the Guards, as you well know, Ivor, were about to blow up.[*] The saga which culminated in The Conroy Commission on pay and conditions was to unfold.

You remember there was the famous meeting in The Macushla Ballroom and the "blue flu" in Crumlin where all the gardai went sick at the same time. I made contact with the Garda Representative Body as it was quaintly known. I suddenly found myself in the middle of a story that nobody else was writing. Here was an institution of the State which had

[*] The author was a member of the Conroy Commission on the Garda Siochana.

been passive almost to the point of supineness, suddenly confronted with crimes, public order - and subversion because the troubles in the North had started at that time; bank robberies were taking place; a Garda, Dick Fallon, was shot - the first time a member of the Gardai had been killed since the 1940s. The rank and file were in revolt. The people who were leading the force were coming to the end of their service. It was a tailor-made story. So, just before I joined *The Irish Times'* staff, I did three articles called, not very originally, "A Policeman's Lot".

I joined as a trainee reporter in 1969 immediately following graduation. I did general reporting, continued to cover the Garda saga up to and beyond the Conroy Commission and I did some local government reporting. I was sent off to London in early 1972. I had a lot of experience packed into a few short years. The North had blown up. We were going into the EEC. There was an exponential rate of growth in all sorts of areas, state and semi-state. Research institutes expanded. The civil service grew. Foreign Affairs was out scouring the highways and byways for young people.

London was hard work. I was there a little less than two years as the number two. I learned a lot in Westminster. One thing I learned was not to be intimidated by scale. I was coming from a small, intimate country and found myself working in the heart of the parliament of a large country. You'd go to a cocktail party and find yourself standing beside Ted Heath or Jim Callaghan. You soon realised the only difference between their society and ours was one of size, they were not any more accomplished than we were. Behind the veneer, the average Westminster MP or minister was pretty much the same as the average Dail Eireann minister or TD. In fact, their good ones were not any better than ours. Their thick ones were thicker than ours - and some of them were very thick. London built my confidence as a journalist.

I had done some time in the North before I went to London and hoped to go back there when my London stint was over but the powers-that-were felt that they did not want me to go.

I was brought back to Dublin. I felt I was kicking my heels around the newsroom. Dublin felt a bit smaller and more parochial but a much more pleasant place to live. It was warm and familiar and, for a journalist, there was a compact network but of course I had a great deal less autonomy than I had in London. It was not that I ever resisted the rule of the news-desk but I hadn't anything specific to get my teeth into. I was marking time.

I enrolled in UCD for a postgrad thesis in the Politics Department. My BA had been in history and politics. I picked the rather obscure topic of *Law Enforcement and Security Policy in the Free State, 1922-32*. This again led back to the Garda thing.

The Guards meantime wanted to revive *The Garda Review*, which had been the force's magazine since 1922. They wanted a journalist to run it. They had an editorial board composed of nominees of the various representative associations. The Commissioner had a nominee. Jack Marrinan and Derek Nally offered me the job. I thought it was a wonderful opportunity to start from scratch as the magazine had been defunct for some years. I found it a challenge - even down to learning how to deal with small printing companies. I had to hire a small team, to involve myself in areas such as typography and design, areas of which I had no knowledge. The revived Review was launched early in 1974.

I had the opportunity to draw on an old-established tradition and to blend in with that a lot of contemporary issues and quite provocative stuff. I proposed to the board - and they had the breadth of vision to accept - that the magazine should move away from the social Christmas-number character it had. It became a professional-orientated magazine that would take it upon itself, for example, to interview the Minister for Justice on policy issues rather than asking him to send his Christmas blessings to all the members and their wives and families. It became quite lively and, in its own way, helped to encourage a sense of professional pride.

Then Mike Burns offered me a job in RTE where they were

expanding the radio news. Radio news had been rather staid up to the late 60s. It consisted largely of a newsreader reading the news and that was it. The interactive interview was a relatively recent thing. They had started a 20-minute programme of interviews after the 1.30 news and a programme on Sundays called *This Week*. They were expanding the news at 6.30 and doing one late at night called *News Extra*. The news unit was made up of highly professional news activists who went out to push back the frontiers. Under Mike Burns were Sean Duignan, now head of the Government Information Services, Kevin Healy, now head of radio, Shane Kenny, who now heads that unit. Then there was myself, Cian O hEigeartaigh, Brendan Keenan, now with the *Irish Independent*, Ella Shanahan and Dick Hogan, now both with *The Irish Times*. We took the day on a 24-hour cycle and had three half-hour bites at it.

We had just moved into the era of the lightweight, hand-held broadcast-quality tape-recorder. You did not have to have two sherpas carrying a big recording apparatus around after you. There was also the huge improvement in global telecommunications. If you had a telephone number and a studio, you could talk to anybody anywhere in the world.

One quiet Sunday a few of us were in the office and there was a story in *The Observer* about Idi Amin. It was one of those very detailed *Insight*-type stories you got at that time in the British Sunday papers: "Idi Amin sat down to breakfast and had two boiled eggs, three slices of toast, and two cups of tea. The telephone at his desk rang. The number was Kampala 67122" - or whatever. One of the lads said let's try and get Kampala 67122. We went into the studio and turned on the tapes and rang Kampala. A deep voice replied, "Yaas". Kevin Healy - I think it was - who was sitting beside me, said, "This is The Irish Broadcasting System. We would like to speak to His Excellency President, Fieldmarshal, General Idi Amin". The voice said, "Yaas". Kevin said, "Would it be possible to have a word with His Excellency?" "Dis is he! Dis is de Principal Father!" There he was on the other end of the line. We got a fine 15-minute interview.

You could now dial any congressman you wanted in the United States. It was exciting, but I had a hankering to go back to print and Fergus Pyle easily lured me back to *The Irish Times* as a feature writer. A feature writer is somebody who works to specific assignments over a period of time rather than someone who works to the news-desk roster. You could not be called upon to do the Courts or the Dail or to attend routine press conferences. You also got the odd foreign assignments.

The Irish Times was in some difficulties at the time - Fergus's editorship was not going well because there was a world economic crisis. The commercial side of the operation was in trouble too. Fergus stood down and Douglas Gageby came back in. Peter O'Hara who was the managing director left and Major Tom McDowell again took over responsiblity for the profitability of the company. He had been non-executive chairman - he became chairman and chief executive.

Douglas hit the paper running. This was 1977 and he had left in 1974 when the trust was formed and he had redeemed his shares. I don't know what he thought he would do when he retired but he certainly wasn't doing it. I think he was glad to be back in harness. He came back for the Second Coming, as it's called inside, completely regenerated. He had had four years of rest and recuperation. He was brimming with ideas and energy. He was in his late 50s, old enough not to make too many mistakes and young enough to put plenty of energy into it.

Shortly after he came back, he asked me to take over as features editor and subsequently gave me the title of Assistant Editor and a bit more money and a motor car. I was given responsibility for what you might call the developmental end of the paper. We'd do the weekend supplement together. We expanded the books pages. We gave more space to business and finance. We gave the paper a sharp kick in the direction of a younger generation which *The Irish Times* had not addressed up to then. In the late 70s there was an assumption that young people would grow up and then start reading *The Irish Times*. That really excluded everybody under 25: the young people would not have the sense to see *The Irish Times* was the sort of paper they should read, a dangerous philosophy. I was strongly convinced that those young people did not see Ireland as a self-contained patch of land sitting in the Atlantic but as part of a wider Europe. It was a time of good employment generally. People were tumbling out of the schools and universities and voluntarily going away and coming back and working for a while and then going away again. I was particularly interested in broadening the paper's international horizons. We also decided that we really needed to address the whole area of educational guidance and career development. We felt the paper needed to loosen up a bit in its design and layout. It made for a much more attractive-looking paper.

Anyway, whatever we were doing, we must have been doing it right. Circulation, which had been climbing steadily in the 60s, plateaued in the 70s. It took off again after the changes we made and climbed to 85,000 before Douglas left for the second time.

In 1980, Bill Shannon who was the American Ambassador to Ireland and whom I knew rather well, asked me to go forward for a Nieman Foundation Scholarship to Harvard. It was - and is - *the* foundation for journalists in the United States. It's a one-year programme for journalists, as distinct from journalism. 12 people are selected for it, you get board and lodging, and they bring the great and the good for you to interview. Douglas Gageby had encouraged me and had arranged for me to get leave-of-absence, when I got a telephone call from Hugh McLaughlin, the proprietor of *The Sunday Tribune*. Hugh had just had his parting-of-the-ways with John Mulcahy and asked me to be editor. Smurfits had bought into *The Tribune* with Hughie. I took the view, rightly or wrongly, I would learn a lot more as editor of *The Tribune* than I would in Cambridge, Massachusetts.

No, I did not see myself coming back from the Nieman Scholarship as Douglas's successor. I had not thought things through like that and, in any event, there were a lot of senior people who would have seen themselves also in the succession. But I had reckoned that Nieman would not do me any harm.

In the event, I went to *The Tribune* and, my God, I learned a lot in a little under two years.

There is a tremendous difference, a difference in kind, between being editor and being anything else in a newspaper. There is no comparison between any other newspaper job and the commitment of 24-hour, seven-day-a-week, 52 weeks a year responsibility which you have to have mentally, intellectually, emotionally with the paper when you're the last man down the line. It may well be like that in most institutions but in a newspaper it is even more so. In every single publishing day there are several things that have to be decided only by the editor.

Back to *The Sunday Tribune*. I was, of course, a bit dubious about leaving a relatively soft berth in *The Irish Times*. I was persuaded to go in basically because the Smurfit Group were in there as joint shareholders. *The Tribune* had a talented team of people. Its first flaw, as I saw it, was that it was endeavouring to be a quality Sunday newspaper in tabloid form. Hugh McLaughlin told me to do what I wanted. In three days we changed it to broadsheet. Andy Barclay was the design genius. We had sent a photographer to Kilkenny to take a picture of Jim Gibbons. The photographer came back with a wonderful picture of rolling acres with Jim Gibbons, his arms outstretched, in aquiline profile. In tabloid form, the picture would have been cropped and ruined. We introduced a little colour supplement. The circulation moved from 70,000 when I went in to a peak of 118,000.

I like to describe the episode in the following terms: the newspaper was a success, the company was a failure. The title is still there, the paper in its essence is broadly the same formula. It brought a new quality ethos to Sunday newspapers in this country. By quality I mean a serious addressing of the issues of the week. The tradition had been for the Sunday papers to leave all that aside and to concentrate on GAA and cooking. *The Tribune* broke that and all of the Sunday papers are the better for it. The other titles have had to struggle up to what *The Tribune* was doing, which is ironic given that the other papers are much stronger than *The Tribune* - certainly the *Sunday Independent* is stronger.

In 1982, we went down in a blaze of glory - the liquidator came in, a searing experience. The paper closed and the liquidator sold the title to Vincent Browne.

You go into work in the morning as editor of a national newspaper and at 3.30 in the afternoon a young man with glasses puts his head around the door and says, "Name? Title? Any property in this office belonging to you? Here's a plastic bag, put it in. The keys of your car please." Searing. The liquidator, John McStay, a decent fellow, let me keep the car for a month.

The worst part of all is waiting for the thing to crash. I am not, as I said, particularly numerate but I could see that the lines on the graph were meeting somewhere off the paper. I had brought together a great team of people, most of them from solid jobs. Jim Farrelly was a strong, energetic deputy. Cian O hEigeartaigh had come in from RTE as my assistant editor, Joe Carroll had come back from the European Community to be diplomatic correspondent, one or two people had come from *The Irish Times*. I found it hard to think they would be out of work. Happily, they all got jobs again rapidly.

The Irish Times had said they would find a berth for me if things went wrong. That was comforting. Tom McDowell said I was not to think of myself as cut off, all experience was useful. Douglas Gageby and I would have had an occasional drink together. So I knew I was not going to be idle. When *The Tribune* went out of operation, I spent six months - recovering I suppose. I was quite exhausted at the end of it all. Our first son had just been born - it was ten years before he arrived and we were just getting used to having a baby around the place. It was a difficult time.

I went back to *The Irish Times* initially on a consultancy basis. Tom McDowell wanted me to look at new technology, at information systems that were just beginning to come on stream at that time, things like remote-access databases and so on. I did that for six months and in 1983 finally went back on the staff of *The Irish Times* as assistant editor.

It was obvious Douglas was not going to go on forever. He was coming up to ten years on his second stint. *The Irish Times* was doing well - the circulation had moved up to 83,000 or 84,000. We had managed to make the transition to the photo-composition technology and had got rid of hot metal. We were the first to do that. We needed a new printing press. We had an old Hoe and Crabtree rotary press from the 1950s. It was clapped out, a Heath Robinson thing that could not do any colour. When I went back to the paper the "Press Project" was the big thing. We did not have any cash reserves. We still owed money to the Bank of Ireland. The only thing we did have was a divvy-out from the Reuters shareholding which had been put into gilts and was just sitting there. For two years we searched for a new press and eventually the decision was in favour of a German one, a Uniman 4/2. It was ideally suited to a medium-run paper like ourselves. It was operational in early 86 and gave us colour and also allowed us to have separate sections. I was back in my old developmental role and was given the responsibility of taking the weekend section out of the paper, having it separate and having colour.

Douglas announced in August 1986 he was standing down. The job was advertised. Two rounds of interviews took place. I was appointed in December.

The Haughey Government came in in 87. There was an almost immediate turnaround in economic fortunes. 87-89 were years of great economic growth. We were well placed to take advantage of it because we had our new press. We developed on Friday a separate property section, a sports section on Monday and we now have a Part Two section to the paper every day except Wednesday. You need one day a week free so that you can drop in the occasional special. The new press also allowed us to use colour for advertising and gave us a strong cash flow. We had three really good years 89,90,9l where we made £2m, £3m, £1m and paid off the bank, paid off and improved the press - when it came in originally it was a five-unit press, now it's an eight-unit one. We brought in our new Atex system which allowed direct input, that is the journalists can put their copy directly into the computer without it going through typesetters. What those three years enabled us to do was to get out of debt, refurbish the premises, kit ourselves out technologically. It also allowed me, as editor, to invest a lot more in the editorial infrastructure of the paper. It allowed us to open a modest but respectable series of bureaux in Moscow, Washington and Brussels and now we've opened in Johannesburg. We've expanded our business staff and our politics. And we've expanded the overall size of the paper.

The Irish Times traditionally was weak on sport and one of the things I did was to ensure that it got a decent crack in the paper. There is a terrific response to the full colour separate sports section on Monday. You remember the anomaly where *The Irish Times* sport was in the front of the paper. For years, nobody could tackle moving sport to the back. You turned over page one and saw hockey notes. We moved sport to where sport should be - at the entertainment end of the paper, leaving the front of the paper free for news. We've also had to expand on the paper-of-record thing. When I became a reporter, there were six High Court judges. Now there are 17. It's a huge task just to keep up with the courts.

You ask me who says *The Irish Times* has to be a paper-of-record and I would reply with a question, is there such a thing as a paper-of-record or is it a myth? Most societies have that which is referred to as a paper-of-record. There is the notion you can look back through the window of the printed medium and see how societies were at a particular point in time. I suppose in that sense there is such a thing as a paper-of-record. You should be able to say that was how things looked to reasonably intelligent people in Ireland on any given day, in a given month, in a given year. Some people think a paper-of-record should give an account of everything important that happens in a society. There are pressures on papers like us to be able to do that but really the objective can never be met. To take a simple example: we give almost a page every day to the

Oireachtas. That's more than anybody else. It is as much as any of the London papers will give to covering Westminster. It is a great deal more than *Le Monde* will give to the National Assembly in France. We know we are going to get into that report only a tiny fraction of what is said in the Dail, yet every TD who stands up expects to find his speech in *The Irish Times*. Similarly with the courts. Someone goes through a traumatic piece of litigation, is vindicated, and not a line appears in the paper. As our society becomes more complex - and it is infinitely more complex than it was 30 years ago - there are many more events which are newsworthy. You can cover only a fraction of them and that creates tensions with readers.

I am convinced that the future of serious newspapers like ourselves lies in analysis and in offering the readers a deeper comprehension of the events that swirl about them. The future is in investigation and in good descriptive writing rather than presenting people with a huge amalgam of nuggets of news.

An example - a facetious example - I give to our staff is that I don't believe *The Irish Times* is the sort of newspaper which necessarily will record the facts about every elderly gentleman who falls off a bike and is injured on the roads of rural Ireland, but it should explain to its readers why there has been an increase in the numbers of elderly gentlemen falling off bicycles because of holes in the road and what is being done to prevent that happening. One of our correspondents telephoned me recently and said he had sent in four pieces about accidents that happened on the worst patch of road in Ireland and the items were never published. I asked him why he had not thought of writing a piece about the most dangerous stretch of road in Ireland and of the number of accidents that had happened over it in the last year: here's what the County Engineer says about it; here's what the local Garda Superintendent says about it; and here's what really should be done about it. Then we'll publish it. This came like a shaft of revelation to him and of course we published what he subsequently wrote. You cannot possibly cope with the avalanche of facts that happen every day. You have to filter through them, classify them and present them in some sort of an orderly whole. Otherwise the reader could never get through the paper.

When I talk about analysis, I am not talking about opinion, I am talking about the sort of stuff our political or our business staff will generate. The signed opinion-pieces are meant to be coat-trailing. They are not analysis in this sense - if you look at the top of the page, you will see it clearly says "Opinion".

Take our overseas bureaux. The function of the people there is not necessarily to give us in precise detail a recent legislative measure: they are there to give people a context within which political decisions are taken, to give a strong descriptive framework and internal, detailed analysis.

I think by and large Irish newspapers are good newspapers. They compare well with their international counterparts at whatever level of the market they operate. Even among the less serious newspapers there is never a problem of conscious distortion. Errors and excesses there may be.

Irish journalists are, I think, a good deal more professional now than many of their predecessors might have been. There is much more consideration and more weighing of issues. There is a sense of accountability to readers which wasn't strong when I started as a young reporter.

I believe that increasingly people get a basic day-to-day diet of facts from television and radio. You don't really have to read the front page any more. Some journalists take issue with me and say, "What about news?" I say to them news is what we decide it is - I am not turning my back on news. A serious newspaper's function is not grounded in the recitation of soft news, formula news, the news which is put out by the spin doctors and the PR people. News is what some fellow somewhere is trying to get suppressed. Everything else is advertising. (I think it was Horace Greeley who said that.) When one of my reporters comes to me and says, look what's happening in Mespil Flats, or in Greencore, or what the Provos are going to do next, or what some politician is planning to do

- that's news. That is hard news. It is the most difficult news to get, when you're telling people something they do not know and someone else does not want them to know. That is where the future of newspapers lies rather than in the routine re-presentation of information which is being disseminated by people who, for perfectly good reasons, are anxious to have their flag flown. There's always going to be a large amount of that. We have to cover the AGMs of the public companies. We have to go to the launch of a new campaign to achieve this or that desirable end. We have to cover crime, fires, crashes, cats caught up in trees etc. We have to cover all the set pieces, but increasingly I think newspaper readers will want to have their understanding deepened, their knowledge of situations given an authoritative grounding, they want to know the background to people's personalities, what is it that makes Albert Reynolds act in a particular way or Jacques Delors or Peter Sutherland or Mary Robinson, what is the synergy between Bill and Hillary Clinton - and they want strong descriptive narrative. But at the same time there is this huge pressure to be a newspaper-of-record and we have to do it. We can't get away from it. The Beef Tribunal is a good example. Day after day after day we had to give that long solid page on it.

Yes, there is an *Irish Times* ethos. There always has been. There is also a great volume of myth which has built up around *The Irish Times* ethos. People tend to see in it that which they wish to see, which they choose to see. People in business tend to characterise us as bleeding-heart populists, soft socialists. People on the left see us as the arm of cunning capitalism, a paper which seeks to put a humane face on the Establishment and retards the ultimate logic of the class-warfare. Protestants tend to regard us as being overwhelmed by and in awe of Roman Catholic influences. Catholics see us as the remnants of the Protestant ascendancy. The myths go back even to the beginning of the paper. *The Irish Times* was not founded as the voice of Anglo-Irish unionism. It did go through a unionist phase but it was essentially founded as a paper which believed in the economic separation of Ireland from England. On economic grounds, it supported a continuing political link between the two islands but it was always a lot closer to Grattan than to Carson.

The ethos of the paper does change but certain things are constant. It is a paper which is liberal, tolerant and which seeks to be as broad a church as it can be in terms of social ideology. It is a paper which certainly believes in the freedom of the individual and which tries to combine a sense of Irish nationalism and pride with a recognition that we live in a wider world.

I was at a retirement party in RTE where someone tried to describe what RTE was about - he said Ireland was a parish and it was our job to report on the parish. I agreed with him so far as he went. Yes, *The Irish Times* reports the parish, but it has always been our view that, while Ireland is a parish, there is a much wider diocese out there - if I may extend the ecclesiastical metaphor. It has traditionally been the paper's function to open the windows on the wider world - and also to the varied worlds which exist within our society.

Where do I fit into all that? The trite answer would be to say my values and the paper's are one. Having been here 25 years, on and off, I would have difficulty in disentangling my own views from those of the paper. People sometimes write to me and say, "Why don't you say what your own view is on abortion or on the North?" I write back and tell them to read my editorials - I write a lot of the editorials myself, especially when we're at pivotal points in political or social questions. Even if somebody else writes them, I will give them their final clearance with additions or subtractions.

I am a fairly typical product of the Irish middle-class educational system of the 60s and 70s. Some people would tend to draw a circle around the fact that I am the first Catholic editor of *The Irish Times*. I suppose that has some significance. It would have been more significant if *The Irish Times* had appointed somebody who was not a Catholic. The decision was made purely on the basis of professional suitability. I take lot of inspiration and values from my education in Roscrea. The Cistercian ethos is a positive one and a practical one, too. In political and social terms, I would be slightly left of centre; in economic issues somewhere right of centre. When I was in college I was briefly in the Young Tigers Fine Gael branch along with Vincent Browne, Henry Kelly and John Bruton. I don't think I'd find myself comfortable in the Fine Gael party today. In fact, one of the great delights of my job is that I am supposed to be apolitical. In European terms, I would describe myself strongly as a federalist. We are going through a period of reversals at present but I believe the European voyage of discovery will ultimately go the whole way - it may take a long time. I have an absolute conviction it is only in that context a way will be found to solve the difficulties between ourselves and Great Britain and between the two communities in the North.

I would certainly describe myself as a nationalist but by that I would not mean I am in favour of territorial conquest - there has to be an accommodation between the two communities. Fundamental to that accommodation is that the nationalists have to be given a permanent and irreversible say in the affairs of their own state, something they have never had. The Ango-Irish Agreement is a half-way step in that direction. It changed all the rhetoric about Northern Ireland. I believe that, without it, such groping attempts at a settlement now being made would not be in currency. I think the only problem with the Hillsborough agreement was that people underestimated the time-scale. I don't subscribe at all to the contention that, if only people had consulted the Unionists, the Agreement would have worked. It was necessary to do it the way it was done, to present a fait accompli. Whatever degree of flexibility there is now, following on the success of the working of the Agreement over the eight years, there was none in 1985. I think it would now be possible to take a further step on the basis of a policy agreed between the two Governments, but it would be only a further step, not a final step because, until you have got community consent on both sides, you have at best a framework that is held in place only by the two Governments and from which the two communities withdraw in varying degrees their consent.

I think we've gone through a bruising time of late in this State. We have seen a sequence in which one institution after another has suffered in reputation and in stature. The inability to create a level of employment to keep our young people together has left a terrible sense of failure. The North has poisoned the island. I don't mean the poison has flowed down to us from the North, it is what we have done or failed to do that has poisoned our values. I think there are few criteria with which we can measure ourselves against the wider world and express any pride. We can't do it in terms of the management of our economic affairs, in terms of coping with social change and disadvantage. We have at best a mixed record. In terms of our ability to live with our own identities - and here I mean particularly the North - we have not done well. And we have not shown any great capacity for preserving the things that are valuable in this society, such as our environment and the quality of life.

And yet, for all that, there are grounds for hope. I think things have got to the point where the ordinary people, the ordinary voter, realises those in power have been playing ducks and drakes with them. I believe there's going to be an insistence on higher standards, on more transparency and honesty. I think there is going to be greater concern for the environment. Health and education policies are going to be much more rigorously tested in the furnaces of public opinion before they get off the ground. We are growing up and probably growing up quickly, which is always a painful process.

The recent elections have been telling us something important. The Mary Robinson election was significant. The fact that the Fianna Fail party failed several successive times to secure overall majorities and has become reconciled to that, the fact of the enormous vote for Labour at the last election, these are things of significance and do indicate that, for much of the hypocrisy and slyness and lip-service, the jig is up. The penny has dropped with the people. The jig is up for a lot of the politicians and the mandarins and the bishops and for certain sections of the business community and for the trade unions - and the media, probably. We have a much more demanding, alert and aware population which is not going to be fobbed off with easy formulae and which insists on knowing why certain decisions are taken or not taken. However much the Labour Party may have gone down in people's estimation for the way they handled themselves after the last election - and I carry no particular flag for the Labour Party - I think the reality is the politicians now know much more is expected of them. People are not simply prepared to take pat answers. The background tragedy to all this is the huge level of unemployment - the widening gap between the better off and those who are not so well off.

There are two points which may give us some confidence and perhaps a small degree of pride: confidence in the sense that the demographics are probably going to take care of the longer term unemployment - and I say that in the bleak knowledge that this society has been able to offer no opportunity to tens of thousands of young people, the lost generation. The demographics will hopefully bring about a closer correlation between the number of jobs available and the people coming onto the labour market. And the thing we can take pride in is that, despite all I've just said, we have managed a good degree of income redistribution. We have at least ensured that people who are in need of some help can get it. God knows, it can't be enough, but we have done reasonably well in comparison with what Britain and France have done or certainly Spain and Portugal. We have, in certain respects, approached almost Scandinavian standards relative to our resources. No matter how we moan and groan about the tax burden, I think we all understand it has been right to divert income to those people for whom we have not been able to provide employment. In years to come we shall take some small pride in that. And that's probably all of the one seamless garment of the tradition of generosity we've had for voluntary giving.

The future is uncertain. It's difficult to run quality

newspapers in a small society because you don't have the economies of scale. It costs as much, for example, for me to keep a bureau in Washington as it costs the editor of a UK daily with a population base of 60m people. That's why you'll always find good newspapers are expensive in small countries - you'll find that in Israel, in Denmark, in Switzerland.

We face other problems too. Mass-media world-wide are concentrating into conglomerates on a scale which makes the barons of yesteryear appear puny. People like Rupert Murdoch or Conrad Black have a frightening concentration of media power. They can mobilise such resources of capital that any target they set their minds to is vulnerable. How can the independent media of small countries like this compete on equal terms with these giants? If they decided to target our small local markets, we would be forced to fight a war of attrition. If you have war-chests like Independent Newspapers, that can be done. *The Irish Times* would have to rely on its quality and the loyalty of its readership.

Apart from the threat of the Murdochs and the Blacks, there is also the threat of what American editors describe as the age of a-literacy - people can read but won't. There are so many other ways of absorbing information, more attractive and less troublesome. This has caused a steep drop in US newspaper reading although there are now signs of it bottoming out. You can be sure we'll follow the same path. We can cope with that by diversification into other forms of communication - data base, electronic archives etc. We have to learn like Mr. Vanderbilt that we're in the information business and not just the newspaper business. He discovered that he wasn't just in the railway business - he was in the transport business.

I consider myself not just the most fortunate person in Irish journalism but one of the most fortunate people in this country. *The Irish Times* Trust is a charter for excellence in journalism and places the editor of *The Irish Times* in an enviable position. I'm responsible to the directors - of which I am one - for the implementation of editorial policy and content. We don't have shareholders in the usual sense so any money we make goes back in one way or another into the paper. That's what allows us to do many things which are not ordinarily within the reach of a relatively small company in a small country.

14

Brian Looney

The Kerryman

*I don't think an editor's values are all that important - they should
not dominate the newspaper. I don't like the image of the traditional
thundering editor telling people what he thinks - and there are still
plenty of them around. The editor should not be seen in his
newspaper.*

The conversation took place on September 10 1993

Brian Looney is editor of *The Kerryman*.

He was born in Cork on December 13 1959.

His father is Thomas Looney, a retired psychiatric social worker.

His mother was Elizabeth O'Brien, a dressmaker.

His step-mother is Joan Higgison, who married his father in 1980.

He is the second youngest in a family of four, three brothers, Michael, Aquinas and Ivor.

He was educated at Presentation College, Cork.

He first worked with a mechanical construction company in Cork, Mechcon, as a personnel assistant, 1978-1980; reporter in *The Limerick Echo* 1980-1984; reporter in the *Irish Press* 1984-1986; 1986 he joined Independent Newspapers as a news reporter, later that year promoted to group industrial correspondent; 1988 editor of *The Kerryman*.

His hobbies are reading, travel, current affairs, politics, talking and cooking. His real hobby is his job.

When you asked me about hobbies for the biographical bit, I realised the huge role work plays in my life. No more than anyone else, I like to get away from things, but working in newspapers offers a job you can really become absorbed in. To an extent, you could say I'm being paid for my hobby. Some people, through force of circumstance, have to do things they hate or at least dislike. I am lucky. I enjoy enormously the diversity of my work. While it would be true to say I drifted into newspaper journalism, I have had a keen interest in the media in general since I was a teenager.

Presentation College, my school in Cork, was an enlightened one with a marvellous principal, Brother Jerome Kelly. He was fascinated with the media and, going back to the 70s, he put media studies on the school curriculum, something unheard of at that time. He had a mini-TV studio in the school. The fifth-years had two hours of media studies every week and then, during a full week in the year, they actually produced a TV or radio documentary. That caught my interest in the media even though I was gearing myself to become an accountant. However, some months before the Leaving Cert, a senior executive from Mechcon - now in liquidation - came to the school looking for young people to train in various management functions. I was offered the position of personnel assistant. I worked there for two years under the personnel manager, Brian Devine, and enjoyed it. It was a good company, employing almost 300 people, and I learned a lot.

At that time a friend of mine, Fergal Keane - a nephew of John B. Keane - was working for *The Limerick Leader*. He always wanted to be a journalist. At 16, his ambition was to work as a foreign correspondent in South Africa and now he's the BBC correspondent out there. He rang me one day and told me a reporter's job had come up on *The Limerick Echo*: "Looney, it's the job for you". I talked my way in and quickly realised that Fergal was right - it *was* the job for me.

While Fergal was passionate about the reporter's role in society, I was always more interested in the editor's role and in the control of newspapers. By the time I was 22, the editor,

Martin Byrnes - a man with a unique personality - had ceded all the organisational side of his job to me. *The Limerick Echo* had been going since 1889. It closed in 1985, a terrible shame after nearly 100 years. I suppose I saw the writing on the wall but that was not the reason I left.

In 1984, I felt that, if my career was to progress, I would have to work on a daily newspaper. Dermot Walsh who worked for the *Irish Press* in Limerick recommended me to the then Group news editor, Michael O'Kane. I arrived in Burgh Quay in November 1984, the week of that dreadful air tragedy at Eastbourne which claimed the lives of all crew and passengers, including four journalists: Niall Hanley, John Feeney, Tony Henegan and Kevin Marron. That was a harrowing story for any journalist to report on.

What I learned in the *Press* was how to write news and how to behave responsibly as a journalist. There were high standards there and a past with the *Irish Press* was a badge of honour. When I announced to my colleagues that I was going to join Independent Newspapers, it was regarded by some as an act of treachery. I was standing in the bar of the Horse and Tram, a pub on the quays, and a senior *Press* journalist came in and put his hand on my shoulder and said, "Brian, why are you leaving?" It was the first time he ever spoke to me. I have since become a good friend of his. What the *Irish Press* needed at the time was leadership and it did not get it. It's a shame to see what's happening now to what were fine newspapers. That was in 1986 and, while the decay started in the *Press* in 1981/82, it had not at that stage damaged morale in the newsroom. Within six months of my leaving, things changed dramatically - including the unexpected departure of Tim Pat Coogan.

Do you know, I feel as if I'm doing my obit!

It's ironic that many of the people I worked with in the newsroom of the *Irish Press* now hold senior editorial posts with Independent Newspapers. There were fine journalists in the *Press*: Paul Dunne, now the Group news editor of Independent Newspapers, was assistant news editor of the *Evening Press* at the time; Philip Molloy, who was in the *Irish*

Press newsroom, is the news editor of the *Irish Independent*. Other journalists in the *Press* at the time included John Downing, now Brussels correspondent of Independent Newspapers; Tim Hastings, now Group industrial correspondent for Independent Newspapers; Michael Woolsey, night editor of the *Irish Independent*; John Spain, supplements editor of the *Irish Independent*; Sean MacConnell, agricultural correspondent with *The Irish Times*; Stephen Collins, the political correspondent who makes *The Sunday Press* essential reading; and Ann Flaherty who now works as a freelance journalist in Johannesburg.

I enjoyed working best on the *Evening Press*. You learned to think on your feet and your journalistic reflexes had to be finely tuned. You rarely had time to write reports - you spent a lot of time on doorsteps trying to get quotes from people or in telephone kiosks dictating news to copy-takers from your raw notes. Someone said at the time, "I've been on more doorsteps than your average milk bottle."

There were journalists in the *Press* who had been there for 20 years and never knew what happened to their copy when it left them. What shocked me more was they didn't really care. If you understand what happens to your copy and if you know the ethos of the newspaper, you will know a particular story will make eight paragraphs or it will make a lead page which will be 16 paragraphs. I would write the stories to exactly the right length so that the subs could not change them. I knew a young journalist who used to fascinate me by turning out 30 paragraphs of a story for *The Herald*. I'd ask him, "Where are you going with that? You know what's going to happen to it? You will be complaining tomorrow it was distorted because you had not done your end of the job."

Michael O'Toole, a columnist with the *Evening Press*, is a great character who was kind to me when I worked there. He advised me about junkets. I told him I had been invited on a travel writers' trip to Yugoslavia, "Well, young man," he said, "Enjoy yourself and, when you return, write nothing and astound your hosts with your ingratitude."

Dermot Walsh, who as I said recommended me for the job in the *Press*, had joined the *Sunday Independent* as a features writer. I met him one evening and he told me there were four reporters jobs coming up with Independent Newspapers. I told him I was happy enough with the *Press* but he encouraged me to apply anyway. I gave it some thought and decided Independent Newspapers was a house of opportunity - it was better managed and there was more movement. The very size and international dimension of the organisation attracted me. Vinnie Doyle was the editor of the flagship, the *Irish Independent*; Aengus Fanning had recently been appointed editor of the *Sunday Independent*; and Michael Brophy was taking *The Evening Herald* from strength to strength. Joe Hayes was the new managing director.* I was 25 years old, felt it was the right move, applied and got one of the four jobs.

After six months as a general news reporter, I was appointed Group industrial correspondent. That was 1987, the time of the negotiation of the first version of the PESP and the major ESB strike which saw the then Minister for Labour, Bertie Ahern, emerge as a peacemaker.

I enjoyed living and working in Dublin but when I was offered the editorship of *The Kerryman* I felt I had to accept and to move to Kerry. It came about suddenly. The then Group news editor, Michael Denieffe - now editor of *The Evening Herald* - asked me over a cup of coffee if I would be interested. He arranged for me to meet Joe Hayes and Bryan Cunningham, managing director of *The Kerryman*. Somebody asked me about my interview with Joe Hayes and I told him he walked around during it. He asked me what I did and I told him that I walked around with Joe. Joe asked me what I thought should be done with *The Kerryman* and I told him jackboot techniques were out, it was a sensitive time for the organisation, what was needed was to bring people together. The last thing needed was that I would be perceived as a young pup down from Dublin.

Incidentally, the first time I met Joe was in *The Kerryman* in 1985. The *Irish Press* was shut for seven weeks because of

* See Epilogue.

industrial relations problems. I was in *The Kerryman* newsroom visiting a friend who worked there, when Joe walked in. He had just been appointed managing director and was on a meet-the-troops presidential tour. The very next time I met him was in 1988 when he offered me the job.

I was 28 years old which must have made me the youngest newspaper editor in the country at the time. I was proud to be offered the editor's chair at a paper which still is the most prestigious of the regional titles. The leadership of men like Dan Nolan - who owned the newspaper before it was bought out by Independent Newspapers in 1973 - and the current managing director, Bryan Cunningham, coupled with the editorial talents of my two immediate predecessors, Con Casey and Seamus McConville, put it in that position. My most difficult task has been keeping it there.

My immediate predecessor, Seamus McConville, had a daunting reputation. He has been embroiled in many controversies over the years. He was under police protection for a while in the 70s. He had got Con Houlihan to write for *The Kerryman*. Con wrote a strong piece about the Price sisters, that they should not be released from jail. At the time, there were a couple of IRA pockets around the country and one of them happened to be in Tralee. There was one in Nenagh and another in Shannon. There was a death-threat on Seamus. He checked it out and it was serious - either Houlihan's column comes out or we're going to get you. Seamus, of course, went ahead. It was under his stewardship the paper achieved its highest ever circulation figures, over 40,000 copies per issue. Circulation today is just hovering under 35,000 copies per issue but that is in line with market trends as new smaller publications - segmented low-cost operations - enter the market. Between 1990 and 1993, l6 new media organisations have entered *The Kerryman's* circulation area. These competitors have made us cost-conscious and innovative in improving the quality of *The Kerryman*.

I have worked hard at broadening the focus of the paper. New sections have been introduced - sports and leisure,

Colourplus, a lifestyle magazine-type section edited by Seamus McConville, a separate features section including, unusually for a local newspaper, a lively letters section. Most of the letters published are from Kerry people. They tend to be in response to articles. When readers have access to the columns of a newspaper, it comes alive. If a newspaper is a nation talking to itself, *The Kerryman* is Kerry people talking to themselves.

There is no public relations ethos in Kerry. People ring up the news desk to complain that there was no photographer at a particular do and Gerry, the news editor, will invariably answer, "But nobody told us it was on." When we tell them we were never invited, they tell us we're supposed to know these things. The Tralee Racegoers Supporters Club have a press conference every year. A huge number attend. This year no journalist from *The Kerryman* was invited.

I don't think an editor's values and views are all that important - they should not dominate the newspaper. He or she should be more like a chairman, listening to the views of the public and journalists and making sure there is a proper forum for them to air their views. I don't like the image of the traditional thundering editor telling people what he thinks - and there are still plenty of them around. The editor should not be seen in his newspaper. Tim Pat Coogan ran a successful newspaper for 20 years and Damien Kiberd has written in glowing terms about him, but towards the end he became bigger than the newspaper. The editor's job is to produce a newspaper for a specific market - I don't see it as a high calling to moralise. That day is gone - you should never underestimate the intelligence of the reader.

I have always argued, I believe passionately, that journalists are too middle-class. Pick any of the people in a newsroom, pick the executives or the news editors, and you'll find invariably they live on the DART, their spouse always works. For your average journalist, the family income could be anywhere between £40,000 and £50,000, depending on what the spouse does for a living. They are comfortable people. What do they do socially? They live in those lovely houses in the suburbs where all the neighbours are like them. When the journalists leave the office, where do they go? They go to Mulligans or the Horse and Tram or to a couple of pubs around that area. Who do they drink with? They drink with themselves. Then they go back out to suburbia and maybe have dinner with their friends. They lead those lovely lives and then, in the newsaper, they have to take decisions on the angles at which they approach particular stories.

People have a lot of faith in newspapers. Irish newspapers are, generally speaking, responsible. When people reach out in the morning for the pint of milk to put on their cereal, they don't expect it to be sour. In the same way, people should be confident their newspaper will be fair, truthful and accurate. A newspaper has a life of its own and, like all living things, it must constantly develop and grow. An editor must have the ability to listen because the most significant stakeholders in any newspaper are the readers - without them the newspaper would not exist. The shareholders make it possible - they bankroll it. The editor, who is only a custodian, makes it happen every day - but it is the readers who give it life. When I hear the rustle of a newspaper, I hear it breathe.

We did a lot of qualitative research last year. Robin Challis, from Lansdowne Market Research, held up a board with animals on it and asked which animal the panel would associate with *The Kerryman*. There was a lion and a lioness lying down very contented and somebody said, "That's *The Kerryman*" - you have finished the week and you know everything that's going on, you're fully briefed, it's contentment. Another identified with a cat about to pounce - you know it's Thursday and it'll be out, I can't wait to get my hands on it to know about the sports.

The biggest change in *The Kerryman* since my arrival has been the introduction of new technology which, I believe, we are exploiting more successfully than any other newspaper in this country. Unlike the situation in the UK, we achieved that without any major industrial relations problems because of the constant dialogue with the unions and with individual employees. The age profile of the staff also helped as we were able to operate a voluntary redundancy programme which attracted sufficient numbers of people. We now have the most advanced pre-press newspaper production system in the country and others come to learn from us. All our pages are assembled on computer screen prior to printing. This is still unusual in Ireland but the norm in other countries. In response to the changing tastes of the readers, *The Kerryman* has been totally redesigned in the past three years. I adopted a gradual approach and subtly introduced new typefaces, a total new house style and a more innovative approach to photography. Visually it is totally different from *The Kerryman* of pre-1988. And it has paid off. This year, against 300 newspapers in Ireland and the UK who were nominated, we won one of the Newspaper Design Awards sponsored by Linotype Hell and the magazine, *Newspaper Focus*.

It hasn't all been plain sailing. The manner of my appointment was met with some resistance by members of the National Union of Journalists - of which I have always been a staunch supporter - who held protest meetings and issued statements to the media critical of the management style of *The Kerryman* and Independent Newspapers. It was a change for me to be featuring in the news rather than reporting on it.

Journalists sometimes forget they are not the only ones who contribute to a newspaper's success. *The Kerryman* is lucky to have enthusiastic staff in every department: the men and women who work in dispatch and circulation, getting the newspaper to the newsagents on time; the printers and camera-room staff; the compositors and typesetters who get the advertising and local notes into print; the administration staff who work the switchboard and pay the bills; and the people who look after our advertisers. The journalists, of course, provide the raw material - the news. They inform and they entertain. They ensure the public is kept aware of what they are entitled to know - whether they want to know it or not. They ensure there is public accountability from public figures - in business, politics, religion or in the community in general. The senior staff are the assistant editor, Gerard Colleran, the sports editor, John Barry, the chief sub-editor, Declan Malone, and the chief news reporter, Conor Keane. They head up a damn good team. I am proud of the role of women on our editorial staff. "Lady journalists" at flower shows and fashion evenings are long gone. I have always been used to strong and competent women journalists on news teams. At the *Irish Press* I worked with journalists such as Maol Muire Tynan, now *Irish Times* political reporter, and Ann Flaherty who I mentioned is freelancing in South Africa. In Independent Newspapers there was Catherine Donnelly as industrial reporter and Dail reporter Lorna Reid. Here in *The Kerryman*, Deirdre Walsh, Breda Joy, Catherine Halloran and Mary Dundon cover anything from a political scandal to a hurling match, from a fashion show to a murder investigation or the first day at an infants' school. It's called professionalism.

It is important that journalists don't think in a censorious way - say to themselves that the editor would never accept that. We carried a story about the Southern Health Board and condoms and about a Kerry priest who was the father of a child - these were news stories. It was what was happening around us. It is not our job to censor. I would rather journalists express their ideas and subject them to debate at an editorial conference rather than not air them at all. If ideas are not in line with editorial policies, they can be tempered. I would not like to be seen as restrictive. On the other hand, I would be furious with a journalist abusing his or her position. If, for example, I heard of one who had a bad meal in a hotel and threatened the manager with writing about it in *The Kerryman*, I would be appalled and would take disciplinary action. That would be a terrible abuse of privilege.

A responsible newspaper has an obligation to provide the public with the information they are entitled to in a democracy. To meet that obligation, it is important to ensure the public want to buy the newspaper. In the modern world, that's where marketing has a real role in newspapers. It means that, in order to compete in a changing media world, we have to put elements other than hard news in a newspaper. There is a need for more analysis, more lifestyles features, plus extended functional information in the form of TV guides and what's-on guides. A newspaper must be an attractive package.

I have always held that view - even in my early days with the *Press*. I was sitting in Mulligans in Poolbeg Street one night having a pint with a senior editorial executive. I was not long in the *Press* at the time. He said, "Tell me, Brian, why do you think people buy the *Evening Press?*" I told him they would buy it for a variety of reasons including to see what was on TV; they buy it because they want to get a flat; they want to get a second-hand car; they buy it because they want to see what's on in the cinema. He looked at me horrified, "You mean you don't think they buy it for the news?" I told him that we gave them the news as well. Outraged he said, "If I believed that, I'd resign now". It is naive of journalists to think that people buy evening or morning newspapers primarily for the news.

15

Michael Keane

The Sunday Press

*In my editorials, what I try to do is to examine a situation and,
if possible, suggest a way forward. I don't like admonishing people
and simply kicking them for having done something I did not
agree with. I believe newspapers have a responsibility
to be positive, not just to knock.*

The conversation took place on June 10 1993

Michael Keane is the editor of *The Sunday Press*.

He was born in Ballytore, Co. Kildare on December 27 1946.

His father was Gerald Keane, a primary school teacher.

His mother, Kathleen Kealy, a housewife.

He is the eldest of a family of three with two sisters, Rita and Mary.

He is married to Jennifer Asquith, a teacher.

Their children are Aoife (13), Michael John (11), and Simon (7).

He was educated at Levitstown National School; Christian Brothers, Athy; and took a Diploma in Journalism in the College of Commerce, Rathmines, Dublin.

1965 copy-boy trainee journalist in the *Irish Press*. 1967 junior reporter. 1970 senior reporter. 1972 Northern editor the Irish Press Group. 1978 assistant editor *Irish Press*. 1979 deputy chief news editor of the Group. 1984 news editor and deputy editor of *The Sunday Press*. December 1986 appointed editor of *The Sunday Press*.

External examiner in journalism in The College of Commerce, Rathmines.

Played football and hurling and won a county medal for football. Now an enthusiastic sports spectator. Theatre and music of all kinds.

I was listening to Rodney Rice on RTE 1 yesterday, and his background knowledge of the topics under discussion was extraordinary. He was able to remember the name of every town in Croatia and what part they played in the Vance-Owen plan. Then he switched over and was talking about Cambodia with equal expertise. Eanna Brophy from *The Sunday Press* does the TV preview on *Today at Five* on RTE Radio and has watched people like Rodney Rice and Myles Dungan at first hand over the years. He is amazed at the skill of Myles Dungan when, for example, a late story breaks. The producer puts someone on live for him to talk to, slips him a few questions and then he is on his own. He takes the interview in his stride as if he has rehearsed it for ages beforehand. Journalists like Rodney and Myles have to be well informed and in general journalists are well informed. They must have that natural curiosity if they are to make it in the business. I suppose it was the natural curiosity which brought me into journalism though there was no background in journalism in my family.

My father was a teacher from Galway who came to a little town called Ballytore. He was from Abbeyknockmoy, near Tuam. They have the distinction in recent years of winning both the hurling and football Galway county championships. They linked up with Monivea. It's extraordinary that two parishes in rural Ireland would unite about anything. Tomorrow I am going down to the 40th wedding anniversary of his only surviving brother and that should be a bit of fun. Coming to the age I am, a lot of my parents' generation have disappeared. At my mother's funeral, only some months ago, one of my cousins said to me, "We have to stop meeting like this. We meet only at funerals. We'll never meet at weddings because none of us can afford to invite all the cousins we have to a wedding." So he decided to have a surprise party for Peadar, my uncle. Anyway, my father was trained here in St. Pat's in Dublin and then went down to Ballytore, which is famous as a Quaker settlement. My grandmother, Mary Kealy, had an emporium which sold everything from a tyre to a ton of coal, rubber boots to a pint of milk, bread to a kit-out for the children. Her shop literally ran the length of the village. It's still there, run by another family. In the late 50s she saw that the car was changing the face of rural Ireland - people were driving to Carlow or Athy once a week to do their shopping. She sold up and bought a pub in Carlow. Unfortunately, the solicitor ran away with the money. She was left struggling.

We lived with her for a while and Daddy used to run the pub for her in the evening. She was a formidable lady - a great poker player, quite stern, respected, liked and feared by a lot of people. She was domineering, wore long black clothes and you did not step out of line. Her husband had been a farmer and she was able to talk to the farmers on their level. As happens, mothers-in-law and sons-in-law don't always get on and my father said we were leaving. My mother had been in hospital, quite sick with TB. Daddy survived TB - the drugs to cure it had come in just in time. There was a lot of TB around then. My mother was in hospital for four years: two years, a break and two further years. We moved to Athy principally because my father had a friend there, Paddy Drennan. Paddy organised a house for us. It was also handy for the school in Ballytore, six miles away.

So I have childhood memories of Athy, Ballytore and Carlow. A child running around in a pub can get away with all sorts of devilment. You have places to hide that you would not find in an ordinary house. On big days, like a football match, you'd run around collecting glasses, delivering sandwiches and having great fun. Peter and Robbie Archbold, sons of one of my grandmother's daughters, have inherited the pub but I must say I wouldn't fancy living in one now - it's a cruel and tough life.

I spent a year in Peamount Sanitorium with TB - it was really rest and some drugs. I was just 11 at the time. I did the old Primary Cert in hospital. There was a teacher in the ward with about ten pupils. The year in hospital had an effect on me in the sense that the whole rhythm of my life was disrupted - I was plucked away from the natural progression of completing my primary education and going on to secondary school. I was late - October, November - arriving into secondary school.

First year in secondary is a big change from primary. It took me at least a year to catch up.

It's fashionable now to kick the Christian Brothers - they are being blamed for all sorts of things. There were Brothers, and indeed some lay people working with them, who were fairly brutal. There was one Brother who was almost a psychopath - he had no idea what was right or wrong. He would beat people around the place. He would line you up and, almost without giving you a chance to find out whether or not you knew your poetry, he would give you a crack on the jaw. But, on balance, the Brothers I came across, and the lay people, were fantastic. I got a great education in that school. They were interested not just in the academic side but in the broader development of the pupils. When I expressed an interest in going into journalism, the then boss, Brother Patrick Dalton, instead of laughing because there was no tradition of journalism in Athy, which had no paper of its own, immediately said, "Right. Why don't we start a school magazine?" He made me editor of it.

In Athy you had people like Liam Ryan, the father of ex-Senator Brendan Ryan. He was a tremendous teacher of English, Latin and Irish. His enthusiasm for the English language was incredible. He engendered a love of it in all his pupils. There was great competition between myself and Brendan and others as to who was going to write the best essay of the week. If you got eight or nine out of ten you'd sing the whole way home.

The summers in Athy were filled with playing tennis, taking part in tournaments in places like Carlow and Portlaoise, and with playing football and hurling. We revived the local soccer team. We called ourselves The Athy Tigers. The Christian Brothers did not like you playing soccer. We went up to borrow a football from them once and their excuse for not giving it to us was the panels on the ball were different.

Daddy wanted to send my two sisters to boarding school because they were at an age when study did not come easy. He said to me, "If you want to go to university, fine, but I can't do both." I said that that was OK, I was going to try and get a job anyway and planned to go to university when I got to Dublin. The two girls went to Cross and Passion College, Kilcullen and benefited tremendously from it. They moved to Dublin afterwards - so we were all here together. I shared a flat with both of them at different times. We are still close.

There was no particular incident or encounter that sparked off my interest in journalism. However, I always had the feeling I wanted to make a difference, that I could look back at the end of my days and say that. And the way I thought I would achieve something was in journalism. It excited me: the idea of getting out there and learning how the world functioned, the people in it - I had an innate curiosity I got from my mother. If you don't want to know things, then forget about journalism.

I wrote to all the newspapers in Dublin and about 20 provincials. None of the provincials had vacancies. *The Irish Times* didn't respond. The *Independent* wrote back and said if I had any relative in the company they would consider interviewing me. The *Irish Press* wrote back and said they were calling people for interview in October and would put me on the list. I thought that was their way of saying goodbye but they did call me.

52 were called for interview with the then chief news editor, Bill Redmond, and Colm Traynor, who ended up as managing director. If we got past that, we were told, we'd be on a short-list of 12. Bill Redmond addressed me as "Mr. Keane" - to this day I can't get over that, "Mr. Keane" at the age of 17! He asked me why I wanted to be a journalist. It was on the tip of my tongue to say I loved meeting people and the usual old stuff that you get at these interviews, when I suddenly said no to myself: these guys have been sitting here all morning. So I answered, "I don't want to die from a heart attack at the age of 40 behind a bank manager's desk." They burst out laughing. It was probably the first laugh they had all day. Bill asked me, "What guarantee do you have, Mr. Keane, that you won't die at the age of 40 behind a reporter's desk?" I said, "None - but at least I'll have enjoyed myself." Then Bill Redmond said, "I see where you went to the Christian Brothers' school in Athy. Did

you know a Brother Kelly?" I answered no and he said, "Are you sure you went to Athy? And you don't know one of the most famous Christian Brothers ever?" I thought to myself that was it. My father was waiting outside and I told him I did not think I had done well. I was called for the second interview. The night before, I was going to the shop to get messages for my mother and I met a man called Frank O'Brien, a local merchant, delivering groceries and coal. I stopped him and asked, "Frank, didn't you go to the CBS in Athy? Did you ever hear of a Brother Kelly?" Frank would have been in his mid-30s and, so far as I was concerned at the time, ancient. He said, "Oh yes, but he was way before my time. He was a great maths teacher and left Athy to go to Wexford." At the second interview I had not got three paces across the floor when Bill Redmond barked at me, "What have you found out about Brother Kelly?" I flopped into the chair thinking I was done for but repeated what little I knew. The rest of the interview, far from being intensive, was almost like reading me my rights when I had got the job. I started on a Monday morning as a copy-boy trainee journalist and Bill Redmond called me up and told me I was a lucky man I knew about Brother Kelly. He wanted to know had I the nose to find out. It's a story I tell when I occasionally lecture in Rathmines or DCU.

My first job in the *Irish Press* was on the Diary where you had to keep a record of all up-coming items, things that might be worth covering - courts where a guy had been charged with murder and been remanded in custody until May 4 at Fermoy District Court or wherever. I got to see how the whole reporting job was done. It was tremendously exciting to be in the newsroom in the middle of the day. With an evening paper, you are depending on the breaking news and, when a big story happens, it's fantastic the speed at which the story can be gathered. I was left on the Diary too long but eventually a vacancy arose and I became a junior reporter.

I was like a pig in muck - I absolutely adored it. They gave you more and more responsibility. There were certain jobs a junior did not do - for example, during President Kennedy's visit, I could be working on it all right but not reporting on his meeting with President de Valera, unless, of course, you happened to be there on the spot and then you had to do it. On a daily basis guys you were working with were helpful - even the guys from the other papers. If you missed something, you could go to the guy from *The Irish Times* or the *Independent* or *The Cork Examiner*, and he would fill you in. Of course, if it was a major scoop for them, they would be off like a bat out of hell and they wouldn't give you anything. If you are covering a County Council meeting and one reporter has to go out to the toilet at a crucial stage, there's no point in getting a scoop over him. All it does is build up bad blood. There are good relations between journalists but they are also competitive. If you were out on a major murder or fire, you made sure you got to the phone box before the *Herald* guy. There are many stories of skulduggery - like jamming a penny in the phone box so that the other guy can't make his call. All in all, there is a healthy competitive environment in Dublin, but not nasty. But, don't get me wrong, the rivalry is intense, particularly between the Independent and the Press Groups.

In 1969, the Northern troubles broke out. Partially on the basis that we were young, unmarried and therefore relatively expendable, and could run fast, we were sent up to cover the riots in Derry and Belfast, principally to help out senior guys who were based up there at the time. Paddy Reynolds was the Northern editor - a wonderful reporter, one of the three best journalists I have ever come across. He is still enjoying good health in retirement in Belfast. Paddy was suffering from fierce pressure. We had a lot of tough experiences covering riots. It was highly dangerous, particularly if you did not know your way around Belfast. You could wander down a couple of streets and find yourself in a dangerous area. I covered everything, including major press conferences with Chichester-Clarke, the Prime Minister, where we were competing with live television. I remember *The Evening Press* being held back a few minutes so that we could get the press conference in. I got great journalistic experience in the North. I was young then and able to take it - the package holidays were just starting so I went off to Corfu or Majorca, had a ball, and got stuck in again.

In the late 70s, they realised the troubles in the North were not going to go away. The fireman approach of sending people up and down just wasn't on - we needed a more permanent arrangement. They staffed up and Vincent Browne was appointed Northern editor. He was there with Paddy Reynolds and Ciaran McKeown. So you had a full staff. There were still occasions when we were required to go up and help out - for example, in the aftermath of Bloody Sunday which was a huge story. It was a traumatic time and extremely sad for the victims and their families. The following Sunday there was a mass march in Newry where everybody expected a repeat, but it passed off quietly.

The one thing that stands out, in the midst of all the troubles, is the resilience of the people there and their sense of humour, often black. It takes an awful lot to knock them down. I have seen whole streets devastated by a bomb and, within half-an-hour, the shop-keepers were out boarding up the windows, fixing their stalls and selling their produce again.

In the aftermath of Bloody Sunday, some of the victims were buried in Derry, some in Donegal. The world's press was there - it was the first time I saw "the world's press". A lot of them were staying in the old City Hotel in Derry - it was bombed out later. There were three days of mourning in all the Catholic areas. We filed our copy, page after page of descriptive stuff on the funerals. We sat down late to have a drink. Michael Hand, now executive editor with *The Sunday Tribune*, was then a high-profile writer with *The Sunday Press*. He marched in and announced that Larry Lyons from *The Cork Examiner* had scooped the lot of us. There had been mayors and dignitaries from all over Ireland and ministers of the Irish Government who had driven up through Donegal to be at the funerals. Michael Hand said, "The lead story in *The Cork Examiner* tomorrow is that the Lord Mayor of Cork led the mourners yesterday at the funeral of the victims of Bloody Sunday". That was getting your priorities right.

Vincent Browne resigned in the middle of 1972. He had a row with the *Press* - not his first. I was offered the job. I was just back from holidays in Greece and had a week of them left when Mick O'Kane, the chief news editor, rang me at home. He said, "Look, I don't want you to say no. Don't say anything. Just think about this. I'd like you to go to the North as Northern news editor." I said, "No. Definitely not." He said, "That's exactly what I did not want you to do. Just think about it. It's a wonderful opportunity. You'll really enjoy it." I said, "How do you mean enjoy it?" This was 1972, the worst year for violence. Nearly four hundred people were killed that year. There were three bombs a day in Belfast alone. Anyway, I did think about it and it took me a while to come round to the idea. I had been having a great time in Dublin, covering all sorts of stories and enjoying a good social life. I went down to Athy - my parents were still there. I went out for a pint with my Dad. I told him about the offer and said I was worried how my mother would react. He asked me what I thought of the job and I told him it was a wonderful opportunity. He said to me, "If you want the job, go for it. I'll look after your mother." My mother was worried all the time I was there - they were both worried, my mother more so because she listened to every news bulletin, but they were supportive and proud of the fact I was doing a responsible job. Once you have the title editor you become an executive in a newspaper and I was told I was the youngest executive ever in the *Irish Press* Group. I was 24.

Up I went to the North, tentative at the job at first - particularly in relation to political analysis. I had Ciaran McKeown working with me at the time and I allowed him to do a lot of analysis because of his experience. I was not so sure of my way. I didn't want to write big high-profile think-pieces which would be a load of nonsense. I organised the coverage for all three *Irish Press* titles and did a lot of the reporting myself. After a year I began to find my feet and was much more comfortable commenting on events and their significance. I developed contacts with the IRA as any journalist worth his salt would have to do. I began to get exposure on RTE. Looking back on it, from a career point of view, the whole experience was tremendous. The *Press* were delighted with the radio and television exposure - I was their man and it was felt that, if that fellow Keane seemed to know what he was talking about, maybe people would buy the paper in the morning.

I loved it in the North. I had planned to stay for maybe a year - I ended up staying five-and-a-half. I made a conscious decision I would leave the North for two or three days every fortnight unless there was something extraordinary happening, otherwise you would run yourself into the ground. On one of those breaks I was in Athy delivering some dry-cleaning for my mother. I met a neighbour and she asked me how I was getting on in Belfast. I think she expected to see bullet wounds and shrapnel scars. I told her it was terrific - terrific journalistically and the people were lovely - except, that is, for those who were trying to blow you up. She ended up, "Ah yes. Sure they say it's not as bad as they say it is." Ciaran McKeown wanted to use it as the title of a book. That goes close to saying, "Sure, it's all the meeja. It's not really happening at all."

Nowhere else could you get the experience: one morning I covered a party political press conference given by the SDLP in the Europa Hotel; in the afternoon I covered a riot on the Falls Road and, in the evening, just when I was leaving, I was asked by the features editor in Dublin to do a review of a play in the Lyric Theatre.

I had a few close calls. I did not tell my mother about them until a long time after. Once there was a gun battle between the British Army and the IRA - three British soldiers and three IRA men were shot dead. The IRA funeral was from St. Patrick's Cathedral in Donegall Street. The start of the Falls Road is close to the Shankill Road and the funeral procession for the IRA men came up in three parallel lines. There was a peace line between the Falls and the Shankill - a big galvanised fence. The coffins had all the IRA trappings, the tricolour, the gloves and berets - I thought that near the coffins would be where the trouble would be and I walked along behind them.

Sure enough, as we passed the peace line, a Loyalist with a machine-gun got up on top of the fence and opened fire. 14 people were shot around me as close as I am to you. Luckily I was not one of them and luckily none of them died. The IRA people in the cortege had, of course, been expecting this and they reached for their guns. They ran up the street blasting at where the Loyalist had been. I shall never forget the way the guard-of-honour, dressed in their black uniforms, never missed step. They kept marking time as the bullets were flying around. I raced to the phone - a lot of my colleagues had thought that the trouble would start at the other end of the funeral - so I had a bit of a scoop. I can tell you, Ivor, I did not have to create any of the atmosphere - it just poured out of me. It made the lead story in the final edition of *The Evening Press* and I got a telegram of congratulations from the editor.

On another occasion I had arranged to meet an IRA contact. You'd telephone, be told to wait for a call back, get a message to go to a certain pub where you might get a message to go to another one. You'd never, of course, be told what the IRA were going to do but you might get the background attitude to some particular strategy. At that time there had been a lot of no-warning car bombs in shops and supermarkets. I had been writing some critical stuff about them. A no-warning car bomb is a horrendous and indiscriminate murder weapon. I made no bones about that in the columns of the *Irish Press*. When I met this guy, he said, "You owe me a pint. In fact, you owe me two pints. You nearly bought it." He told me there had been an application before the last meeting of the Belfast Brigade to have me given a head job. A head job is exactly what you think it is. He told me the Third Battalion were not happy with the way I was writing. He said, "You are lucky you had a friend in the Belfast Brigade". I asked him how many pints he wanted. The difference between the IRA and the Loyalists is the Loyalists would not bother applying for permission, they'd just knock you off. Both are brutal outfits.

The IRA people knew I was opposed to their campaign of violence: anyone who works in the North has got to look at the violence and make up their mind where they stand. Once you can justify any violence, you have to justify the whole lot. So, while the IRA were well aware of the fact that I opposed them, they also knew I was someone who would report straight down the line. And, in fact, those were the instructions I got from the late Vivion de Valera when I first went to the North. A tremendous man in many ways, he called me over to the then head office in O'Connell Street. He talked to me for 45 minutes about everything and anything. I was beginning to ask myself why I was there. As I was walking out the door, in rapid fire, in the space of about 35 seconds, he told me why. He said, "Michael, you are going to the North now. I want the news straight. I don't want it varnished. If I want your opinion, I'll ask you for it. You leave the editorial column to Tim Pat Coogan and myself - we'll decide what goes in there. When I read what you have written on page one, I want to know that it is straight and fair. You are to resist any possible pressure to change or twist the truth. If you don't resist it and I find out about it, you'll be fired. If you are under pressure, I want you to come to me." Later on, I did come under pressure and I resisted it, confident in the knowledge, if it became heavy, I could walk into Vivion's office and ask him to do something about it. However, it never got to that stage. "The Truth in the News" is the slogan of the *Irish Press* and that's the line we followed.

I had my life saved by a British soldier. I was driving from the city centre up the Grosvenor Road to meet my Deep Throat. The Grosvenor Road comes onto the Falls Road at The Royal Victoria Hospital. It was eight o'clock at night in the middle of winter. I was suddenly aware there were not many cars around. Next thing this soldier jumps out with a gun in his hand, screaming and roaring at me - I nearly drove into him. He yelled, "Get the bloody 'ell out of here - there's a bomb in that car". Just 30 yards up the street a car was parked at a drunken angle. I did the fastest U-turn you've ever seen. I had gone only 50 yards when up it went. I don't know who that squaddy was but "Thanks".

During that period we had the Queen's visit, Secretaries of State coming and going, elections to Stormont and the Assembly and Council elections - after about four years I began to tire of it. It was a steady diet of violence and politics. Unfortunately, the newspapers down south are not interested in the cultural life of the North or in business stories. When you've had your fourth Secretary of State and you hear him making the same statements as his predecessors - "My priority here is to give security to the people of Northern Ireland and ensure that a political path - blah-blah-blah" and you've reported on the nine millionth confrontation between the SDLP and the Unionists and you have heard repeatedly Paisley and Hume in megaphone diplomacy, you say it's time to move on.

My colleagues in Belfast threw a dinner party for me in the house of the CBS correspondent, Peter Martin. We were just sitting down when word came through of the La Mon disaster. The IRA bombed a restaurant-bar where the members of a kennel club were having their dinner - scores of people were burnt to death. Our dinner party was abandoned as we went off once again to chase another disaster. The next day I got into my car and drove back to Dublin.

While in Belfast I met a girl called Jennifer Asquith. We went out together but had parted when I left the North in early 1978. She came down to Dublin to visit mutual friends, Conor and Della O'Clery, and we met up again. During that visit I realised I couldn't let her go back. I proposed on the morning she was to return. She accepted, I am glad to say, and we married in 1979. We have three great children.

When I came back to Dublin the idea was I would be in charge of a small team of reporters who would do news and news analysis, working specifically on the *Irish Press*. Negotiations to set up this unit broke down and it never happened. As a result, I was assistant editor in a function where I did not possess any sub-editorial skills. I now think all young journalists should spend at least six months sub-editing, even if they plan to have a career as a reporter. And vice versa - all sub-editors should spend at least six months as a reporter learning what to do and what not to do. You can make life easier for each other if you understand the different roles and don't do stupid things. I was not able to do layouts and I did not know typography. I ended up subbing letters to the editor and writing leaders and organising some features. I was trying to do the job I had come back to do but without any staff. Coming back to Dublin was always going to be difficult but coming back to what was effectively a non-job was frustrating. It was also five nights a week and I was a single man. It was not the best year of my life.

The chief news editor at that time, Michael P. O'Kane, had Group responsibility with 50 or so reporters. He would allocate his team between the three newspapers. I was appointed deputy chief news editor and Michael gave me a lot of freedom. I got, for example, the job of drawing up a plan to cover the Pope's visit. The same with President Reagan's visit and then also with the three elections we had in succession around 1981. I was able to bring on people like Stephen Collins and Stephen O'Byrnes - Stephen O'Byrnes is now an important backroom strategist and press secretary with the PDs. Stephen Collins is our well-respected political correspondent. At the end of that period, which lasted about five years, Vincent Jennings came down to me one day and said, "Would you like to be deputy editor and news editor of *The Sunday Press*?" Gerry Fox, a talented and popular journalist, was retiring.

I have been lucky because, after a certain number of years in the one job, the excitement may go out of it and I have always been able to move on within the Press Group. I did not plan it that way. I never thought, when I started out, that I would remain for so long with the one company. However, I have never had any reason to leave because the jobs were so varied and came at the right time. I have had other offers but the Press has been good to me and I have felt a certain loyalty.

Being editor of a weekly paper is quite different from working on a daily. You are trying to judge what will be of interest in a week's time. On a daily paper, the news almost generates itself - you have a list of what's going on that day: the Dail, the courts, commissions, press conferences. Then, of course, you follow up your own stories - somebody rings you up and asks if you have heard about so-and so. On a daily paper it's: get the story, get it in, now. In a Sunday paper, on the news end, you are trying to get a good story that won't die on you on Friday. It's heartbreaking if you have been working all week on a story and suddenly the opposition have it. It could be dead on Saturday - a body is a body and you can't pump it up into a living creature again. You scrap it and that's it. You have to decide whether it's worth investing time and money in a story. Some you take a chance on - you think they'll hold.

In features people want more in-depth, more background than they get during the week. In a Sunday paper you not only reflect on what happened but why it happened and what its significance is for the future. Sunday papers are leisure-orientated. While the daily and evening papers have five or six issues to deal with, say, TV criticism one day, theatre the next day, fashion the next day, then food - it's all spread over the week, with a Sunday paper it's all on one day. You're gearing up to give a good package with all those elements in it - to giving a good read to all the family.

I would like *The Sunday Press* to be as interesting and relevant to a person living in a rural town as it is to a Dubliner - the difference between Dublin and rural towns is now slim. You're also trying to ensure that page one is as newsy and up to date as you can make it. In *The Sunday Press* we give you news, but we also give you the background, the analysis, features and leisure. The *Sunday Independent* on the other hand have taken a decision that they don't really care about the news - it's page after page of comment and analyis by high-profile, highly-paid writers. People must like that because it's doing well. My decision - and the company have gone along with my view - is that there is still a need for a Sunday *newspaper*. I don't think the company would be comfortable with the Terry Keane-style material, suggestions of various friendships and who's having it away with whom, although Terry Keane is widely read and has had an impact on the *Sunday Independent*. *The Sunday Tribune* is more like the traditional Sunday newspaper was but it's geared to a narrower market.

In a Sunday paper you have to pace yourself. Many of the pages are finished on the Friday - colour has to be done well in advance. We once decided to do a colour front page on Mother Teresa. We got John O'Shea of Goal, who'd met her in Calcutta, to write a good piece on her. Unfortunately, she broke three ribs and at the last minute we could not be sure she'd come and we could not wait because there was a three-week lead-in time to colour. We had to scrap it. I would love to have our own printing presses where we could print our own colour on the night - so if you have a spare £6m or £7m there, I'll take it off you.

In December 1986 Vincent Jennings became managing director and I was appointed editor. I learned an awful lot from him - he is very talented. Having been a deputy editor for two years, I thought the job would not be much different. I had not realised what it was like to bear ultimate responsibility. I was not prepared for that. There are so many decisions to be taken and you are involved in every one of them. As news editor or deputy editor you had defined responsibilities - you did not, for example, have to worry in detail about what the sports department was doing. When you are editor you have to worry about every section of the paper plus the promotion, marketing, budgeting, planning, recruitment - the whole nine yards. Six years on, I am still learning. I said to you that after five years you might get a bit bored with a job but the editor's job is so multi-faceted that I'm not bored. The job has also been frustrating because of all the problems we have had in The Press Group right throughout my tenure. The last ten years in fact have been difficult.

In my view, the fundamental problems in The Press Group began 20 years ago. Vivion de Valera did not bring his son Eamon in early enough and he and Jack Dempsey did not stand down early enough and let a younger team take over. The company was doing quite well. The philosophy was not to change a winning number. *The Sunday Press* was a runaway success - at one stage it was selling 450,000 or so, way ahead of the *Sunday Independent,* which is a much older paper. Times were different, of course, there was no real competition. Why change when particularly *The Sunday Press* and *The Evening Press* were doing fine? In the 1970s Vivion tried to bring in new technology and, when the unions said no, he backed off. Perhaps it would have been better had he pushed ahead and hammered home an agreement, even if at that stage it would have been costly. In the long term, it would have been cheap. The unions had seen what was happening in Britain and were wary of new technology - it does mean the end of the printing trade. In my view that was a major opportunity lost.

The *Irish Press* was failing and Tim Pat Coogan revived it a little in the late 60s, early 70s. Then it began to decline again. Change was needed in the whole approach to our products. There was no market research such as the *Independent* were doing. There was no marketing at all. The *Independent* were spending a lot of money on it. We spent none: we just went our way saying things would be fine. They were not - the company was in trouble. Then, eventually, when they tried to bring in the new technology we had a dreadfully damaging three-month strike. We were off the streets for a prolonged period - our credibility was seriously affected.

We had trade union problems on a number of fronts. The workers wanted to keep pace with workers in other companies and the *Press* did not have the money to pay them. It was a vicious circle. You had trouble both with the printers and the journalists even though the NUJ had got in 1974 a productivity deal which doubled their salaries.

Things got worse. We were almost in free-fall. Vincent Jennings took over as managing director and did a lot of things to try to stem the tide. He and Eamon de Valera recognised that, to develop the papers, we needed capital. That's where the Ingersoll organisation came in. They were introduced to us by a later director of Ingersolls, Roger Nicholson. At the time they seemed to be an ideal partner: Ralph Ingersoll II had a huge number of mainly provincial newspapers in America. He also had a couple of big ones and on the surface a reasonable track record. We did not know at the time that he was involved in the junk bond market - that led to the collapse of his US empire. He also invested $24m in the *St. Louis Sun*, a tabloid morning paper. It tried to take on an established paper, the *Post-Dispatch*, but did not last long. Meanwhile, he bought *The Birmingham Post and Mail* and *The Coventry Evening Telegraph* - they cost an arm and a leg just at the wrong time when the recession was at its worst in Britain and advertising was terrible. Ingersoll bailed out of there and, meanwhile, relations with the Irish side deteriorated badly. Ingersoll was, first, trying to get out of America and Birmingham and, second, trying to get rid of Vincent Jennings as chief executive.

I had been hoping to develop *The Sunday Press* - in the early part of the relationship, the Americans had helped redesign the *Evening Press*. It was relaunched with a fanfare - unfortunately, their redesign was a disaster, totally unsuitable to the Irish market. The relaunch was reversed within weeks and we are still suffering from the damage. The *Evening Press* lost a huge amount of circulation and advertising revenue. I am just glad that *The Sunday Press* was not the first one into the mill.

At the end of 1990, the Ingersolls, who had been preoccupied with Bermingham and had hardly come near us, turned their attention on Dublin. When they came back in, the editors of the three papers had their development plans on the table. They were not interested in our plans. They wanted to talk "with you Mr. Jennings - we want you out". A protracted battle followed, lasting from October to the end of January. Eventually Vincent Jennings had to go because it was written into the agreement that the Ingersoll Group had the right to hire and fire the chief executive. There seemed to be no way around that. That led to terrible bitterness. However, the balancing part of the contract was that Eamon de Valera is not only chairman, he is also editor-in-chief. His right is to hire and fire the editors - the Ingersolls have no function there but they must be consulted.

The Ingersolls put in an Englishman, Pat Montague, as chief executive - he was never accepted by the Irish directors.

Dan McGing, Chairman of ACC Bank, had come in as chairman of Irish Press Newspapers PLC, on the Irish side. He switched sides and became a supporter of the Ingersolls. I have never asked him why he did that but I understand he thought they were more together than the Irish side. His changing sides again led to tremendous bitterness.

However, once Vincent was gone they did give me the money partially to develop *The Sunday Press*: we increased it in size, put in more colour and a number of new features, expanded the business section, put in a kids' page, got in some new staff and, generally, in May 1992 we were able to bring out a far better paper, partially catching up on the opposition. The Independent Group had been steadily improving their products over the years while we did not have the money to do it. The Independent Group, in my view, have gone out of their way to do serious damage to us. When they launched the Fortuna scratch card game, we had to spend £250,000 launching our own counter-game - rather than putting the money into the development of the *Irish Press* as a tabloid and marketing the colour in *The Sunday Press.* They also poached key personnel from our news division - they took six or eight of our best journalists: news editors, crime correspondents, people like that. You don't become a news editor overnight - it was like taking away the first mate on a ship. The Independent Group's objective was to put us in such a weak position that we could not pose any threat to them.

I got through the first part of my development plan but it was a three-part plan and parts two and three have not yet happened because of all the disputes at board level. The more time goes on, the worse things get, and the more difficult it is to catch up.

However, despite the unbelievable problems we've had to put up with, it is a high tribute to the staff of the newspapers that the three of them have continued to come out. They come out on time and are of a reasonably high standard without the money to develop them. We are under continuous pressure to *save* money.

Eamon and Vincent were advised not only that they should take a case against the Ingersolls but that they *must* take one. That case now, of course, has become a monster and Dan McGing has been appointed chief executive by Ingersolls. Eamon challenged the appointment in court. As I speak, in the immortal words of George Bush, "We are in deep do-do".[*]

Despite all that, I am tremendously optimistic. We have a big problem with the daily paper and the *Evening Press* has been badly damaged but I don't think the problem in either paper is irretrievable. *The Sunday Press* has fantastic potential but it needs huge development. We have a company with a £28m or £29m turnover - I think we can make a profit out of that. It's a company with three strong identifiable franchises - just think what it would cost you to come in to try to start a morning, evening and Sunday newspaper.

The tradition of The *Irish Press* Group alienates a section of the population because it is associated with de Valera. There are other people who don't give a damn any more about who your antecedents are so long as they get a good product. However, as of now, we are not competitive. Whereas I am optimistic, I wish to hell all this conflict at board level was resolved. In the circumstances, my colleagues and I in *The Sunday Press* have been bringing out a good newspaper but it could be a lot better.

We need new printing presses. The technology we have is not "new" any more. We have £1m worth of computer technology lying idle in Parnell House because the transfer of staff from Burgh Quay never took place. We're now operating on 19 interactive terminals for three newspapers - it's lunacy. The move to Parnell House could have given us a new start.

In my editorials, I try to examine a situation and, if possible, suggest a way forward. I don't like admonishing people and simply kicking them for having done something I did not agree with. I believe newspapers have a responsibility to be positive, not just to knock. There is an awful lot of knocking, of the

[*] See Epilogue.

confrontational approach which seems to be geared mainly to boosting the egos of the writers rather than to providing any beneficial contribution to the overall debate. As a country, we have been badly let down by a lot of our politicians who seem more intent on getting elected than on running the country. Instability was a problem particularly in the 80s when politics degenerated into faction fighting.

The role of a newspaper is to give an independent view of what is happening in all walks of life, not just in politics, and to give a forum to people to express their views. I try to be part of the debate on all aspects of a developing country. Newspapers are part of the Establishment but independent at the same time. I used to love going to the Dail where you could see the political process in action - you were a witness to it but yet you could walk away from it, be independent of it.

We have lost a number of opportunities as a country because of political instability over the last 20 years. We have failed to get a united approach to many of our problems. There has been no concerted effort to deal with the unemployment problem - it's been haphazard. What's happening to the Culliton Report on Industrial Policy is a perfect example of that. You have a Minister saying we are doing such and such because Culliton recommended it and Culliton rings up and says that he did not recommend that. That is nonsense. We are bottling the unemployment problem. Emigration allowed us to have a safety-valve. We are still creating huge difficulties - we have built up a monstrous black economy where it will be difficult to get these people back into the mainstream. Who is going to work for £250 when the dole is more attractive? The recent misbehaviour in the business world has contributed to a deep-seated cynicism - it sends the message you are a fool to pay your tax, you are a fool to abide by the law, you won't get caught and, if you do, sure maybe you know someone. I believe that's pervasive now. I don't envy anybody standing up in a Leaving Cert or degree class trying to instil civic values. While, some years ago, we may have turned out in our thousands for the Pope, I would say there were an awful lot of people around then who would have said his views on some subjects were for the birds. The average young Catholic married would have thought, sure, it was a magical moment but, so far as contraception was concerned, the Pope was talking through his tiara: "I don't agree with him on divorce or on contraception - but a grand fellow, a lovely visit, really inspiring." There are also people who were reassured by what the Pope said but they tend to be in the older half of the population - and it's the younger half you need to convince. There is an appalling vacuum of leadership. With Charles Haughey, half the country loved him, half the country hated him and everybody wondered what he was at. If he had put half the energy into running the country that he put into screwing his enemies we would have been a lot better off. Now you have Fine Gael in total disarray, the cynicism of the Labour Party is boundless and Fianna Fail are at their lowest electoral ebb. Where do we go for the dynamic leadership we require?

As against that, there are a lot of young people who are resilient, enthusiastic and have shielded themselves from all that carry-on. They do their own thing, they have their own standards - standards which are instilled principally in the home despite all the stuff at the top. We still have enough people out there who are idealistic to see us through a reasonably good future. But it is difficult.

16

Geoff Martin

The News Letter

*I don't have answers. If I did I would plaster them over
The News Letter every day. We are burdened by our history here.*

The conversation took place on September 20 1993

Geoff Martin is editor of *The News Letter*.

He was born in Ballymena, Co. Antrim on August 14 1953.

His father was James Martin, a building sub-contractor.

His mother is Agnes Woods.

He is the penultimate member of a family of seven, three brothers and three sisters: Gwendoline, Raymond, Robert James (Roy), Joyce, Pauline and Stephen.

He is married to Susan Forty, a child-care supervisor.

Their children are Suzanne (18), Paul James (16) and Catherine (5).

He was educated at Gracehill Primary School and Ballymena Boys' School.

His first job was with the Health and Welfare Department of Antrim County Council in 1971; 1972-1976 *Ballymena Guardian* from office junior to local government correspondent plus sports editor; 1976-1978 reporter and ultimately sports editor on *The Newbury Weekly News*, England; spent a year in Canada living the life of Reilly 1979; sports editor for *The Berks and Bucks Observer* Group 1980; founding editor of *The Windsor Observer* l983; group editor of *The Berks and Bucks Observer* Group 1985; editor of *The News Letter* 1990.

Founder member of The Slough and Windsor Breast Screening Charity. Winner of the UK prize for editorial excellence for *The Windsor Observer*; 1993 UK Press Gazette's Journalist of the Year for articles in *The News Letter* on Somalia; 1993 Newspaper Society's Feature Journalist of the Year. Several awards for newspapers of which he was editor.

His hobbies are golf and music of all kinds.

My father used to contribute to a magazine in England. Those were the days before electronic communications. On a Sunday evening I was despatched to the nearest letterbox that would ensure delivery to the publisher on time. The magazine would come into the house at the end of the week and I would see my father's piece written large. I was impressed by that. He wrote about pigeon-fancying. He was one of Northern Ireland's leading pigeon-fanciers - something he inherited from his father. I think he hoped I would inherit it from him - it was the writing I inherited. He was meticulous with his contributions and keen to arouse a bit of controversy, if it is possible to arouse controversy with pigeon-fanciers. However, he managed to cause front-page articles and angry letters. The whole magic of the thing intrigued me: going off with a letter in my pocket, putting it in the letterbox, then seeing it come back with beautifully crafted headlines. That was my first real interest in newspapers. The second thing was my love of English literature at school where I distinguished myself by being a bit rebellious. Thankfully I had a teacher, Danny Fleming, who spotted whatever talent I had and encouraged me. He contributed to the local newspaper. Though I did not see it that way myself, he believed I had a gift for writing. By the time I was 15, I was helping him out with his newspaper contribution, doing the odd event he could not cover, earning a penny a line, a bit of pocket-money for a young lad. You felt an achievement when you saw in print what you had written. Then you got the feedback from people who thought your article was good or bad. I suppose, before I knew it, the whole thing caught up with me. When I started to wonder what I would do after school, the only thing I could think of was newspapers. I have found that with a lot of people. It gets under their skin and they can't let go of it. When I told my headmaster all I wanted to do was to be a journalist, he said, "You'll end up making the tea". So I had one teacher urging me on and another, well let's say on the cautious side. My headmaster warmed to the idea after I won a competition to go on Ulster Television and do a live report of a football game - Linfield 5, Portadown 0. It was nerve-racking but I was famous for a day!

I was determined and just when I had finished my O-Levels, at age 17, a new newspaper started in our area. They had vacancies for village correspondents. I went in to see the editor, Maurice O'Neill, told him I lived in Gracehill and asked if I could be his village correspondent. He was in his early 30s - he is still there - and I don't think he was too convinced. He said he would phone me back, that there were several people keen on the job. I think in fact I was the only one. A couple of nights later when I was out seeing the girlfriend he actually arrived at the house and told my mother I had got the job. I was impressed by that - I was only the village correspondent, yet the editor had arrived at the door and parked his Rover outside. Even though the job was only part-time, I took it as a sign I should go hell-for-leather for a career in journalism.

During the summer I took a temporary job in Antrim County Council. Their headquarters were just around the corner and I could walk there in the morning. I stayed for a year all the time contributing to the Ballymena newspaper. Because the Council had only just set up, there was no communication with the local press but one or two of the officials noticed my name in *The Ballymena Guardian* so they started to come to me with things they wanted to get into the paper. I became more than village correspondent for Gracehill, population 750. As I got better-known, people with interesting hobbies would talk to me about them and I would write a piece. Rather than being a down-table clerk in the County Council, I would be summoned up to see the head of the Department of Education. For a 17-year-old it could be intimidating. All this led to Maurice O'Neill offering me a full-time appointment. I had to take a pay-drop - that was a harbinger of things to come - people are not in journalism for the money. I was quite miffed when about six months later Antrim County Council decided to appoint a press officer - on four times my salary.

Six months after I joined *The Ballymena Guardian*, the

sports editor, Billy Graham, left. I graduated up into Billy's job and was not really qualified to do it but the paper was new and the editor was making the best of the resources he had. For me it was a lucky break because over the next three years as well as being sports editor I covered major stories and became virtually the local government correspondent - those were days' of great change in local government.

Quite young I married my schoolyard sweetheart and we decided to try something different. We set off for England after I got a job on *The Newbury Weekly News* simply by applying. We ended up in the fair town of Newbury, in West Berkshire, set in the heart of an agricultural and racing community. We felt at home. Six months after joining there was a carbon copy of what happened in *The Ballymena Guardian* - the sports editor left to join *The Scotsman* and I applied for a job with a bit more responsibility and a bit more money, which was important then. I stayed there as sports editor until we got the opportunity to move to Canada.

At *The Newbury News* I had the dubious honour of being the Father of the Chapel. That gives me a bit of an advantage now when I have to deal with FOCs - you know where they are coming from. You can see through the union patter and get down to common-sense discussions. The position on *The Newbury News* was fairly innocuous but suddenly we found ourselves caught up in a national strike which was part of the Winter of Discontent. We were on strike for seven weeks and over the Christmas period - dark days. There was a great deal of antagonism building up between managements and journalists. The NUJ was militant and had far more influence in the industry than it has now. Through no fault of our own, we found ourselves out on the street on picket lines. I was in the difficult position of having to negotiate with a management who were asking us what they had done to deserve all this. A lot of us at that time wondered why we were doing it. It was a lesson in how easy it can be to be caught up in mass politics. Someone on the management side made a statement that, if the employers had been able harness the same loyalty as the union, there would not have been a newspaper strike. It was a loyalty that got us out on pickets in rain, hail and snow at a most unfortunate time of the year when we needed the money. There was a lesson there for both sides. Although the journalists won many of their demands and the NUJ hailed it as a great victory, it was really the beginning of the end of the Union. It never again succeeded in getting its members to take that vital step. It was a valuable lesson to me when I became game-keeper rather than poacher. Now I am a great believer in the open-door approach - the FOC has immediate access to me. Little things that needle away at people can be aired before they become major problems.

When we went back to work - this was 1979 - the atmosphere was a bit murky and we decided to make a break one way or the other. We went to Canada where I had a brother living. Had I gone straight from Ballymena to Canada, I would have been bowled over and might never have returned. We were mainly in Quebec and Ontario - fabulous country. The standard of journalism there was either very good or very bad and I am sure I could have carved out a career but we were just not ready to commit ourselves. We decided to come back rather than apply for full immigration status. It turned out to be the right decision. You look back on decisions in life and wonder what-if, sitting around a barbecue in Canada having a beer . . . Within a month of coming back I landed a position in *The Bucks and Berks Observer* Group. There I stayed for the rest of my working life in England.

Life in southern England is good. We still have many friends there. We had fallen in love with the city of Montreal but it was then going through the partition thing. Your children had to go to a French-speaking school. You had to be bi-lingual for certain positions. That created problems for people - a lot of businesses were moving out. One of the two major daily newspapers in Montreal closed down overnight. There were 200 journalists on the street looking for jobs. My opportunities were going to be limited. I had a sister in Montreal who put up with the situation for another 15 years but is now back living with my mother in Gracehill. She would say that Montreal is a great city and Quebec a great province but they have been spoiled by the French Separatists.

I became sports editor of *The Slough and Eton Observer,* an interesting combination of papers covering industrial Slough and up-market Eton. I worked away there for three years and then there was a conflict in the office about what we should do with a fledgling newspaper called *The Windsor Observer. The Windsor Express* was the established newspaper. It ruled the roost with all the readers and advertisers and was delivered every day to Windsor Castle. The Queen was said to be a reader - I am not sure if she was. We had never been able to get a foothold in Windsor. Just about that time, free newspapers, of which I had some experience in Canada, started. Peter Lawrance, the owner of the *Observer* Group in Slough, decided this might be the way into Windsor. It was not a popular idea with journalists who felt that the only way you could measure reader-feedback was by the number of people prepared to pay for your paper. Anyway it was done, but for the first two months it was not having much impact. There was considerable expense involved in putting 12,000 papers into homes in Windsor. Kids in Windsor won't deliver papers for a penny-a-time - they're all too well off. The people of Windsor saw it as a paper coming from the industrial town, Slough, across the river. Peter Lawrance asked me what I felt was going wrong and I told him we were cheating the people, we were telling them the paper was something it was not, only bits of it had Windsor news. It needed to be a Windsor paper in its own right not hanging on the coat-tails of the other papers in the Group. He felt that was the right way to go although the then group editor did not. I ended up in the middle of the conflict. When eventually they decided to establish *The Windsor Observer* in its own right, I was given the job as editor, a job nobody wanted. I think they thought I was more open to what they wanted to do than most of the other journalists who were quite hostile. I was allowed to take three people with me and I took three of the best which again created divisions in the office. We never looked back - from doing four pages of Windsor news, we were doing 14 and then 20. Within two years the newspaper was winning awards for editorial excellence. It was leading major campaigns - from a paper that was of no importance we were blamed when leading councillors lost their seats because of unpopular decisions that were prominently covered in *The Observer*. All the time the poor old *Windsor Express* sat idly by and treated us with contempt. In three years we had taken from them their readership and their advertising market - they ended up in hideous difficulties. One of the leading weekly papers in the south of England was taken to the cleaners by a team of four journalists.

The group editor became seriously ill and died and, largely because of the success of *The Windsor Observer* in 1984, I got the job. It was difficult to target the different markets - there is little similarity between industrial Slough and its immigrant population and Gerrard's Cross or Henley or Maidenhead - or Windsor. The river is a snob divide. You could stand on the ramparts of Windsor Castle and the view is Slough but there is a ring-road of five miles to get from one to the other. From my house I could tell whether the Queen was home because I could see the Royal Standard fluttering over the castle. A story that's never been told is that another way I could tell she was home was when the aircraft from Heathrow were diverted over my house. In any event we made *The Windsor Observer* acceptable in Windsor and *The Slough Observer* acceptable in Slough. It was my big chance to edit a group of mushrooming weekly newspapers. There was always something happening - new editions, forays into the magazine business, some spectacular successes and failures, but a vibrant group of newspapers with a chairman who gave me complete autonomy. That's something I have cherished and have always been able to find. Wherever I have worked there has been no heavy pressure from management for the editor and journalists to take a particular line. I can say hand-on-heart that I am not subject to the pressures other editors feel, particularly from the commercial side. I have many friends working in Fleet Street who have to make stories fit a particular policy. I was talking to one recently who was earning £35,000 a year and who said, "When Kelvin McKenzie, editor of *The Sun*, offered me a job I thought he was buying my talent. I found he was buying my integrity." I have the greatest admiration for Kelvin McKenzie, for what *The Sun* sets out to do, nobody could do better. They tailor their paper precisely to their readership. At times you wonder what journalism has sunk to but they know what they're doing from a commercial point of view. They have brilliant headline writers, there are a lot of talented people, but it's not for me.

I got word on the grapevine that *The News Letter* was looking for an editor. At the time there was a degree of turmoil here - the paper seemed to have lost its direction. There were new owners - the Henderson family had severed their long connection. There was an attempt to sell the paper to *The Belfast Telegraph* but that was blocked by the Monopolies Commission. People were writing *The News Letter* off. The new owners were a London-based consortium, Century Newspapers, with whom our present chairman, John Barrons, was involved. He succeeded in giving the paper a stability and direction again. In Slough I guess I had a job for life if I wanted it. Perhaps I was getting a bit complacent and was not advancing professionally. Everything was rosy, we had achieved amazing things. I was 37 years old and wondered if I was still going to be there at 57. Finding out that *The News Letter* job was vacant started me to think along those lines. I did not want to go to Fleet Street. I was disenchanted with the popular press. Here was a chance to come back to a newspaper which really meant something to me in my formative years.

I remember when I was working on *The Ballymena Guardian*, Maurice O'Neill and I going out one midnight to meet a train coming back from a seaside resort. It had been smashed up by hoodlums, ripped apart, hysterical young girls on board. We sold our story on to *The News Letter* and saw it in headlines the following day. It was a real achievement to get the lead story in *The News Letter*. It was a paper I could remember as being hugely prestigious, authoritative, having a voice in the community, highly respected among journalists. That was not *The News Letter* I came back here and found but it was *The News Letter* nonetheless.

It was not really a difficult decision to make. I would give it a go and it could last six months and then go down the plughole - but I wanted to make a success of it. In the last two or three years the circulation of the paper has stabilised after years of constantly dropping. We have just put on a small increase and hopefully we will put on another in the next six months.

The first Sunday night I was working here in 1990, three IRA men "on active service" were shot by the security forces. It was a story that created the usual shoot-to-kill furore. The IRA buried them with military honours - their way of saying fair dues, on this occasion the army got the better of us. Then everything began to go haywire. Protestants were not then shooting people the way they are now. The bombing campaign by the IRA seemed to be part of history. The talks were just starting to kick into gear after years of impasse. Then there was a return to the worst times of the 70s. I have found myself editing *The News Letter* in one of the most unsettled periods in the last 25 years. It's ironic because 20 odd years ago I made the decision to leave the Province because of the troubles just as a lot of young people did at the time.

I got the job after a series of interviews. The most interesting moment was when I met the entire board who had flown over from London. Somehow I had the courage to say to them that, if *The News Letter* was going to return to its long-standing policy of bigotry against everything that was not Unionist, then I wasn't really interested. There was a silence and some glances exchanged. I thought that was it, the interview was over. Much to my relief it continued and afterwards I was told by one of the board members that was precisely what they wanted to hear. *The News Letter* has retained its Unionist bias - there is no doubt about that. That is where the newspaper is placed but we have made an effort to get rid of the dogmatic approach to Unionism which came from its close association with the Unionist party. Now I don't see it allied to any party. In this very room I have had deputations from the DUP that they were not getting a fair crack of the whip and from the Ulster Unionists saying the same thing. Maybe we're getting it right. We feel free to criticise wherever criticism is deserved.

We are unashamedly Unionist - for the union in the broadest sense. We have tried to encourage the Catholic Nationalist population to see that is in their interests. We have approved of cementing links with Dublin on a whole range of issues: agriculture, industry, commerce - cross-border cooperation that would have been anathema to *The News Letter* ten years ago. It is up to us to reflect the feeling in the Unionist people now that we cannot isolate ourselves on the island of Ireland. While we hold firm to our constitutional position, we are all for opening up dialogue with the rest of Ireland. That's been a reawakening among the Unionist population. The IRA has damaged that - I often wonder how far the cause of Nationalism would have got without the IRA. There is a school of thought that a lot of Nationalist concessions have been won on the back of the IRA terror campaign. There is also the school of thought, perhaps equally valid, that Unionists would be far more open to cooperation North and South if they did not feel they were being bombed and bullied down that road. The IRA will say they are winning all these things for the Nationalist population. On the other hand, they are holding things back. The Sinn Fein vote, one-third of the Nationalist population, is often trotted out. Compare it with the vote for the Scottish Nationalist Party - it's not that impressive. There is a view the IRA campaign has damaged the Sinn Fein vote but you can never separate the two.

The day will probably come when the Nationalist community is able to out-vote the Unionists in Northern Ireland. The demographic trend has slowed up as Catholics begin to have fewer children but I am not sure that when the Northern Ireland population is 51 per cent Catholic and 49 per cent Protestant it will mean there will be a vote for a united Ireland. I am aware of a lot of Catholic people who do not see themselves as Republicans - they may have the romantic notion of a peaceful united Ireland but equally they know it is impractical. Unity won't necessarily bring peace. A lot of them have done well under the British system - a lot of them are open to seeing themselves with a British or Irish identity. If, however, there was a vote for a united Ireland, there is a large number of Unionists, including myself, who would try to make it work, who would see themselves as part of a new entity, who would do what they could to keep their own standard of living alive and retain their identity. They would go into a united Ireland in a positive state of mind if it were achieved democratically. If it is seen to be achieved because of IRA terrorism, then the shadow of the UVA or UFF is always going to be there because it will be seen that terrorism has succeeded. That's the great danger about concessions being made at the moment. It's part of the reason why Unionists are so incensed with what appears to be the pan-Nationalist front: John Hume and Gerry Adams sitting down and issuing joint statements. Unionists are starting to think again there is a huge conspiracy involving all the strands of nationalism. They would see the Dublin Government as part of that conspiracy.

We are no more privy to what's going on than anybody else - we hear just bits and pieces. I had a feeling that Charles Haughey was developing an open relationship with the North. The present regime is holding on tenaciously to these bloody Articles 2 and 3 of the Irish Constitution. It's got political designs on an All-Ireland Council which would still be anathema to Unionists. If it were laid on the table as one of Dublin's objectives, it would certainly get a hostile reaction here. When the shift in power happened in Dublin, it set back the progress that was being made here. The new team are more adventurous in promoting Dublin's role in Northern Ireland affairs.

Perhaps the Anglo-Irish Agreement would have had more success if Unionists were involved in it. No, I can say that emphatically. Unionists have had to go along with it because they had little choice - or because there were some good things in it, for example the Ulster Prod was hostile to things like Co-Operation North which does a lot of good work, and Unionists are beginning to see the benefit of the funding that is coming in from America. In the early days we used to call it blood money. Some of the institutions that have been set up are now tolerated, for better or for worse, as what we have to live with. I am against all of that - I think it is a false form of democracy. It does not exist anywhere else in the UK. The original agreement did not give Dublin the rights to which it now aspires. It gave them a consultative role but it seems to me it has become more than that. Then it's an invidious position to be in to be told somebody is doing something and you are supposed to feel better because you know about it. Perhaps it opened up dialogue. Maggie Thatcher in her memoirs was not too enamoured of it. I think we all have to accept it has not worked in terms of bringing an end to violence. People who should know better were floating the Agreement as some great thing along the path to peace. The Anglo-Eire Agreement was actually called a document for peace. I think the whole thing should be thrown out and we'll start again with Unionists involved.

Unionists have learned the lesson that their extravagances will not be tolerated forever, they have to have dialogue with their political cousins on this island, they have to have some degree of concern for what the rest of the UK wants. The Anglo-Eire Agreement taught them they can't live in splendid isolation. A tenacious and ruthless lady like Margaret Thatcher felt she had given them every opportunity to engage in dialogue and they did not want to know - I think Unionist politicians are a bit wiser now.

When I was young, if you went down to the Republic you felt you were going to a foreign country. That was before any of the troubles. As part of my Unionist Presbyterian upbringing I always viewed the Republic with some degree of suspicion. I felt there were people down there who wanted to take us over. On the Twelfth, you had a great day out and then, when it came to the speeches, they were about what Dublin and Rome had in mind for us. Now, going down there is the same as going to England or Scotland - I still see it as a separate country but I don't feel intimidated. I don't feel I am a stranger there. I enjoy what everybody enjoys about the Republic, the warmth and the hospitality. I think the political set-up there is rife with corruption but what political society is not? I feel we Ulster Prods have not given the Republic enough credit for the way it has come on. There is a greater understanding now in the Republic of the Unionist position than there ever has been. There has been some brave journalism in Dublin - to take issue, for example, with Mary Robinson over her handshake with Gerry Adams. I see the Republic as a country close to our own which we can do business with. My wish would be that at some stage there should be a declaration from the Republic that Northern Ireland is a constitutional entity. That may change in 30 years time for the demographic reasons but, in the meantime, let us respect Northern Ireland.

Here we have the SDLP who will give only grudging respect to the security forces and who won't support the Constitution. They are loth to work with the political representatives of the majority population. They feel they should achieve things around our politicians rather than with them.

Gerry Fitt has made the interesting point to me that, when you read the Irish translation of the Anglo-Eire Agreement, there are subtle differences allowing the Dublin politicians to see it all as part of reclaiming Ulster. Gerry Fitt was horrified at the Irish version. It gave him a few clues as to what it was all about. Dublin politicians have a different agenda for Northern Ireland and you can't fault them for pursuing it by any means they can. If I have a complaint, it is that they are insensitive to the situation here. While it did not have official sanction, the Mary Robinson gesture of shaking hands with Gerry Adams showed that. I honestly don't believe she realised how big a mistake it was. Neither did the Dublin politicians. The same thing happened with Peter Brooke. On the afternoon several

Protestants were murdered, we were trying to get a statement from him. It was a singular atrocity - the blowing-up of the workmen at Teebane. Peter Brooke was appearing on the Gay Byrne show and what was he doing? He was singing. *The News Letter* was the first paper to carry that. On the front page we gave a harrowing account of the Teebane incident and in a small paragraph we said that, the night this happened, Peter Brooke was on television singing "Oh My Darling Clementine". The reaction we had in the office here was one of disgust. I don't think Gay Byrne consciously set Peter Brooke up - it was just total insensitivity. Dublin every now and then is guilty of that.

I don't feel the Republic is an enemy - I do feel politically challenged by what Dublin is up to. I feel Unionists have to make their case in a far better way than they have managed up to now.

The Republic says it is the guarantor of the Nationalist community in Northern Ireland. Gerry Adams says he is the same thing. The IRA say the same thing. If Dublin were to say that it wanted what was right for the Nationalist people, it would be different but I find it difficult to take that the Dublin Government is the only political arena in which the rights of the Catholic population of Northern Ireland are being safeguarded. There is a realisation at Westminster that there is a sizeable minority here - in many ways it's not even a minority. They should have the same rights as anybody else and legislation has been introduced to make sure that happens. I had this conversation with Brid Rogers of the SDLP when I said to her that Nationalists were doing well here. She said, "That's only because of legislation". I said, "Whose legislation? It is the British Government's legislation." Nationalist Catholic interests are being safeguarded by the Westminster Government.

If Articles 2 and 3 went, that would be a gesture of enormous goodwill from the Dublin Government. I think the Unionists would be expected to show an equivalent degree of magnanimity, of concern for the Nationalist population. I don't think the Articles will disappear in isolation, they would be part of a bargaining process which cheapens things anyway.

The Telegraph's positioning is purely commercially-led. Fundamentally, it's as Unionist as we are. No doubt about that. Some years ago, they said they were bridging the divide but their politics are firmly Unionist. Their office is the only one in central Belfast that still flies the Union flag all year round. We had a discussion here as to whether we should fly it just for the Twelfth of July. Our support is for Northern Ireland in a United Kingdom but we do not support dogmatically the DUP, the Ulster Unionist or the Alliance Parties. Insofar as we have a line, it is: what is best for all the people of Northern Ireland within the confines of the United Kingdom. More money goes into the Republic from the EC than comes into Northern Ireland but a lot of money comes here from the UK. Few countries of our size, or even of the Republic's size, could sustain themselves nowadays.

A country is its people and there is a difference in the two ways of life. You will find here a lot in common with Scotland going back to the Plantation. We have strong links with the English - even though we don't always like what they do. The majority of people here don't have that with the Republic. Some Catholics may have a bit of an identity problem - they do well out of the situation here but feel some sort of romantic attachment to the Republic. I don't really know what is going on in the mind of a Nationalist who has lived here for 30 years and feels that the British are here by default.

Nationalists and Unionists here could work together to build up a thriving economy if the Constitution were respected. There is a lot of investment coming in and it's being spread around in areas of greatest need. Both Unionists and Nationalists have benefited.

However, things are happening in the background that we don't even see - the rundown in our National Health Service; changes in our education system; the rundown of local hospitals and their replacement with centralisation - a good thing in some ways, a bad thing in others; the onset of commercialism in education where schools have to pay their way as increasingly they do in the UK. A large company funds a local technical school in the belief it will supply them with young engineers. The company goes through a recession and the funding is withdrawn and the college suffers severe hardship. That's not too far away here. There are environmental things going on in Northern Ireland that people should be up in arms about, Unionists and Nationalists together. It's difficult to rally them. We have an Order in Council system in Parliament which is unsatisfactory - it puts us at a political disadvantage. The media are obsessed by the constitutional debate to the detriment of major issues that affect all of us in our daily lives.

Let me give you an example of that. When it was known that a fellow over in England was getting the job as editor of *The News Letter*, I had a lot of calls from fellow journalists, including some from Dublin, asking if *The News Letter's* stance on the Anglo-Eire Agreement would be the same. How would I position *The News Letter* in terms of the Nationalist population? They were totally politically-orientated questions. After two or three weeks of that, I wondered if I was coming over here to be a politician, not a journalist. When I got here, and met the man-in-the-street, he talked to me about the Roamer column, the best folksy column in newspapers here. He wanted to talk about the sports columns. Why it was always Glentoran and Linfield and not Ballymena United. Incidentally, we covered the recent All-Ireland final in which Derry won, on our front page, on our back page and in the leader column. We have the best GAA columnist in the whole of Northern Ireland.

We broke through a barrier when we did a series called "Answers for Ulster" where we invited 30 people of all shades of opinion to contribute, including TDs. An article from Paddy Harte TD set people talking. He warned the Unionists that if they did not get their act together, they could face the prospect of dual sovereignty, an interesting article to read now in the light of events. That was not the sort of article people wanted to see in *The News Letter* but I got around that by inviting contributions from all sides, including John Hume, Gerry Fitt and David Andrews who was then Foreign Minister. They set out the Nationalist position alongside articles by Dr. Ian Paisley and people even farther to the right. "Answers for Ulster" became a special edition of the paper - people sent in for copies. There was a request from a school in Dorset. It was a publication in which we showed our readers all shades of opinion. We are constantly trying to provide a forum for Unionists to find out what makes Nationalists tick. We interviewed Gerry Adams - when I mentioned that first at a management meeting people buried their heads in their hands in horror. They felt our readers were not ready for that - our readers were ready. I had one or two hostile phone calls but when I chatted with the people they calmed down considerably. The ultimate reaction I got was that the paper had been brave to do it and people were interested in hearing what Gerry Adams had to say. In the event, I felt he missed an opportunity. He was defensive and probably thought we were trying to stitch him up. Effectively what he said was Northern Ireland's problems would be solved when we learned to hate the British as much as he did. It's an increasingly empty rhetoric. It's even more empty now that republicanism has a political voice here in the Dublin Government.

None of that has changed Gerry Adams' view that the British are here to do us all down. If you lived in West Belfast or Newry or Crossmaglen all your life and were used to the army in the streets and your grandfather was interned in 1920 and your son in 1970 - there's hatred and bitterness there to feed on. Gerry Adams is feeding on that resentment. The fact is his influence is with only one-third of the Catholic population concentrated in areas like West Belfast. The vast majority of Catholics don't believe it. But he has a fair constituency who believe the British are bastards and let's get them out of here, that is the only way forward.

I don't have answers. If I did I would plaster them over *The News Letter* every day. I think it would be a great help if all the population could accept Northern Ireland as a constitutional entity and work together at a grass-roots, social level, on things like housing and jobs - the SDLP and Alliance and the Unionists all working together to achieve a better structure for the country. The isolation of the terrorists is important. They are not isolated on the Nationalist side while Gerry Adams and John Hume are meeting. There are still some Unionist politicians - I won't name them - who show themselves to be anti-Irish, anti-Catholic. While they are around, that will fuel the Loyalist terrorists. Having been away for the best part of 15 years, one of my greatest disappointments was that, when you come back, where are the new politicians, where is the imagination? Clever young Unionists have either been shot as a deliberate policy of the IRA or the Unionist cause has been so tainted with bigotry that good people don't want to get involved in it. The politicians who were making war 20 odd years ago are now trying to make peace. It must be more difficult for the likes of John Hume and Ian Paisley to reach an agreement than it would if we had two new able energetic and imaginative people who did not carry around a weight of history. We are burdened by our history here. Paul Brady wrote a line in a song about trying to write our future on tombstones.

17

Colin McClelland

Sunday World

The public's great misconception of journalists is that, if you work for
The Irish Times, *you could not work for the* Sunday World *and vice
versa. That is totally wrong. A journalist, if he's professional, can
adapt to whatever newspaper employs him.*

The conversation took place on June 22 1993

Colin McClelland is editor of the *Sunday World*.

He was born in Belfast on February 14 1944.

His father was William Thomas McClelland, a telecommunications technical officer for the Post Office.

His mother was Frances Fitzsimmons, a housewife.

He is the younger of a family of two with an elder brother Bryan (now deceased).

He is married to Helen Ross, a company director, his second marriage.

The children from his first marriage are Gavin Richard (22) and Tanya Frances (19).

He was educated at Belfast Royal Academy.

From 1962 until 1965 he worked in Belfast Central Library, then for Easons in their book department, for a shipping company, in rock and roll managing bands, and in pop journalism. His full-time journalistic career began in 1972 when he worked for *The Sunday News*, Belfast, as a reporter. In 1978 he left there, as chief sub-editor, to join the *Sunday World* in Dublin as chief sub-editor. 1980 deputy editor. 1981 editor of the *Sunday World*.

He is a director of Sunday Newspapers Limited.

It goes back to school because English and art were strong subjects. It was something to do with communication before it had to do with words. If I could explain. When I was ten, a hobby I shared with some friends was to collect the badges of exotic cars. Porsche and Mercedes and Jaguar used to make little enamel badges you could pin on your lapel. These were high-quality and so rare that to collect them was like collecting stamps. You had first to get the *Observer's Book of Automobiles* - you then had to write to the manufacturer expressing an interest in the car. You had to compose an adult letter so it did not look like a child writing. We had a competition to see who could get the rarest badge - but what I got the real buzz from was composing the letter, sending it out into the void, and waiting for a reaction. I never identified what that buzz was until I came into journalism and saw what you were doing there was sending out a fact or an opinion or a photograph and waiting for the reaction. I succeeded in penetrating the USSR in the Iron Curtain days. Even the *Observer's Book of Automobiles* could not get any information on the Russian cars - all they had was the address of the manufacturers. I wrote and eventually got a letter back in a strange blotting-paper envelope with a Russian stamp and my name written in purple ink. The letter inside was in Russian and a teacher in school translated it for me. I sent the brochure and photographs that came with it off to the *Observer Book of Automobiles* who published their first ever specification for a Russian automobile and I got a credit in the book. I was 13 at the time - it was the first time I had seen my name in print. The buzz was in the communication, in writing to a remote place and then, months later, getting a reply.

However, art was my strong suit and I was to go to art college. My father died when I was 14. That turned everything upside-down - my mother immediately felt we were poor. It was an automatic reaction for somebody widowed at a relatively young age - but we were not half so poor as she thought. It was suggested to me that going to art college was no longer an option, that, when I finished school, I would have to go out and earn a living.

I had a reasonably good Senior Certificate and, with it, work was fairly easy to come by in those days. Your options were to join the civil service, to join City Hall or to take up a trade - I got a job as a clerk in the City Hall, Belfast Corporation. I then moved into Belfast Public Library as a library assistant, arguably one of the dullest jobs in the world - except that I got into the reference library where you have access to a vast databank. If you are curious at all, it is a great place to work. People come in and ask for the most unlikely things and your job is to find an answer for them. You trip into all sorts of areas of expertise that you never knew existed.

My first confrontation with journalism was when I worked in the Irish section of the library - not only did it have lots of books about Ireland and by Irish writers but it had a vast collection of newspaper-clippings. One of my jobs was to take cuttings from newspapers and paste them into a cuttings-book. The two middle-aged gentlemen in the library took me under their wing. I was always a talker and they felt that I should also be able to write. The first thing they did was to point me to a typewriter - the Irish Library was never very busy so I was able to teach myself to type. Then they said, "Look around you - there are thousands of subjects. Pick one." I looked at cuttings from the *Belfast Telegraph* to see what sort of things they published. Aspiring journalists today will send totally inappropriate articles to newspapers. The *Sunday World* is not going to publish an article on Quantum Theory. I am sure *The Irish Times* gets the same in reverse. So my first lesson was: find your marketplace, understand who it is you are writing for.

The first article I ever got published was about Irish ghosts. I must have written about 16 drafts - one of the librarians would come over to me and point out that I had too many adverbs or adjectives. When it was pared down to the bone, I sent it to the *Belfast Telegraph* who published it immediately. I did a follow-up and they published that. I was paid £3 per article, quite a lot of money. Then I learned my second lesson, because I got too smart. I went back 20 years in the *Belfast Telegraph* files and found an incredible article by a journalist whose name meant nothing to me. It was about the sinking of the *Lusitania*, or some similar disaster, and I felt that nobody was going to remember it. I pirated a lot of the descriptive stuff, sent it in and got a letter back from the chief sub-editor who said, "Thank you for your contribution. Unfortunately it bears a remarkable resemblance to a piece written by J.W. Watson in 1946." A good sub-editor is worth his weight in gold. I did not try that again.

For some reason, it never occurred to me you could make a career out of journalism. I felt it was something people either did in their spare time or needed a degree to do full-time. After three or four years, I left the library, mainly because I became a square peg in a round hole. I never discovered why I did not get on with the authorities - in hindsight it was because I was too rebellious, I was always questioning. The civil service mentality will not brook that kind of employee. I never did anything wrong - I just got too aggravating for them, so, after my two-year probationary period, it was intimated to me I might look elsewhere. That was a terrible period in my life because I could not understand why they did not want me. I had turned up on time, had broken no rules, was not handling money, there was no question of dishonesty. It took me some time to realise organisations like that do not like people who are curious or inventive or who ask too many questions. I was probably a little upstart, rocking the boat. I asked why things were done a particular way, why a system could not be operated with fewer people. The experienced hands spotted a trouble-maker.

I then had a succession of non-jobs but I learned a few things - I now know how to import bulk grain and can write out bills-of-lading and customs declarations. I know it's a cliché but you do learn something from everything - working in the library gave me the ability in later life to retrieve information quickly from unusual sources.

The non-jobs lasted for two or three years and then I started to hang out in a music pub. They were then rare in Belfast. It was a place called The Pound, a jazz club. The owner, Arnie

Knowles, a young entrepreneur, asked me to do some posters for upcoming events. That's where my art training came back. My father had been a distant person, withdrawn, certainly not a role-model. He used to spend his time in an attic room in the house doing strange things like building a television set from blueprints and an RAF radar tube - he did it in 1953 in time for the coronation of Queen Elizabeth II. The picture came out translucent green. He was really an inventor. I suppose Arnie Knowles became a father-figure. If your father dies when you are 14, he can't have become a real father-figure and you tend to look for other male figures on whom you can build your incomplete character. My brother was one of those - he was the elder brother everyone dreamed of having. He was charismatic, talented, popular and handsome, well-dressed and fun-loving and crazy in his lifestyle - fast cars, fast women and drink. It was like having a film star for a brother.

If he was my first role-model, Arnie Knowles was the second. Arnie ended up employing me full-time, much to my mother's horror. We ran a rock club called The Marquee. It was incredibly popular. Arnie had a great gift for making money and an even better one for spending or losing it, so the club, after making a phenomenal amount, went bust. At the age of 22, I was out on the street. This was coming up to the end of the 60s and the only thing I knew about was pop or rock. I was there with the flower-power and the rock groups and the drugs, the girls in mini-skirts and the sexual revolution - I had a great time, I thought it was the most wonderful couple of years of my life.

Father Brian Darcy reminded me recently that Albert Reynolds in a perverse way gave me my first job in journalism. There was a magazine called *The Musical Gazette* published in Longford. Jimmy Molloy was the editor - in desperation I wrote to ask if I could write a column. Looking back, it was a peculiar little two-bit country-and-western magazine. Unknown to me, Albert Reynolds owned it - so my first journalistic job, even though part-time, was with an Albert Reynolds-owned publication. I had to cobble together a career writing freelance for different magazines and newspapers and I was still doing that when I first got married at 26. I was writing for *The New Musical Express* in London, *Spotlight* in Dublin and *City Week* in Belfast. *City Week* was folding - it was not getting advertising and was losing money. They put in a caretaker editor who was younger than me. We got the permission of the owner, Jim Morton of Lurgan, who owned Morton Publications, to stage a revolution. We turned it into a pop magazine called *Thursday*. We got money from Morton to advertise it on television - circulation and advertising revenue went back up. But we must have been victims to some larger game-plan because it was closed within a year of its regeneration. That was the closest I got at that time to editing a paper - assistant editor, unpaid.

I never went on the dole. Even though I was living on a shoestring, and married, I had to work, to try something. My total income from bits and pieces was £17 a week. It was below the tax threshold. There was a baby on the way when the editor of *The New Musical Express*, Nick Logan, with whom I remain on fairly friendly terms - he now runs *The Face* magazine - phoned me to say they were cutting out all the provincial columns, Irish, Scottish and Welsh. A third of my income disappeared overnight. It struck me, enjoyable though it might be, it was not a clever way to live. Like most young men with wife and child, I felt it was time to get the act together.

Throughout my life I have been lucky in finding the right person at the right place at the right time when I needed help. That person was John Trew, the features editor of *The News Letter*. I was writing a pop column for the sister paper, *The Sunday News,* and John took me under his wing and gave me features to do for *The News Letter*. I was still a freelance. One day I was on a pedestrian-crossing outside the City Hall and John, who was by now managing editor, was coming towards me. He was a man of few words and dramatic delivery. As he walked past me he said, "Do you fancy a staff job?" and kept walking. I turned round and asked, "Where?" He said, "On *The Sunday News*". My next question was how much it would pay. He said £2,000 a year, £40 a week, twice what I was earning. He told me I could continue to write my other columns so long as it was not for competitor papers. So I became a reporter in Belfast in the worst days of the troubles, 1972. I went straight from writing about pop and rock to writing about bombs and bullets.

My first news editor was Jim Campbell who, many years later, became the Northern editor of the *Sunday World*. Jim took an immediate dislike to me. He thought I was brought into the place because I was a friend of somebody's and, oddly enough, things are not as a rule done like that in Belfast - it's not who but what you know. Jim sent me into the worst places in Belfast at the worst times to do the worst stories. He'd send me to Artillery Flats where neither the RUC nor the British Army could enter because the Provos had the place locked up. He'd tell me to go up to the 13th floor to talk to the people about why the lifts were broken and they could not get their prams down. I had to go in cold, nobody to ask for, my only protection my press card. I found the best time to do it was early in the morning because all the guys who had been out rioting the night before were asleep. I developed a great rapport with the housewives in these deprived areas. These were neglected people with rats in their houses and no running water.

If somebody says to me, "You'll never be able to do that", I will kill myself to do it. What Jim proposed for me became a challenge. I became a bit of a hero with the housewives because nobody else was going in to do the stories. Finally, they'd phone up looking for me - Belfast is a small city and the word got round that there was this bloke in *The Sunday News* who, if you had a problem, would come out and see you, get the story into the paper and maybe get something done for you. Much to Jim Campbell's credit, after I'd been through my baptism of fire, he accepted I was a reporter. He then subjected me only to the odd murder or riot or gun-battle. They were always scary but high-adrenaline stuff. That's one of the problems about the North. Adrenaline is a drug - the ever-present danger keeps people high. Reporters who have moved out of the North go through withdrawal - they find it difficult to adjust to anything like a normal pace of life. The scariest experience I have had was to be caught in the middle of a riot. Whether it's the British Army coming in with batons or people chucking bricks, you have no neon sign to say, "Don't touch me - I'm press". To be right in the middle of mob hysteria is a peculiar feeling. Belfast was always blade-running. I had my share of it.

As with most jobs, if you get too good, they promote you. I became chief sub-editor, responsible for newspaper design and layout. I didn't actually go looking for it but it became available and it was a big rise in salary. It took me off the streets. I had no real training but I suppose my artistic skills came into play. But, removed from the adrenaline, the job became boring. I was reading the stories others had to go out and get. One half of you said that you were relieved to be behind the safety of a desk and earning more money, the other half wanted to be out writing those stories.

There is always a pivotal time in a job when you start to reconsider your position. This happened to me when somebody left a bomb outside *The News Letter* building. There was an appalling fire. A warning had been given and there was an evacuation. We all ran across the road. Some brave souls formed a human chain with buckets and hoses. You saw the place where you worked going up in flames. They saved the printing press. We moved back in - all our offices were water- and smoke-damaged. We got a paper out but I said to myself this was stupid, I could find myself on the dole because terrorists had decided to blow up the place I worked in. It started me thinking I did not like what was happening any more. My second child had arrived. My first idea was I would like to go to America. I thought it would be a good place to work in journalism. Now I can't think why - perhaps it was to make a big move rather than a small one.

Around that time, my then sister-in-law, Judy Hayes, was active in the Ireland Fund. Her home in Dublin was a place where heavy political people would meet. You could find a bunch of senior politicians from North or South sitting round the dinner table. I used to visit her and, on one occasion, she asked me to come down because she would value my input as a reporter. Among the well-known people there was Tony O'Reilly who was heavily involved with the Ireland Fund. The North was then so parochial, so cut off from the rest of Ireland, that I did not know who Tony O'Reilly was. I knew he had played rugby but I did not know he was a significant player in world commerce. When the political discussion had ended, Judy said to me, "Didn't you mention to me you were thinking of going to the United States? Why don't you talk to Tony? He's based in Pittsburgh and knows some very influential people." I spoke to Tony and he told me to ring him later at Castlemartin, his home outside Dublin. He asked me to send him a CV. I thought I had better do a good one because it was going out to the States. It was like an ad agency presentation for myself. The problems getting into the United States were substantial at that time - I would have had to wait for a year-and-a-half before anything happened.

A year later I had a call from Sammy Smyth, an old friend from Belfast, who was then working on the *Sunday World* - the editor was Joe Kennedy. Sammy told me the position of chief sub-editor was going. I had met Joe once or twice and he told me he knew my work and would like to consider me for the position. I discussed it with my wife. The salary in Dublin was £3,000 a year more than I was getting in Belfast. It probably was a fortune but I had not taken into account the high price of housing in Dublin on top of the income tax. When I did get the job and came down, I found I was not much better off at all, but I had not come for the money - I wanted to get my family out of Belfast.

The *Sunday World* was at that time the only colour paper in existence except, I think, the *Sunday Mail* in Glasgow. I predicted - I suppose anyone could have predicted - that would become the norm for newspapers. If you learned early about colour you would put yourself in a strong position. So the move not only took my children out of the appalling atmosphere of Belfast, it was good for my career. I never thought I would stay with the *Sunday World*. I would find out all about colour and then look for the next place to go. But circumstances changed. Within a short while, the deputy editor, Tony Fitzpatrick, had left to start *The Sunday Journal* - it lasted only nine months. *The Sunday Journal* was a bit like the *Sunday World* but directed at the rural community. Tony misjudged the incredible reader loyalty outside Dublin. In my wildest dreams, I did not expect to be offered his job - I had been there only a year. Kevin Marron, the editor, came down and stood beside my desk and said in his laconic way, "You know Tony's going? I've put you up for the job." I thought I had misheard him. He said, in his quick Dundalk accent, "Do you want it?" Gerry McGuinness, the chairman, then put me through an exhaustive quizzing about my capabilities and I took over as deputy editor. It's probably the best job in the newspaper. You can do all the work but, if there is any trouble, you pass it on up to the editor. It was a creative and enjoyable period when I didn't have the burden of budgets, meeting targets and the administrative duties an editor has. Kevin, to his credit, was an editor who would give you a free rein. He left design, colour and features to me. His area was the news stories and the TV and entertainment side - he still did his television column. Quite unexpectedly, he got a brain haemorrhage one night in Dundalk. To my horror, I found myself two wet weeks in the place acting editor. Kevin was in hospital and no one knew if he was going to recover completely. I worked night and day - I was determined not to let anybody down. I was due to take my first ever trip to Florida with my wife and children - I had to say to them this was one of the times where the job had to come first.

The paper was moving fast during the six months I was acting editor and we pushed the circulation up. When Kevin came back he was able to preside over the first issue to proclaim we were the biggest-selling newspaper in Ireland, number one. Four months after he came back, he telephoned me one night at home to say he had just come in from his walk - part of his regime was now regular exercise - and he was thinking of giving up the job. He told me he did not want a second brain haemorrhage. He said he was going to talk to Gerry McGuinness and recommend me as his successor. Gerry McGuinness was faced with promoting to the editorship somebody he had not known for long. The Independent Group had taken over a large percentage of the ownership of the *Sunday World* and the story I heard was that Gerry felt he should discuss my appointment with Tony O'Reilly in Pittsburgh. Tony, or so goes the story, told him to hold on while someone got out the CV I had sent him several years before. He read through it and allegedly said, "Yep. If *you're* happy, give him the job." It goes to prove things you do in the past sometimes come back to your credit. Gerry took the gamble and appointed me. The contract was tentative at the beginning. I found myself in a job which I had not been expecting - but it worked out. I was 37.

The relationship between Kevin and me turned strange. I can understand it now - I have seen it happen to other people. He was the editorial architect of the *Sunday World* - he was the one there in the deeply creative period. He passed it over into the hands of a friend, as I was at the time, but, like all editors, I started to change things. Kevin resented this. He would send me memos as if he were still editor. I would send him back equally snotty ones telling him it was now my job. On one classic occasion, I cut ten lines out of one of his columns so that we could fit a picture into the page. He refused to speak to me for six months after that and insisted his byline be taken off the column. I suppose it was his baby and I had taken it off him. We were never great friends after that and then, very sadly, he was killed in the Eastbourne air crash in 1984. Niall Hanley, the editor of the *Evening Herald*, was also killed. There were nine killed altogether. It was devastating - none of us had known anyone who worked with us who had died in such violent circumstances. There was a series of funerals. I still can't articulate what I felt. If we had patched up what looks now like a petty quarrel, I would have felt differently about it but it was unfinished business. Kevin's death left a big gap in the paper because he was still an incredibly popular columnist. He had written about television with tremendous humour and I felt no one could replace him. I split the television and the humour into two different parts, gave them to two different people and put them at the two ends of the paper so that no one could make the comparison. Now I was on my own - my mentor, even with the difficult relationship, had disappeared, and 12 years later I am still there. I still feel I'm on probation - if you work for Gerry McGuinness you're always on probation.

The excitement of working on the paper came from the fact it was colour and it was iconoclastic - it was upsetting all the sacred cows of that time. It introduced an awful lot of things that hitherto had been unthinkable. It became the brand leader, the great paper of the 70s and 80s. Our circulation hit an incredible peak around 1985. At that time also we opened up the successful Ulster edition. Predictably and inevitably, other papers started to print in colour, especially the English Sunday tabloids. Then the "quality" Sunday papers began to ask the obvious question: which is the most successful Sunday paper in the country and what is it doing? Let's steal some of it. We'll dress it up in slightly different clothes and put it into our paper. With the possible exception of *The Irish Times*, every national newspaper in Ireland has stolen some of the *Sunday World's* magic. The *Sunday Independent*, for example, has done a bit of this with great success. I have to take my hat off to Aengus Fanning and his colleagues because what they have done skilfully is what I would have done in their situation. They looked at their readers who are increasingly television-viewers and saw which newspaper was servicing them best. It would be no use taking on the *Sunday World* on its own ground but there were several things it was doing that could be adapted to the *Sunday Independent's* format. The *Sunday Independent* is the *Sunday World* in a pinstripe suit. That's an oversimplification and, of course, they do many things we would never do, but into their mix they have skilfully fed the sexual content of the *Sunday World*. They have also fed in the gossip format and the controversy they did not have previously.

They have consequently attracted part of a generation of young readers whose parents may have read the *Sunday World* - I believe a lot of children read out of protest newspapers different from those their parents read. A generation of educated kids has grown up which will find a lot of the *Sunday World* in the *Sunday Independent* alongside heavier topics. They are getting the best of both worlds. The *Evening Herald* has also adopted a lot of the *Sunday World's* sex, drugs, rock and roll - a razmataz that was not in the *Herald* before. What I have said is not a criticism of either newspaper. To ignore the *Sunday World* would have been bad business and bad journalism. If you see a car that is outselling all others, you get your people in to take it apart to see how it works. We broke the ground, established the format.

The recipe for the *Sunday World?* It's like baking a cake all your life, you forget what the ingredients are. We have, in fact, strayed from it on occasion because we imagined people were changing their tastes. Only in the last year have we come back to the original formula. Circulation has slipped for a whole lot of reasons but mainly because we are not the only player on the playing-field - there are about 20 others now, all wearing coloured jerseys. People's newspaper buying habits have changed and we are in a price-sensitive section of the market. At a time when the National Lottery came on the scene and unemployment grew to vast numbers, everything was nibbling at our base. People in advertising and market-research have told me it is an absolute miracle we are selling as much as we are, now just under 300,000. The highest we ever sold was 356,000. The *Sunday Independent* is beginning to bite at our heels. That does not illustrate the strength or weaknesses of either paper - it is a reflection of the changing marketplace out there. There are apparently many people who require something that looks more like the *Sunday Independent* than the *Sunday World.* Fortunately, the majority still prefer the *Sunday World.*

The recipe - I said sex, drugs, rock and roll. That's a cliché. Sex certainly you have to accept as one of the great motivators for anybody to be attracted to a product. It's not a reason for buying it - it is a reason to become attracted to it. We are blatantly sexual. People are basically sexual - men are interested in looking at pictures of pretty girls in bikinis or less; women are more interested in reading about sex. There are loads of data to back that up. Our recipe would span all that - from the agony pages where sex is discussed by readers and answered by experts, to pictures of pretty girls wearing very little. Where we score over other papers is we don't pretend to do anything else - we don't say this is a feature about lingerie or about holiday swimwear. We simply say: here is a picture of a pretty girl, we think she looks smashing. We don't put coy captions under the pictures - if anything we put humorous ones: here is Maria in biker gear and a black leather jacket and she causes accidents - she never crashes but everybody else does. I don't think the girls who work at being pretty take it any more seriously than we do, although they make a lot of money out of it. Sex is a cornerstone of the paper. It's amazing the number and availability of girls whose profession this is. For a long time we used agencies in England. We have been doing an occasional series, "The *Sunday World* Girls - Where Are They Now?" There were a lot of girls in the 70s who used to model for the *Sunday World*. They got snapped up by modelling agencies and became "proper" models. The advertising agencies would not let them do glamour work any more. It came with the feminist wave - appearing with your clothes off in the *Sunday World* was the next worst thing to prostitution. Only about six months ago we said let's try it again and we put an entry form in the paper for a Miss *Sunday World* competition: you don't have to be six feet tall, you just have to look good in a bikini. There was a top prize of £1,000, not a huge one these days. When we tried that five years ago we got three or four replies. This time we got 110 the first week and there are now 500 replies in for it: 500 girls living in Ireland who want to be glamour models. There are so many of them our photographers are finding it difficult to make the time.

I think things move in cycles. People have got over the idea of taking the *Sunday World* seriously. They don't say any more that you don't buy the *Sunday World* because it's sexist. They accept the *Sunday World* the way it's presented to them. We suffered when feminism was Politically Correct. Now young girls think that feminism is old fashioned, like hippies. They are expressing their freedom by saying, if they want to appear in the *Sunday World*, they will.

The rest of the recipe is sport with which people are becoming increasingly fascinated as they have more leisure time and as Ireland becomes a greater sporting nation. The only sport I am really interested in is equestrian, something I came to late in life. It does not fit into the *Sunday World* formula. I listen to Mozart and Chopin and Beethoven and I go show-jumping - a total reversal of my running rock clubs. But no editor knows everything about everything. I am not expert in sport - I had to force myself to pay more attention to it. We have a strong sports section but we thought it needed to be stronger, and we are working heavily on this at the moment.

In the middle of the mixture of sex and sport, you have to put in what was always our forte, heavy investigative reporting. We would go out and find the evil men, the drug dealers, the criminals, the guys who were pulling cons, fraud. That was always the *Sunday World's* big stick. The libel laws have forced us to pull in our horns. We have been punished severely in the libel courts - many times, I would argue, unfairly. Unless you believe what you wrote was absolutely right, you don't go into the High Court with all its costs. The Defamation Act itself is seriously flawed. It is against newspapers and in favour of plaintiffs. We have paid out an awful lot of money. Our teeth have been drawn in going after the criminals. There comes a point in a commercially-driven newspaper like the *Sunday World* where you have to say we can't do this to the same extent any more. Gerry McGuinness said recently what he was afraid of was the £1m libel action. We were being hit for libel as much in the North as in the South - up there we were perceived in some quarters as an alien newspaper anyway.

I talked earlier about Jim Campbell. We put him, a firebrand, in charge of our newspaper in the North. He has always been outspoken. We knew that was the kind of journalist we were hiring to look after the Ulster edition. We knew also he opposed paramilitary violence just as we did. He is a ferociously good newsman, intrusive and fearless. In 1984 he was shot on his own doorstep by Loyalist gunmen. They represented a Loyalist paramilitary figure whom Jim had been singling out for attack. Jim recovered - he still has one bullet in his spine - and went back on the attack because that's the way he is. We did not want to put him in danger. We told him that if he wanted to turn his face away from the paramilitaries, that was OK with us, but he's not made of that material. Trouble erupted again in October of last year when Loyalist paramilities placed a bomb in our Northern Ireland office. Thankfully it did not go off. Jim's courage will never cease but, by this time, the trauma of the first shooting had affected him physically. He had a series of stress-related illnesses. With his family he moved out of the North and is living in Donegal. He continues to report and to write his column. How Jim lived for 25 years with the kind of continuous pressure the paramilitaries can exert, I don't know. He has paid his dues. We continue to sell strongly in the North and to maintain our editorial policy.

Gerry McGuinness, in your last book, Ivor, referred to the *Sunday World* as Sunday Night at the Palladium. It's a print annex to the television world. It's an acceptance that television is the medium that rules most people's lives. We replicate television in newspaper form - as well, of course, as telling you everything that is on television. Pretty pictures, snappy stories, controversial columnists, sporting action, some business news - you could compare it to the Sky News channel. Take an hour of Sky News, segment it, analyse it, put the ingredients into printed form. It is what we have always done best. Any time we have veered away from that we have suffered for it. What you see is what you get, we are what we are - all those phrases could be used for the *Sunday World*.

I have to say that over the years, sometimes it has been difficult. Journalists grow older and get married and live in middle-class areas as their careers progress and they prosper. They mix in different social circles. It's been necessary to pull them back and remind them they are working for the *Sunday World*, not *The Sunday Times* or *The Observer*. I have to remind them that, if their friends are buying our paper, there is something wrong. The professional people you have to your house to dinner are not the readers we want.

The comments I hear at a dinner party now go over my head. The most common one is, "That dreadful rag - I would never read it. How could you possibly work for something like that?" The answer is, "I am glad you don't read it because, if you did, I would be doing something wrong. You are not the sort of person I want to read my paper." They will attack the paper by quoting something that has appeared in it in the last three or four weeks. The *Sunday World* is the paper that nobody buys but everybody reads. If people say it is sleazy or vulgar, I say, "Correct". It is pointless to defend oneself against those perceptions - it is better to agree we are pure and utter filth if that is what they want to believe. The only thing to do is to accent their prejudice. I have no problem at all dealing with people who turn their noses up at it. I am proud of the product. It is what it is.

Other papers can be a bit coy or hypocritical about sex, using the old *News of the World* formula - we deplore this but we think it should be published in the public interest.

The *Sunday Independent* could alienate a core readership if they went too far. They have a readership which will accept a level of sexual content provided it is presented correctly, but they can't become too blatant about it. We all walk that tightrope. We did some market research targeting women of all ages and all socio-economic groups. We asked them, on a scale from one to ten, what would most offend them in a newspaper. Up near the top would have been something like lesbians kissing or graphic descriptions of child-abuse or details of rape cases reported in courts. Then we showed them pictures of girls with big busts in bikinis and asked them where they would score them in terms of offensiveness. They scored just below one. The message was women have become so used to seeing those pictures they are no longer offended by them. However, the written word can be offensive if you are going too deep into subjects they find hard to take.

The boundaries are difficult to define. I will give you one example. People say the *Sunday World* has got topless girls every week. We put topless girls in about three times a year. Our boundary is we don't put topless girls in every week. A girl wearing some clothes is a lot more exciting than a girl wearing no clothes. That has been amply illustrated by *The Sun* which every day has a picture of the same pair of boobs with a different face over them. The best glamour photographers don't do that. They can make a girl wearing a full-length dress look sexy. Glamour photography does not mean getting somebody to take all their clothes off. It would become boring or offensive. No matter what people think about it, it is an art form. The guys who are experts in it are hugely talented photographers. I could tell you from looking at four different transparencies which agency produced them - they all have their different style. So, the boundary on sexy pictures is they should look as nice as possible - when I say nice, I mean as appealing, pretty, seductive as possible. Ad agencies use that kind of photograph all the time to sell a variety of products. With us, they are an integral part of the package. Another boundary would be child sexual abuse which should not be exploited to sell newspapers. That would be deeply upsetting for most people. You can make people laugh or giggle, you can make people raise their eyebrows but, in a Sunday newspaper, our function is not to upset them deeply. It may be the function of a television documentary - I don't know.

From time to time, we take a political stand. We ran a series of front pages on the current Government before and after it was formed. You pick up a popular mood and people look to somebody to say something in their language. We had a headline, "Just a Couple of Bowsies", about Albert Reynolds and Dessie O'Malley who were acting like spoilt children. It was our country they were kicking around. They forced a general election because of petty bickering. But then look what we got in return - we attacked quite viciously the Fianna Fail/Labour alliance saying it would not work. That remains to be seen. That's the mood of the people - let's wait and see. They made some terrible mistakes at the beginning. They are trying at the moment. We had a lash at a time when we thought it was appropriate. You can't editorialise every week about subjects people don't really give a damn about. People would prefer a picture of a pretty girl to one of Albert Reynolds and Dick Spring.

In our occasional editorialising, we don't always reflect a current mood. We did a series on dirty Ireland. Our reporters and particularly our photographers were coming back from tourist areas with pictures of dumps with old cars and sheeps' heads. When you get that from hardened professional newsmen who get offended, you can believe people are quietly fuming about it but think nobody is going to do anything. We would take an issue like that and push it for a while. Before it became a popular cause, we took up street crime in Dublin. Why should we have to live in a society where you can't walk down the capital's main thoroughfare? We have always been a big law and order paper.

The public's great misconception of journalists is, if you work for *The Irish Times*, you could not work for the *Sunday World* and vice versa. That is totally wrong. A journalist, if he's professional, can adapt to whatever newspaper employs him. In recent years, some of the Rupert Murdoch papers have dragged journalism into the gutter. They have given all journalists a bad name. But a totally professional journalist should be able to transplant him or herself into a different product and pick up what that product is doing. I'd have a crack at being editor of *The Irish Times*.

18

John Cunningham

Connacht Tribune

*Readers of provincial papers have a tremendous loyalty. I know
families who would buy five* Connacht Tribunes - *four of them
would be posted on a Thursday evening to sons and daughters living
in England or America.*

The conversation took place on September 11 1993

John Cunningham is editor of the *Connacht Tribune*.

He was born in Tuam, Co. Galway, on June 2 1945.

His father was John Cunningham, a maintenance man.

His mother was Mary Leonard, a housewife.

He is the youngest in a family of five, two brothers and two sisters: Gerry, Mary, Padraic and Thérèse.

He is married to Nuala Dolan who worked in advertising in the *Tribune*.

They have four boys: Shane (23), Ivor (22), Gary (19) and Enda (17).

He was educated at The Christian Brothers Primary and Secondary Schools in Tuam.

1964 junior reporter on the *Connacht Tribune*; later senior reporter and then assistant editor; 1982 editor of *The Waterford News and Star*, part of *The Cork Examiner Group*; 1984 editor designate of the *Connacht Tribune*; 1985 editor of the *Connacht Tribune*, the *Connacht Sentinel* and the *City Tribune*.

Part-time lecturer in journalism at UCG and works occasionally for RTE Radio and for RTE and BBC Television.

Member of the Broadcasting Complaints Commission for eight years.

1979 Provincial Journalist of the Year.

His hobby is golf (lowest handicap 3) - played Junior Cup for Galway Golf Club.

My brother, who is now in publishing in America, was a printer in the *Tuam Herald* - Jarlath Burke was then the editor. Jarlath died last year - he was one of the great figures in Irish provincial journalism, renowned in his day for producing young journalists. There is a solid tradition of the provincials grooming people for the dailies. Under Sean Fahy's editorship in the *Connacht Tribune* there were Joe Fahy who was the pol corr in RTE and then went on to the European Commission, Sean Duignan of RTE, now head of the Government Information Services and Dick Walsh of *The Irish Times*.

When I finished school I was, like all my contemporaries, under pressure to get a job. If my father saw anybody idle, he would drive you around the twist - you had to pretend you were doing something. He had me applying for jobs in places like Potez in Galway. His idea was that a job in Potez was a job for life, little thinking it was about to go forever. It was the last place I wanted to work and I did my best to make a hash of the interview - I wanted to be in newspapers. To pacify my father, I took a job in CIE in Tuam issuing dockets for the beet lorries for the sugar factory. My only interest in the job was it kept my father off my back and gave me the time to go to the convent during the day to learn shorthand and typing from Sister Lourdes. I was the only guy among 24 girls - I'll never forget the embarrassment. Shorthand was not seen as a manly thing - it was like learning to knit. If your shorthand outlines were bad enough, Sister Lourdes had the happy habit of bringing a ruler down across the back of your hands. You quickly learned how to survive.

My father saw an ad in the *Connacht Tribune* for a reporter - he took my application apart and made me rewrite it and rewrite it. He had been a schoolteacher up to the time he dropped out in the 20s because he hadn't the necessary Irish qualifications. I am glad now I wrote that letter 20 times.

I was interviewed by Nellie O'Reilly who was part of the folklore of Irish provincial journalism. I think I told her I wanted to write a book - I have always wanted to write a book - and, after my appointment, she went up to tell the hardened souls in the newsroom she had appointed young Mr. Cunningham who wanted to write a book. I got a bad time for that - 20 years on Sean Fahy would ask me how the book was progressing. It's very hard for a journalist to write a book because he spends all his time writing - my father gave out to me for not writing letters to him. You don't need writing for relaxation.

Being a child of journalism in the 60s, my attitudes are probably a bit old-fashioned. I would still try to put myself in the shoes of the people about whom I am writing. Out of 13 inquests, seven were definitely suicides, four of them involving paraquat. We have an obligation to report those suicides but we also, so long as I am editor, have to be sensitive to the people at the other end of a human disaster. Maybe that's a cop-out - I would like to see it as rather more than that, as caring for the ordinary person about whom you are writing. So we don't use the names of the people who have committed suicide, but we do cover the suicides and fulfil our social responsibility. Newspaper people have to ask themselves occasionally: are they exploiting human tragedy? If somebody is murdered, the *Connacht Tribune* will cover it at length because the *Connacht Tribune* is trying to sell newspapers. I am not saying we're holier than thou. If the father of a family goes out to the barn and hangs himself or drinks a bottle of paraquat, you can be sure that will be known the length and breadth of his parish. I draw the line at the local newspaper coming along three months later and giving the gory detail and the name. That's one of the differences between the dailies and the provincials - the provincials are closer to their readers. We are in the business of selling newspapers, of reporting the news, and of competing against radio and television which have changed provincial and national journalism so much. We are not in the business of making worse the misery of people, intentionally or otherwise. One of the nicest things that happened to me was when we covered on our front page the death of a child who was run down. We did not do it in a mawkish way. It was reported factually but not over the top.

One of the parents came to me and said, "Thank you for the way that was reported".

Readers of provincial papers have a tremendous loyalty. I know families who would buy five *Connacht Tribunes* - four of them would be posted on a Thursday evening to sons and daughters living in England or America.

The single biggest hassle I have, apart from the libel laws, is the instant phone call following a court case. I simply say, "What do I say to all the poor divils who do not have your social clout, or even the courage, to come in and ask to have their court case kept out of the paper?" In the *Connacht Sentinel* we covered a London court case where Bishop Casey was had up for drunken driving. A man came into the office and demanded to see a copy of the *Sentinel*. He looked at it on the counter and said, "I am happy. My son's court case is in the *Sentinel* but so is the Bishop's."

I don't for a minute believe newspapers can fall back on the old excuse that "justice must be seen to be done". Newspapers are there because some poor divil is in trouble and that makes news. I am not codding myself about that. We report these things, sure, because it is socially responsible to do so and sometimes it can make a difference that newspapers are there. Remember Nell McCafferty's consistent verbatim reports of what happened in the District Courts in Dublin? That stopped strange things happening. If a District Justice is a bit erratic, to say the least, it's important that a newspaper be there. It's important where the case of a big shot is being quashed or held over or being heard in the early hours of the morning. It's important the newspapers be there to ensure the same justice is applied to everybody. But any kind of injustice happens only in a tiny minority of cases and you have to remember you are writing about people. It's the same as reporting the fact that Mrs. Murphy got the first prize for a clutch of brown eggs at the Oughterard Show. Newspapers are in the courts primarily because it's news. Hopefully they are there too if something is happening that should not and they are there too because courts are great levellers - the greatest in the land is there as naked before the law as the ordinary five-eighth who has no money or influence.

I don't have an easy answer to the phone call where you are told, "My mother's 87 and she has a bad heart and she does not know about the court case" or "My son is 17 and he will never get a job after this". It's unfair to put the onus on the newspaper to save a young man's career or the distress of an aged mother. I sometimes find myself saying, "This will be a one-day wonder. In a week's time your neighbours will remember it. In a fortnight's time it will be forgotten. You will remember it clearly but everybody else will slowly become hazy about it." At the end of the day, the only fair way is to cover the courts fully - or not at all.

The other area of concern is the libel laws. It's an awful business for an editor to sit across the table from a Senior Counsel who asks you, "Is this story correct?" "Yes." "Can you prove it?" "No." Then it's hands-up time - the kind of proof that satisfies a court is different from what the man-in-the-street will accept. You and I might know something is true but proving it is a different thing. There was a story running recently that money from the National Lottery was disbursed without the proper documentation. The first thing I had to ask myself was, if we use a name, and everybody thinks they know that name, can we prove that was the person who was actually involved? It's so different from even five years ago where there was nothing like the same level of litigation involving newspapers. Whoever heard of the Taoiseach of the day threatening libel actions on a number of newspapers and making settlements? Newspapers are having to become more cautious and, because of that, are afraid to use particular stories they know are correct but could not prove in a court of law. It's not unusual for us to have a solicitor come in and scrutinise a story - the *Independent* have one on a full-time bleeper. It can go off at four o'clock in the morning and he has a fax in his house. It's now arriving in sports stories. If we say Ivor Kenny, at centre-half-back, played absolute crap, that is potentially actionable. There are potentially actionable things in film or television critiques. I saw an apology to the Australian film star, Mel Gibson, in *The Sunday Press!* That means somebody is reading *The Sunday Press* on Mel Gibson's behalf and has instructions from Australia to slap in an action. I am not saying newspapers that are wrong should not be caught out - of course they should. The best defence against tough libel laws is to be right but being right and being able to prove you are right are totally different. Unlike criminal actions, newspapers have to prove they are innocent. And you're looking at awesome money - it's like getting in a taxi with the metre running and going nowhere. Though you know you are right, and *might* be able to prove it, it's often best to settle. I remember a case where the plaintiffs got £15,000, the costs were £166,000. Not only is it leading to newspapers becoming ultra-cautious but, as Ben Bradlee has said, what with wall-to-wall radio and television and CNN, newspapers are going more and more into the entertainment business.

Bradlee says it's film stars, video reviews and the latest disaster to strike a particular person. I tend to think of it as industries - the John F. Kennedy industry, the Marilyn Monroe industry, the Michael Jackson industry, the Woody Allen industry and the Mia Farrow industry which goes with it. There is the Bishop Eamon Casey and Annie Murphy industry where you take a particular story of the day and the people involved in it and you analyse it until you are blue in the face. That's fine provided you're actually getting somewhere but not if you're just bringing in the fellows with the coloured pencils. Kevin O'Connor in *It Says in the Papers* on RTE drew attention to it lately when he said on a Saturday morning, "Today on page four of the *Independent Weekender*, we have the usual picture of Marilyn Monroe". Marilyn Monroe still sells newspapers. The same pressure is on the provincials.

Do you remember the *Topical Talk* on Radio Eireann? There was a ten-minute news bulletin at 1.30 p.m. followed by a five-minute topical talk on April showers or the first daffodils or I heard the cuckoo today. It shows the different pace of things not so long ago. Now you have news bulletins from 6.30 a.m., business news and sports news; 8 a.m. *Morning Ireland* with a review of the papers and commentary; on to Gay Byrne who is current affairs dressed up as something else - last week it was all about Telecom and the Telecom charges; 11 o'clock Pat Kenny, there's a slight break with John Creedon at noon, 1 p.m main news followed at 1.45 by Marian Finucane covering current affairs in a soft-focus way. There's a respite until *Nuacht* comes on at 4.50, 5 p.m. news and *Today at Five*. News at 6, farming news at 6.15 and main news at 6.30. Meantime there are several news bulletins on television including the 6.01 News which goes on until 6.50 and which broke the Brian Lenihan story. You can get 24 hours of Sky News. Newspapers are left in the situation where they have to come out the following morning with a scoop, which is almost impossible to get, because, no matter what it is, radio can be on the air two minutes after it happens. That's why more feature and profile material is appearing in the newspapers.

Not alone is television reporting the news, it's making the news - television schedules are the most read page in newspapers. Who shot J.R. Ewing? Newspapers, and provincials with them, have to respond to that.

In the old days in the *Connacht Tribune*, if you misbehaved you were punished by having to do obituaries. You had to get on the bus, go out to Salthill to the house where the wake was and get the details. Obituaries were regarded as the pits. Suddenly they are becoming, once more, the strength of the provincials. If ten people die in a week in a provincial area, you can carry the obituaries. Radio, television and the dailies can't do that. Local radio might give you a line but you could not imagine an announcer on local radio reading out ten comprehensive obituaries. Anyway, when you do it on radio, it's gone - when you do it in the *Connacht Tribune*, it's cut out and put into the missal or whatever. We're getting back to our old strengths which is covering our area in depth with understanding and with links into our people.

If there's a murder, three reporters and two photographers will arrive down from the dailies, into the house, "Have you a photograph of your husband, Missus?" The local reporter will go in, "How are you, Mary, I am sorry for your trouble - isn't it terrible about poor Jack." These are people we are living next door to. The local reporter will end up doing the same job as the daily newspapers and getting the photo, but with greater sensitivity and without people feeling exploited by the media.

The boundaries are shifting. If, 20 years ago, somebody were to tell me you could get semi-pornographic videos in Galway, I would have told them they were out of their tree. Michael Browne, the Bishop of the time, would have blown that shop off the face of the earth. If somebody said to me you could buy condoms in chemists' shops, or homosexuality would be legalised, that it would be fairly commonplace to read about allegations that priests were involved in child sexual abuse - I would have said you were out of your mind. I don't really think it is that the boundaries have moved for newspapers - it is society that has changed. You can have a discussion on radio about masturbation at 2 o'clock in the afternoon - it's not a question of saying we'll discuss it after 9 o'clock at night as the BBC do - no nudity before 9 o'clock. A newspaper can decide today not to publish something and, in five years time, the decision will look fuddy-duddy. Even five years ago if somebody told me we would have to handle the Bishop Casey/Annie Murphy story, I would have quaked in the face of having to write it, and of its social consequences. We wrote it in full, plus feature pieces and editorials, and now must await the final social outfall from the undermining of one of the pillars of Irish society.

You can't avoid reporting the facts. I have no problem with that. What I would not countenance is something gratuitous or voyeuristic. Some of the extracts published from the Annie Murphy book were voyeurism. You and I have a fair idea of what happens between a man and a woman in a bedroom - unless you have unusual needs - and at some stage you close the door. At some point newspapers and radio and television do have to close the door and say this is as far as I am prepared to go. Maybe "good taste" is a better expression of where the boundary should be. If that sounds pernickety and old-fashioned, I can't think of a better definition. In the end it comes down to the judgment of the individual editor and what the "house" stands for.

What was widely unacceptable 20 years ago is now commonplace and is written about in a commonplace way. Most provincials stand mainly for what the person in charge stands for. It would be unusual in a provincial to have a policy guideline from a board of directors. That just doesn't happen. I'll tell you one thing the *Connacht Tribune* stands for. If you go to Brussels and ask for £8b because of Ireland's peripherality vis-a-vis the golden triangle, then you can't come back with that money (or part of it) and walk in precisely the opposite direction within the country itself. People argued against the Tuam sugar factory because the Irish Sugar Company was losing £Xm a year - that is to divorce Irish sugar from what it was originally intended to be, a Government vehicle for economic development spread throughout the country. When he was announcing it, Sean Lemass stood up in the Dail and said, "If an accountant were doing this, he would not build a factory in Tuam". When the Tuam sugar factory closed, somebody took the Government's thinking of 1935 and turned it on it head. Why should we have good roads out of Dublin to the West, if that's going to happen? Why not write the West off? Over a ten-year period I witnessed the workers in the Tuam sugar factory being softened up by the politicians. Their jobs were bought off. They knew the jobs were going to go anyway and, when they were offered large redundancy money, they found it best to shut up and protest no more. On the other hand, I did not argue for the retention of the Shannon stopover, now gone, on economic grounds, because the situation would inevitably overwhelm it. What I did argue is that you must have a regional policy, it can't be a question of a series of ad hoc decisions. Shannon and the Tuam Sugar Factory were regional planning. Father McDyer recognised the state of mind of the people in Dublin, a city which just gets bigger with all its attendant problems. There they question the validity of regions like ours - why should we have high-risk ventures in the gaeltachtaí, for example? The answer to that is, if we don't, you write off an entire geographical area in the country. *There are people here who want to live here.*

I felt a personal sense of being stabbed in the back by the Tuam sugar factory closure. The Minister for Finance sent the Irish Sugar Company a note telling them they would have to live within their means. They responded by saying their greatest loss-maker was the Tuam factory and it would have to close. For ten years Governments lived a lie of saying the Tuam factory would remain and issuing the opposite instructions to Irish Sugar. That was the biggest single industry in a West of Ireland town. From November to February the night sky in Tuam was red from the furnaces of the factory. At its peak, 700 people were working there in a town of about 4,000. The entire hinterland depended on it - not just the people from the town who worked in the factory, but the farmers who grew the beet had 16 weeks' work. It was their only cash income other than selling stock in autumn. The facts of the situation were lost in the hopelessness of it - the main fact being that from 1932 to 1982 the total Government investment in Irish Sugar was less than £10m and for that it got damn good value over 50 years.

Crusades in the paper? You might as well be idle. People are now preoccupied with day-to-day things. There was an enormous campaign run against the Telecom Eireann charges. On the day the protest march was held in Galway, 200 people turned up. The only time I saw a substantial protest was the PAYE march in 1979. 250,000 people took to the streets. I became friendly in his latter years with William Cahill, who was a former revenue commissioner and a chairman of the Labour Court. He ran a campaign that the PAYE sector were fools, they would accept anything, that self-assessment would not work - and he said all this as a former revenue commissioner. He came to factories in Galway and spoke to hundreds of workers - and got no response. People are just too hassled with their day-to-day concerns.

News is manufactured? Up to a point. The people in a newsroom will be keeping an eye on what's happening - they will also be generators of news. If the application for planning permission for Clifden Airport is due to come up again, it would be a bad news editor who would not check it on a particular week. Editor, news editor, assistant editor in provincial papers are always one and the same - if they don't have a list on a Monday of potential lines for stories, it has the making of ulcers. The only time newspaper people are happy is when they have a list. From the list, you say that and that will work and that won't. But, if I did not approach the planning authority to find out about Clifden Airport, that story would never see the light of day - so in that sense it *is* manufactured. "Manufactured" is perhaps too crude a term. In the case of features, then it's manufacture. If there is nothing happening, and you get hold of Mia Farrow because she's making a picture in Wicklow, then that's half-manufactured. You are talking with people who are newsworthy in themselves or who have information. Yes, "manufactured" is too crude a term.

Local politicians read the local paper. They believe it is desperately important to them. When a politician goes from opposition to Government, his needs from the local newspaper change completely. When he's in opposition, it's comfortable to be against everything - he doesn't have to deliver. If there is a major issue, say the Telecom charges, he or she will ring up with a minor twist to it. Health cuts are a great regular - the opposition politician will tell you he has a woman out in Claregalway, 83, she needs both hips replaced, she's confined to bed and she's going to have to wait five years. The local politician in opposition will often particularise a general problem. When they're in Government, they don't want to know about health cuts. Then you hear from them to the effect that they're going to open a new factory and they're sending you a statement by fax or the development agency will ring or they will be painting a Garda station or there will be £750,000 for a local water scheme. They will be significantly embattled on certain issues. Those who were in Government will have put on the opposition's clothes and be out there screeching about health cuts. Their needs change diametrically. When you're on the opposition benches, you can rail against stroke politics, when you get into Government you become part of the system. One of the great boasts of Labour at the moment is that Eithne FitzGerald has grabbed most of the £8b to spend it as the Labour Party would wish - this from the party that was against clientilism and gombeenism - now they're claiming to be better at it then Fianna Fail. The boot is on the other foot. Some politicians get a bit lofty when they get power and it can become more difficult to get in touch with them. But most keep a close watch on their provincial newspaper - Bobby Molloy, all the years he was a minister, constantly worked his local provincials. You would not see him that often but he remained accessible. They become far more accessible as an election looms. We had one TD and you knew, if he walked into the newsroom, there was an election coming.

Now you get into journalism as a post-grad or through the College of Commerce in Rathmines. Before that, people got into journalism on the hunch of the people who were in charge because it was felt you had a flair. I did a snow-job on Nellie O'Reilly. At that time it was unusual for somebody to be studying shorthand and typing - that was regarded as evidence of the seriousness of my intent. I give the occasional career guidance lecture in schools. The kids gather round you and say, "I'd love to be a journalist. It's so exciting. You meet so many people." It may be unfair, but I ask them to write me a two-page note on why they want to be a journalist. Out of 60 pupils, I get zero notes.

The way you learned in my day was monkey-see, monkey-do. You watched the copy as it was being edited by somebody like Sean Fahy or Jack Fitzgerald, his predecessor.

I had regular shorthand tests in the *Tribune* because they were paying 3s 6d an hour for my continuing lessons. I was coortin' hard at the time and did not attend all the lessons. Jack Fitzgerald would bring me into his office and read out something like the Garda Siochana Guide. Now you have some chance if what you are taking down makes sense to you, not the Road Traffic Act, Section 3, Sub-Section 2, paragraph 4. Then he'd say, "Go out now and type that". I was only a kid and I had a real fear I would be fired if I did not pass the test. One of the reporters, John McHale, who has died since, went into Fitz's office when he had gone home and found the book and we typed it out of the book, with a few judicious mistakes. I think Fitzy copped on, because the following morning he told me I had remarkable shorthand.

You would be sent to a court in Derrynea where the court was totally through Irish. I had Christian Brothers Irish but you quickly learn conversational Irish when your job is dependent on it. We didn't regard it as unusual but there we were as reporters listening to the court proceedings in Irish, translating them on the trot into English and writing it down in shorthand.

We worked until 2 p.m. on Saturday at the time and one of the big markings was the local market. I wrote solemnly a piece about carrots, 2d a bunch, potatoes, so much a stone. This was regarded as news. It was a punishment detail, the youngest junior in the place did it. John McHale and I often did a fiddle - we lifted the figures from the previous week and varied them slightly but we always had a problem because Nellie O went to the market on a Saturday and if the price of carrots was wrong, she knew.

Before my time, Fitzy used to cycle from Clifden to Galway with the district notes - that's a good spin on a bike over bad roads. It gives an idea of the kind of things that were regarded as the norm. There was no question of overtime - there still isn't - if you were covering matches at the weekend, that was your tough luck.

Jimmy Walshe, the photographer, was driving the van - it was a Volkswagen and the engine was in the back. I used to sit on a shelf over the engine and I'll never forget the fumes. Every time the van braked, you flew off the shelf. I remember clearly, on the way to matches, opening the back door and puking out as Jimmy drove on. And this is not Oscar Wilde's crack about the older a man gets, the farther he had to walk to school.

When I lecture to the post-grad journalism students in UCG I am always amazed at the number of them who want to be specialists before they start. Everybody wants to write socially-concerned pieces and colour pieces and features. Nobody wants to do news. Most of the stuff that appears in newspapers, I tell them, is *not* literature. You are working against time trying to get across what happened without trimmings - unless it's a colour or a feature piece. Boil it down to its basics - what the hell happened? A story for the front page has to be competently written and comprehensible to the ordinary punter. It does not have to be like *The Dandy* or *The Sun* or *The Star*. Years ago, Jim Fahy (RTE) and I compiled a list of ten phrases which could form the introduction to any story. "Top" and "Major" were essential words. "Slam", with "Slated" as an alternative, was another. "Slammed" with two ems took more room in a line of type so you might have difficulty getting it in. Sub-editors are always looking for the quick or lazy way out. There were other key words like "Anger" and "Pall of Gloom". I can't remember happy ones - like Erskine Childers going to produce a good news newspaper - "It didn't rain yesterday". Erskine never got past the planning stage. Anyway, we figured a maximum of ten would cover every eventuality from winning the Lotto to a disaster. Newspapermen think in clichés all the time. Jim Fahy and I resolved that, as a discipline, we would not use any of the words in our list of ten and soon found ourselves in grave difficulty - there you are "grave difficulty"!

Johnny McMahon in *The Galway Observer* - he was a great character and died young - produced headings that nobody else could think of. Once a guy scored a number of penalties for Corinthians - he was known as Pepper. The heading in *The Galway Observer* was "Pepper Pots Perfect Penalties". A former county manager, C.I. O'Flynn, was involved in a row with CIE and Johnny did a heading, "CI Doesn't See Eye to Eye With CIE".

On Friday in the *Connacht Tribune* there was a regular meeting between Fitz and Jimmy Walshe. Jimmy had to type out the diary: what's on next week. Once Jimmy did not include in the list the Mountbellew Show and shows were a big thing, you took pictures and carried the results. Fitzy said, "Mr. Walshe, this does not include Mountbellew Show. You'll have to go there." It was a two-day event and Jimmy went out there on the Saturday. There wasn't a sausage doing in the town. Finally he went into a pub and was told that the show was not on until the next weekend. The following Friday he brought the diary into Fitz and said, "Mountbellew Show *is* on this weekend - I suppose I had better go". Fitzy said, "You will not - they got their chance last weekend".

The pace in those days was totally different from what it is now. Junior reporters doubled as proof-readers - it was an awful pain-in-the-neck. You had copy and proof side-by-side and you read line-to-line which is taxing and slow. However, it was a great way of learning your area. If you were from Tuam, you would not know a village down in South Galway like Kilbeacanty. You also learned what was going on in those areas because you read every line in the paper. Very often journalists don't read their own newspapers. As a young journalist, you are wound up to do great things and find yourself correcting misspells but it was a big part of learning how to write properly. Nellie O would come up to me on a Thursday and say, "Mr. Cunningham, you were reading proofs this week? How do you spell parallel?" You had to sign each proof and were held responsible for it. Occasionally, late at night, Jimmy Walshe would come in and ask me what I was doing. He would take a batch of 20 of the proofs and sign his name, sight unseen, at the bottom of each of them. He was too long in the *Tribune* for Nellie O to do anything about him. Jimmy had pity on the junior reporter who might not get out until midnight and who wasn't being paid for it.

You'd go to the Oughterard Agricultural Show and have to go around each stand marking off on the catalogue who came first, second and third with the caged hen or the brown bread.

I felt there must be a better way and mentioned it to the show secretary who said, "Don't worry - I'll mark up the catalogue and post it in to you". On a Friday we used set up what was called "early copy", that is stuff that would have to be in the paper the following week but that did not change - like the Oughterard Show results or the radio and television programmes. Nellie O arrived up to the newsroom and asked where the Oughterard Show results were. I told her they were being posted in. She went down and came up again and said, "Mr. Cunningham, I see you have claimed 4s 6d for your expenses when you have failed in your assignment".

It was a rough schooling but you had no illusions about the game. You learned to be right, the importance of a name and address, spelling. It was a good grounding - if a slow, grinding one.

If you were lucky enough, you would be let do stuff for the daily papers which gave you a few extra bob. You could be involved in huge stories for 2d a line per line published. Four fishermen were missing and were recovered. Through the good offices of the RMS, Nicky O'Beirne, I got into the intensive care unit and spoke to the fishermen. Next day the story was splashed over the front page of the *Independent* with my by-line on it. I got £7.10s. The money may have been lousy but you learned to work to a deadline which was not your own. If something happened in Galway on a Monday you knew it did not have to appear in the *Connacht Tribune* until Thursday - for the daily papers, you did things on the spot.

The Customs and Excise Officers once raided a travellers' encampment. They found quantities of radios and televisions and videos. There was a pitched battle between the Customs Officers and the Guards and the travellers - the travellers used slash-hooks and rocks, and whatever they could lay their hands on. I had been tipped off by the Guards and was there. I went to the telephone booth in Renmore and phoned through to Dublin 20 paragraphs verbatim without having written any of it, just using my notebook. It teaches you how to write a running story. Once you get the intro, you follow the story chronologically. You have no time to treat it in any other way. Very often it reads better anyway.

A junior reporter did not become senior until he was 26 and did not become full-senior until he was 29. Most of them started at 18 - it was a long time. When I got married, the top rate was £11 a week - that was in 1969. I remember the NUJ got an interim award from the Provincial Newspapers Association of 2s 6d - we juniors got 1s 10d and were over the moon.

I saw an ad for the editorship of *The Waterford News and Star*, applied for the job and got it. I was about 37 at the time but felt I wanted to broaden my experience. I had been 20 years in the business and had not moved outside the *Connacht Tribune*.

I had an old Renault 20 with all the kids in the back surrounded by sheets and things. A CIE lorry had gone out the road ahead of us. As I passed by Renmore I cried quietly. I didn't look around to see if anybody else was in the state I was in. My youngsters regarded it as a huge adventure. But there we were heading off with everything we owned to a new place and a new job and new people, leaving behind our familiar town, our house, our friends. To me it was trauma. 20 minutes after we were there, the kids were coming in saying, "This is my friend so-and-so".

Waterford worked well - in the year we turned the paper around from a fairly staid provincial to something quite bouncy. We changed the production schedule and discovered that by going 20 minutes earlier we would miss the rush-hour traffic in Cork and get to *The Cork Examiner* printing presses. You got in, got printed, got out again and back into Waterford two or three hours earlier than we had been doing. It made an enormous difference to sales. Circulation increased significantly. It's nice to get the paper to the shops before the competition. You can get caught trying to get a story perfect, waiting and waiting for developments, but nowadays radio will always beat you to it with a rolling story.

I never got to know Smokey Joe Walsh. I tended to stay out of his way. I did not want to be perceived as this high-profile whiz-kid who was in to knock the crap out of *The Munster Express*. First of all, I wasn't sure that I'd be able to knock the crap out of it, it had been a long time there. Secondly, that's not what the business is about - the business is about producing the best product you can. It could have been personalised - here is an alleged hot-shot from Galway down to take on Smokey Joe. Life is too short for that. It would have been corrosive for me to worry about trying to best a guy who had been there for 50 years, who had been successful as a result of his idiosyncrasies as much as anything else, a multi-millionaire, limitless funds with which to take me on and a newspaper that was selling more than mine. Why should I think about him and worry myself to distraction when all I had to say to myself was - better product? In any event, it's a slow process to wean people away from their familiar paper. We had a super story about a drug-bust that never came to trial. We had got the documents - when the ship was coming in with the cannabis they would send the message "Happy Birthday". I went to the newsagents the evening our paper came out with the headline "The Happy Birthday Gang". People would ask for ten cigarettes, lean across our paper and take home a copy of *The Munster Express*.

I came back to Galway when Sean Fahy decided to retire. I came back effectively as news editor but marked for the succession a year later. Part of the reason I was returning was they were going to launch the *City Tribune* which was the *Connacht Tribune* with all the county news dumped and 16 completely new pages. I was responsible for working out, not so much staffing, as areas of responsibility which would make things possible without driving everybody spare. I was news editor for the *Sentinel*, the *Tribune* and the *City Tribune*. In two years you could be in the looney bin.

I now have an assistant who is essentially responsible for the *Sentinel*, which comes out on Tuesday and he has access to our ten reporters. I am editor and news editor of the *Connacht Tribune*. I go in on Monday and, so far as the *Sentinel* is concerned, I am a reporter if something comes my way. The early days of the week I act as news editor effectively for the *Connacht Tribune*, the main product. I will have my list of possible stories from the weekend and I allocate them. When I give out the stories I tell the troops I want to hear from them by Tuesday lunchtime on how the story is developing. They may well have stories of their own which I add to my list. I would see that product right through till the end on Thursday lunchtime. By the time it hits the street, I will have seen every page of subbed copy. Two senior people - Michael Glynn and Brendan Carroll - have been withdrawn from news earlier in the week and they take responsibility for the 16 new pages for Friday's *City Tribune*. The *Connacht Tribune* sells 23,000 and the *City Tribune* 6,000, so we've a total circulation of 28,000 or 29,000 and the *Sentinel* sells 6,000 or 7,000 on top of that. At the end of the day, if something goes wrong, the buck stops at my desk for all three papers.

You ask me if there are any vestiges of your father in the *Connacht Tribune* now. There are none. There was, I think, a photograph of him in an oval frame in Fitzy's office which was the old boardroom. In my early days in the newsroom there was talk of him as a tough operator, a super news man, the guy who produced *the* news story of the century and locked it up - the Alcock and Brown landing near Clifden. In 40 years time, who is going to remember Cunningham as editor? I used to say you're only as good as last week's newspaper. John Devine in the *Independent* used to say, "You're only as good as next week's".

Epilogue

On December 16 1993, following on a High Court hearing lasting 35 days, Mr. Justice Barron ordered the Ingersoll organisation to sell its 50 per cent shareholding in Irish Press Newspapers and Irish Press Publications to Irish Press PLC, the company of which Dr. Eamon de Valera is managing director. The Ingersoll organisation was ordered also to compensate Irish Press PLC for the drop in share values since November 1991.

In January 1994 Michael Brophy relinquished the position of editor of *The Star* on his appointment as managing director of the *Sunday World* and editorial director of *The Star*. He was succeeded by Paul Drury.

On January 11 1994, the Government decided to allow Section 31 of the Broadcasting Authority Act 1960 to lapse on the expiry on January 19 of the then current order. The order banned interviews on radio or television with, inter alia, members of Sinn Fein. Members of Sinn Fein, including Gerry Adams, have since been interviewed on both RTE and independent radio, but subject to the stations' own guidelines and to a Government prohibition of broadcasting anything which might reasonably be regarded as being likely to promote or incite to crime, or as tending to undermine the authority of the State. British Government broadcasting restrictions, which prohibit live interviews - an actor's voice or subtitles may be used - continue to apply in Northern Ireland.

On January 20 1994 the board of Tribune Newspapers PLC dismissed Vincent Browne as editor of *The Sunday Tribune*.

Joe Hayes resigned as managing director of Independent Newspapers (Ireland) Limited with effect from February 1994.

In the first investment by an Irish company in a British national newspaper, Independent Newspapers PLC, on February 4 1994, bought for Stg £18.4m a 24.99 per cent shareholding in Newspaper Publishing, publishers of *The Independent* and *The Independent on Sunday*. It subsequently increased that stake to 29.99 per cent. On February 9 1994, Independent Newspapers PLC announced that it would acquire a controlling 31 per cent stake in Argus Newspapers, the largest newspaper group in South Africa.

Index